America's Money
America's Story

Richard Doty

Published by

krause
publications

700 E. State Street • Iola, WI 54990-0001
Telephone: 715/445-2214

Please call or write for our free catalog.
Our toll-free number to place an order or obtain a free catalog is 800-258-0929
or please use our regular business telephone 715-445-2214
for editorial comment and further information.

Library of Congress Catalog Number: 98-84438
ISBN: 0-87341-618-X

Printed in the United States of America

Note: A number of the coins, notes, and other items contained
herein have been enlarged in order to show greater detail.
Unless otherwise credited, all photos contained herein were taken from the
Krause Publications photo archieves.

Dedicated, as always,
to my wife Margaret.

Table of Contents

PROLOGUE

PART 1: BEFORE EUROPE
PART 2: THE SPANISH CENTURIES
PART 3: INTERLOPERS!

PROLOGUE

PART 1: BEFORE EUROPE

The majority of this book will focus on the importation, adaptation, manufacture, and spread of a variety of monetary forms by the European colonizers of America and their descendants. But it must first render an accounting of earlier peoples and the monies they created.

It must do so for several reasons. First, historic pride of place demands as much. These were indeed the "first Americans," and their monetary forms deserve discussion for that if for nothing else. But there is more. A number of the types of trading goods which they devised were ingenious, interesting commentaries on the fact that man is a commercial animal at all times and in all places. Furthermore, many of these goods enjoyed a double life: devised prior to European colonization, they remained in use after that event, finding continued popularity in transactions between Native Americans and a new employment in those between Native American and European and between European and European. And there is a final point of interest for us: the primary, preferred European trading medium paid very little attention to surrounding realities, but trading media among Native Americans always functioned as a part of the larger environment.

In the sixteenth, seventeenth, and eighteenth centuries, the main period of European expansion into the Americas, the preferred Western trading object was the coin. This monetary form held sway even in those regions where lack of precious metal made its elaboration impossible, where poor communications rendered its circulation unlikely. No matter, because the coin stood as the ideal monetary form and in some cases as the only legal monetary form—and as we shall see, those areas which were coin-short would go down many paths to make up for the deficit.

Native Americans were more practical—their monies were rooted in immediate experience, their proximate environment. While Europeans remained wedded to one particular monetary form (and some of their transplanted cousins dithered about its lack), native peoples used what was there and did quite well.

It might be argued that native economies could function without coinage because they were more "primitive" than their European counterparts. But this argument would be shaky indeed: until the coming of the Industrial Revolution, the percentage of any given population which absolutely required coinage for buying and selling, for payment of wages and rendering of taxes, was quite small. Even in Holland, which in the seventeenth century stood as a paragon of economic, urbanized development, the majority of the people lived on the land and were not dependent on coinage for every transaction required. In many parts of central and eastern Europe, serfdom was still the rule in the early modern period, and while payment of money was being substituted for payment in labor in many cases, "money" frequently took the form of kind rather than coin. In sum, the presence or absence of coin usage is an inadequate, incomplete definer of which society is advanced and which is not.

Regardless of time or place, any exchange medium must satisfy a number of requirements. If it does so, it is viable money, likely to remain in fashion; if it does not, it will soon be replaced by something else. To be money, an object must be **durable**. It must be **practical**, either directly or indirectly. It must be **easily quantifiable**. It must be of **moderate scarcity**, rare enough to carry an aura of desirability, plentiful enough so that everyone can see it and have a minimal chance of obtaining it. Finally, **attractiveness**, either for display or for other reasons, gives some potential trading objects an advantage over others—without being an absolute requirement for any of them. With these conditions met, any object, either natural or manufactured, can become money. In practice, relatively few objects have gained the consistency in usage which admits them to consideration as "real" money. We know what the Europeans preferred for exchange, but what of their contemporaries in the Americas?

This depended on their location, at least to a degree. That is, peoples occupying an area rich in furbearing animals would probably incorporate pelts into their monetary exchange practices. But so might adjacent peoples who occupied areas where game was scarce. And while shells would certainly form trading objects for coastal tribes, they might be known and utilized in the interior as well—at least in areas connected with the seacoast by reasonably easy communication.

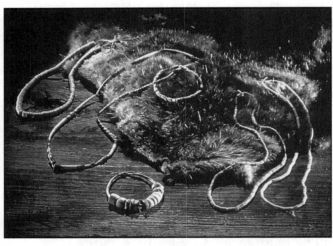

Early North American monetary mainstays: a beaver pelt and wampum. Courtesy the National Numismatic Collection (NNC), Smithsonian Institution, Washington, D.C.

Hides and shells became the backbone of native monetary systems in what would become the United States and Canada. In time, particular types of pelts and particular varieties of shell came to gain a special regard and became units or standards of value. The beaver gained such a role, perhaps because it was regarded as a sacred animal by many peoples. From Alaska, across Canada, and through much of the United States, the beaver held sway. Skins of other animals were traded as multiples and fractions of this one, and when European commodities came to the tribes, the new goods too were tariffed in terms of so many to one "made" beaver (that is, a properly skinned and tanned pelt). In Canada in 1748, such a skin was worth two pounds of sugar, a brass kettle, or a pound and a half of gunpowder.

Shells, clams, and conchs were extremely important, for they were the raw materials behind the most important single type of precolonial currency in all of North America. This was *wanpanpiage, wampumpeage,* or *wampum.*

Wampum is an Algonquian word which means "a string of white beads." Another term was used for strings fashioned from purple beads, *suckauhock,* but the earliest European settlers tended to use the shortened term wampum indiscriminately, and their practice survives. Wampum consisted of short beads, cut from the shells of clams and conchs, drilled by hand, and strung. It appears to have originally seen employment for conveying messages (was it related to the *quipu,* a knotted string used by Andean peoples for the same purpose?), and it only gradually came into use as a display of wealth and finally as a unit of wealth. We know that it had achieved this final, crucial stage, and was now indeed a form of money before European settlement, for the explorer Jacques Cartier found it so employed in the mid-1530s. And we believe we understand why it achieved popularity as a monetary form: under preindustrial conditions, wampum was difficult to manufacture. In other words, it served as a unit of value because of the work and skill required to make it. In this, it has much in common with the stone money of Yap whose value was based on the time, effort, and danger involved in transporting the raw material across the open ocean by outrigger canoe. Both monies show a degree of sophistication quite surprising on the part of peoples often called primitive by outsiders.

Wampum was popular on the Atlantic Seaboard of North America, both among Native Americans and among European newcomers. There was a parallel monetary form on the Pacific Seaboard, based on the shell of a different sea creature, the dentalium, or tooth shell. The popularity of this money was not as widespread as was that of wampum, and it was never as hard and fast, for while wampum only came in two colors, many different species of dentalium were traded, resulting in a fluctuation and confusion over value. Unlike wampum, these shells were never used for display, and indeed they do not appear to have had any function beyond the monetary. They never captured the attention of the European newcomers in the way that wampum did, and they played little role in post-contact economies.

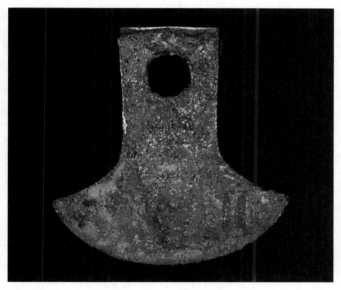

Aztec siccapili *or* tajadera, *an axe-shaped trading object from Mexico. Courtesy the NNC.*

To the south, other trading objects held sway. In Mexico, copper axe-shaped objects called *siccapili* (in modern Spanish *tajaderas,* chopping knives) found great popularity among Aztecs and their contemporaries— so much so that the earth is still yielding large numbers of them to the plows of modern farmers. These pieces were cast, and most of them were probably manufactured late in the pre-Columbian period. They bear similarities to Chinese pieces cast in the form of knives and

spades and like them probably represented a translation from the purely practical, original object to its symbolic, economic representation. In the case of Mexican axe money, a fixed relationship appears to have existed between this trading commodity and another, for one siccapili equaled eight thousand cacao beans.

Cacao beans—eight thousand beans were worth one siccapili in Aztec days. Courtesy the NNC.

The latter were mainstays of the Aztec monetary system, and they afford one of the earliest instances of the debasement of a non-coin monetary form. It is recorded by early explorers that the contents of the cacao bean were sometimes scooped out and replaced by earth, the skin carefully replaced, and the extraction cleverly hidden. The theft might go unrecorded until the bean's other purpose, and the origin of its money value, were put to the test, for mud makes an indifferent cup of hot chocolate!

The peoples of pre-Conquest Mexico employed other exchange media. Maize was one such commodity, and so was gold, either cast into bars or traded in transparent quills, so that its purity could be seen by all. Tin, cut into small T-shaped pieces, also served in exchange along the Mexican Gulf Coast. Cortés found that metal circulating as money in several of the provinces through which he and his tiny band marched on their way to glory—and to the creation of a new chapter in the monetary history of the Western Hemisphere.

His compatriot Pizarro found much less to the south. The economy of the Inca Empire was paternalistic, socialistic, and so planned, in fact, that commercial transactions (and thus the employment of money) were largely unnecessary. But it has been suggested that leaves of the coca plant—the source of a modern, international currency called cocaine—may have enjoyed a limited monetary function prior to the Spanish conquest, although our testimony for this comes from José de Acosta, a Spanish priest who came to Perú after the event. In outlying areas (such as central Chile and the disputed borderlands to the southeast and far north) some normal monetary trade very likely took place, as the control of the Inca grew faint.

Elsewhere in the Americas, tribes in what became Venezuela appear to have used strings of shells, a form of money somewhat similar to wampum although probably not inspired by it, while some of the Brazilian peoples used arrows and others stringed beads of snail shells. The latter practice persisted in Mato Grosso until well into this century.

The longevity of this particular form of money should alert us to an important fact about "primitive" monetary forms: they did not all obligingly disappear when the first Europeans arrived on American shores. While few of them displayed the persistence seen with the shell money of Mato Grosso (in part because few places in the Americas were as impenetrable as this jungle area in western Brazil), many of them were found as useful by new settlers as old, and they formed essential links between old economies and new. Indeed, it is difficult to see how the numismatic history of the United States could have been written in the absence of the skins of furbearing animals and the shells of creatures of the sea. Along with commodities known to and developed by Native Americans but not generally used for trade, along with scant supplies of coinage and other trading objects brought from Europe, they would form most of the basis of our early money—but not all. A final ingredient was being created to the south, one whose influence would be so persistent and ultimately so potent that it would shape the very way we reckoned and fashioned our symbols of wealth.

PART 2: THE SPANISH CENTURIES

This final ingredient was the Spanish conquest of most of the Western Hemisphere. It began with Columbus' first voyage in 1492, and in some ways it is still going on, as the spread of Spanish language and culture across many areas of today's United States suggests. But it was far more active, and far less peaceful, four or five centuries ago.

At that time, nothing less than the wholesale exportation of one way of life (and a snuffing-out or radical transmutation of many others) was going on. We have no idea how many millions died in the process—from new diseases, new and merciless labor systems, and perhaps from simple despair—but it certainly stands as the greatest of all holocausts, the most massive change of population in all of human history.

While it was running its course, a hybrid society was being created. It was a mixed one in the most literal sense, for a new racial group, the *mestizo*, had been created from the forcible interaction of Spaniard and Native American. The earliest mestizo children began appearing in the streets of Tenochtitlán and Cuzco by the 1520s and 1530s; their descendants would in time become the dominant, "typical" Latin Americans.

While Spaniard and Native American were co-equals in the creation of the new race, the Spaniard would dominate what that race wore, what it was taught, what it believed, where it lived, and how it worked. That is, Spanish folkways, ranging from a particular brand of Catholicism, to the names for days of the week, to what was edible and what was not, took an early and permanent hold in the Americas. We should not overstate this: there is overwhelming evidence that native peoples managed to sustain elements of the old religion *within* or *beneath* the new faith, and the Spanish language was enriched by many hundreds of new words from Native American languages, just as it had been by its own centuries-long immersion in another culture, that of Islam. But in the final analysis, the Spanish world view would predominate, first by force, later by tradition.

One of the key elements in the Spanish world was the coin—and the concept that this small metallic object and wealth were

Iberian antecedent: Spain, double excelente of Ferdinand and Isabella, 1474–1506. Courtesy the NNC.

American response: Mexico, four reales, c. 1538. Courtesy the NNC.

essentially interchangeable, simultaneous. The concept did not originate in Spain or indeed even in Europe. But when Spaniards carried it to the Americas, a number of interesting events took place, all of them stemming from a central fact: the new lands contained vast quantities of silver and gold.

These metals were of course one of the primary reasons Spanish colonization began and was maintained. At first, the newcomers were happy to merely appropriate what had been collected by someone else. For example, Columbus obtained gold from the indigenous peoples he encountered on his voyages, while Cortés and Pizarro did the same (for silver as well as gold) on a much grander scale in Mexico and Perú. These metals were sent back to the homeland and were quickly turned into coinage there. Indeed, the first concrete numismatic indication that something important was happening takes the form of plentiful Spanish gold and silver coins, now struck for the first time, from metal which could only have originated overseas. The employment of the new metal was not confined to Iberia, though: mints on and near the Atlantic coast of France may have been using American silver as early as the 1520s.

But Spain's people soon began finding raw sources of gold and silver, just as they were running through the last of the finished product. At first, this metal was simply re-fined on the spot and sent back to Sevilla (home of the Casa de Contratación, the organization set up to oversee transatlantic trading in 1503) in ingot form. Ingots would obviously benefit the King, who got his share of the loot (the royal fifth, or *guinto*); turned into coinage at Sevilla and other places, they would soon benefit commerce in Spain and eventually all of Europe. But metal in ingot form would be of no particular use to those who had actually found it. These people, in the Caribbean islands, Mexico, Perú, and particularly in what became Bolivia, were developing expanding consumer economies well before the middle of the sixteenth century, economies which must have coinage if they were to continue to expand.

And so an obvious though epochal solution was devised: let the colonials make their own coinage, following Spanish forms, denominations, and designs. It was obvious in part because of the primitive minting technology then in force, for virtually anybody could make a creditable coin, provided the metal were at hand. But it was epochal because this was the first time anyone had ever done so in the Western Hemisphere. For the first time in human history, the concept and the making of coin spread beyond Europe and Asia, the lands of its birth. This fact changed the Americas, but it changed Europe as well.

Santo Domingo, copper four maravedis, c. 1550. Courtesy the NNC.

By 1625, no fewer than eight mints had been set up in Spanish America. Several of them were ephemeral: Santo Domingo (1542–1564, 1573–1578), La Plata (1573–1574), Panamá (1570s), and Cartagena (1622–34, 1653–55). Two were sporadic: the mint at Bogotá was created in 1620 and struck coinage from time to time, eventually becoming a more consistent and organized moneyer after 1750; while that of Lima was a major player from 1568 to 1588, but was then closed and only reopened in 1659 (after which its output was consistently heavy through the remainder of the colonial period). The final two mints were unqualified successes: Mexico City, which struck its first coins in 1536, and Potosí, which entered production about four decades later. These two facilities were extremely active through most of the colonial period, and their aggregate production was simply gigantic. In time, New Spain got a second mint, at Guatemala, as did New Granada, located in the southern town of Popayán. And a small facility at Santiago de Chile, surely the world's southernmost mint at that time, would complete the roster. No final reckoning of the coinage of these mints will ever be made, but the combined output of Mexico City and Potosí alone was several billion pieces.

Decade after decade, hand-struck coins of an increasing barbarity clunked their way from Mexico City, Potosí, and the other mints, entering the pockets of local burghers, pausing there only momentarily, then making their journey to Spain, and flowing out of that country as soon as they had entered it to pay for wars, to furnish luxuries, and even necessities that a local population, enamored of the instant wealth and good life promised by the coins, either could not or would not elaborate at home. Those coins traveled in strange directions and found strange resting places indeed. Recently, hordes of them were discovered along the coast of China, suggesting that the commerce of the seventeenth century was far more complex, and American-Asian connections far more widespread, than we had previously imagined.

We call these crude coins "cobs," the name perhaps derived from *cabo de barra*, end of a bar. The name affords a clue to their manufacture. A rough ingot was cast, then crudely sliced into coin-size planchets or blanks. The blanks could be adjusted down to their desired weight by means of a file, after which they were struck by hand, in a

Typical Mexican "cobs." Above: eight reales; below: two reales. Both c. 1630. Courtesy the NNC.

fashion which would have been familiar to the Attic Greeks, but with far less impressive results. These are incredibly crude coins. But those who made them, and those who would use them, had other matters on their minds besides esthetics. Cobs were struck in both gold and silver, but silver predominated at most mints. Within the coinage of that metal, one denomination in particular came to overshadow all the others. This was the Piece of Eight.

Atypical Mexican cob, pre-1700. The bizarre shape inspired someone to put a hole in it for wearing. The coin was later countermarked for use in Central America around 1840. Regardless of its shape, it was good Mexican silver, and that was what mattered. Courtesy the NNC.

Never was there a coin whose creation and flowering were more closely linked to empire and trade. The coin could not have been created without the silver stolen by the *Conquistadores*. Nor could it have been struck in sufficient quantities to make it what it would finally become, the most successful, longest-lived trade coin in all of human history, without the silver ore soon to be unearthed by pioneering miners. But the silver was there to be stolen and unearthed, and thus the Piece of Eight fulfilled its destiny.

Between its introduction (probably in the 1530s, although one opinion would place the event in the later 1490s, only half a decade after the Discovery itself) and its demise, some four hundred years would elapse. The Piece of Eight would be struck at half a dozen mints in Spain, and in well over two dozen mints in Spanish America and the independent successor states. The final examples would not appear until 1949, when the Nationalist government of Chiang Kai-Shek (which was coming to the conclusion that it might be well to leave the Chinese Mainland), asked the Mexico City mint to strike several million of the pieces on its behalf. Chiang reasoned that suspicious Taiwanese merchants would more readily accept the Piece of Eight than his own inflated currency. He was right, and another ten million members were added to the roster of the coin.

Its brothers were the *Joachimsthaler* and its Middle European descendants, the Danish *daler*, the French *écu*, and the British *crown*, all of which came into being because of the greater abundance of silver during late medieval and early modern times. The Piece of Eight overshadowed them all because it was able to draw on such a larger source of metal than any of its competitors. So while the daler's name may remind us of another American coin, the Piece of Eight would soon provide the metal from which to strike it.

Its persistence, and that of the other members of the series, surprises us when we least expect it. The New York Stock Exchange quotes securities in terms of an eighth of a point because the real—the eighth of a Piece of Eight—was once the lowest increment allowed on the Wall Street bourse. And when we refer to something as "two-bit" (a bit of slang which describes something of negligible importance), we are unconsciously harking back to a time when two bits referred to a real coin, the two-real piece. The Spanish never called their silver reales bits, but a number of enterprising interlopers did so. We now turn to these uninvited guests at the Spanish fiesta.

PART 3: INTERLOPERS!

The Spanish conquest did not occur in a vacuum. In Europe, honest amazement over Columbus' success turned quickly to envy, denial, and very soon to determined attempts to match it. Many of those efforts would take place on the site of the original success; when they had finished, the map of the Spanish Empire would be greatly altered, and the seeds of a new country would have been planted. Those seeds would grow in time into the United States of America.

Those who planted these particular seeds were Britons, but they were not the first to dispute Spanish exclusivity in the Americas. The first non-Spaniards to do something about the new transatlantic possibility were Spain's Iberian neighbors, the Portuguese. Lisbon had been sending explorers down and around the African coast since the mid-1480s; in 1500, one of their captains, Pedro Alvares Cabral, just happened to get blown so far off course that he arrived at a new land altogether, on the far side of the Atlantic. This was named after a rosy-red dyewood found there—Brazil. By the 1530s, the Portuguese were making a determined attempt to settle the vast new land which their captain had discovered.

Some believe that Cabral was not the first Portuguese to reach Brazil, but that other sailors may have made landfall there about the time of Columbus' first voyage, or perhaps even prior to it. The Lisbon authorities were notoriously closed-mouth about the matter, but it is interesting to note that in 1494, the Treaty of Tordesillas was signed by Portugal and Spain. Under the treaty an imaginary north-south line was drawn some 370 leagues west of the Cape Verde Islands, with the new lands east of the line being consigned to Portugal and those west of it to Spain—Cabral's "new" discovery conveniently fell on the east side of the line. While non-Iberian reaction to the agreement was less than enthusiastic (the King of France growled that he had never seen a clause in the last will of Adam conceding such exclusive control to Kings Manoel and Charles), the happy winners in the first lottery of new lands got on with the business of colonization.

But other Europeans were soon doing more than mere carping. They were biting off bits of Spanish and Portuguese wealth. And they would soon be biting off bits of Spanish and Portuguese land as well.

The wealth was appropriated first, probably because it involved less of an outlay on the part of national governments. The original Iberian conquests had largely been affairs of private enterprise for public gain; so were many of the early efforts to redistribute the loot.

The first targets of attack were those Spanish vessels which carried home the rich American cargos of silver, gold, and other desirable commodities. By the 1520s these vessels were being attacked and taken, their contents being triumphantly carried into French harbors. The Spanish (and we are generally talking about Spain here: not much of obvious value would be found in Brazil until the late 1600s, when gold and later diamonds would give the drowsy colony a new beginning, the fusty Portuguese Empire a new lease on life) retaliated as best they could. They began arming their merchantmen, and they very soon created a convoy system with two main parts. In one of them, vessels brought Spanish (and increasingly other European) goods one way, and carried gold, silver, and other American products the other. In the other, convoys crossed the Pacific, voyaging all the way from Acapulco to the Philippines (on the Portuguese side of the Tordesillas line but

Dutch "lion dollar," made from Spanish-American silver, 1617. Courtesy the NNC.

taken by Spain anyway in the 1560s) and back. This Pacific *flota* (fleet) carried Pieces of Eight to Manila, where they were traded for Chinese products, especially spices and silks. The flota system made sailings much safer, and it also made matters easier for royal bookkeepers back home, because all legal trade was conducted and controlled through a single channel. Of course, there was a growing volume of illegal trade as well, connived at by local Spanish authorities—and we shall eventually see a surprising result of this clandestine commerce to the north, in the pious town of Boston.

The fleet system protected much Spanish trade, but certainly not all of it. Raids on outlying vessels were common, especially when the scourge of hurricanes scattered members of the convoy. The weather sent more vessels to the bottom than did Spain's enemies, although the most enterprising of them did achieve a record of sorts: in 1628, the Dutch managed to capture an entire plate fleet, an accomplishment never equaled before or since. The production of the silver *leeuwendaalder*, the "lion dollar"—Holland's answer to the Piece of Eight—rose accordingly.

There were other ways of capitalizing on Spanish good fortune. A series of increasingly audacious captains, ranging from Hawkins to Drake to Morgan to Anson, conducted raids on Spanish-American cities. These were coastal sites, where rich cargos were gathered together prior to shipment to Spain. One could move in quickly, pick up anything of value, then decamp before the Spanish navy hove on the scene in these seacoast cities. To this day, we are impressed by the massive walls of Campeche and Cartagena—those walls had to be thick if they were to keep out the likes of Sir Francis Drake and Company!

In time, a curious sort of historic repetition began taking place. Nearly a thousand years before, sea peoples from Scandinavia began raiding rich towns on the coasts and rivers of England, Ireland, and France. In time, they began doing more than simply raiding: they began wintering over, and what had been a target for loot became a place for permanent settlement. So Dublin became Danish, as did York, and northwestern France became Normandy, the land of the Normans or Northmen. Nearly a millennium later, history began repeating itself.

Britons, French, Danes, Dutchmen, and Swedes began nibbling away at lands which Spain was unable or unwilling to defend. They did so from a variety of motives, including revenge (in the case of the Dutch), religious exaltation and exclusivity (again the Dutch, and the British), the heady chauvinism of the new nation-state (the Dutch again, under William the Silent; the British, under Good Queen Bess and those who followed her, including the Lord Protector; and the French, under the Houses of Valois and Bourbon), and greed (everybody).

The enemies of Iberia turned up in the strangest places. We might expect the English to occupy various islands in the Caribbean, although we are somewhat surprised to learn that one of the greatest additions to the First British Empire took place during the tenure of a gentleman who was not even a monarchist. This was Oliver Cromwell,

during whose dictatorship the rich isle of Jamaica was taken in 1655. And we most certainly would not expect to see the enterprising Dutch in Brazil. But they were there, nevertheless, occupying the area around Recife for nearly a quarter of a century—for the record they were striking the first true Brazilian coins there in 1645, precisely half a century before the Portuguese got around to setting up their first real mint at Rio. The French had been in Brazil a hundred years before, but had struck no coins to mark the occasion.

So the islands and bits of the mainland were eaten away. In time, the useful theory of "no peace beyond the line" was conceived by Spain and its enemies. It was a way of ensuring that, regardless of peace treaties in Europe, warfare might continue in the Indies as Spain's competitors attempted to take, and Spain attempted to defend and retake, lands and property as the opportunity appeared.

We are especially interested in the fortunes of one particular group of interlopers, the English, and we shall devote most of the remainder of this book to exploring what they and those who followed managed to do with their particular share of the booty, centering on the future United States of Amer-

Interlopers! Dutch Brazil, six florins, 1646. Courtesy Joseph Lasser.

ica. We shall be particularly interested in how the coinage and currency of this British sphere and the independent state which succeeded it reflect the land and the places where its history was made. But before we conclude this final portion of our prologue, we might glance briefly at some of the monies produced by other places where the interlopers came to stay.

We have already mentioned the Dutch coinage in Brazil. It was unique in one way, unusual in another. First, it consisted entirely of gold: the Dutch appear to have been unable to secure silver bullion for moneying. None of the other coinages of the interlopers consisted entirely of gold, although a number of them were only made in silver. And it was distinctly unusual in another way: the Dutch in Brazil made their coinage from start to finish. They got the gold, refined it, beat it into a thin sheet, cut planchets from that sheet, and then struck the square bits of metal with round dies (they lacked the equipment to make normal, circular blanks—this was an unplanned, emergency coinage). In-

terlopers elsewhere almost always used somebody else's coinage, cutting it up, punching holes in it, removing or adding bits of metal until it came into rough tolerance with legal standards imposed either locally or by the metropolitan governments. In other words, they were cutting and countermarking extant coinage, recycling it for their own commercial purposes. And the coins which they were using were generally Spanish-American and Brazilian.

How could it have been otherwise? The days of a regular supply of coinage to a colony would only come in the nineteenth and twentieth centuries. In the seventeenth and eighteenth, the prevailing concept was that colonies existed to benefit the mother country: money was supposed to flow *to* England or France, not *from*. So if the interlopers wanted a currency, they would have to provide it themselves.

They could not do this from native metallic sources. While Sir Francis Drake may have singed King Philip's beard, he and his successors never succeeded in picking that

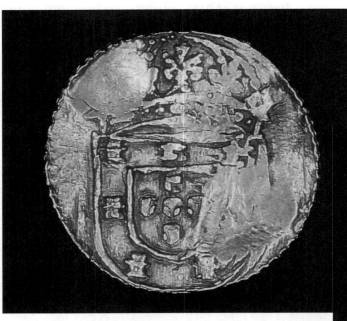

Portuguese gold coin countermarked for use in Brazil during the 1660s. Courtesy the NNC.

gentleman's pocket: the King retained the sources of his gold and silver, even if he lost bits of it after it came out of the ground. And the islands where the English and others settled had no precious metals, for what little had ever existed had been cleaned out by the first two generations of Spanish colonists. In sum, there was only one source of coinage metal to which the latecomers could turn, and this was coinage which already existed. Consequently makeshift mints were set up all across the Caribbean and on the fetid coasts of Guiana, and Englishmen and all the others created a rough and ready monetary supply, one which might have been sneered at at home, but which worked well enough in a local setting.

In a sense, the Portuguese led the way. While they only began minting normal Brazilian coinage in 1695, they began countermarking Portuguese and Spanish-American coinage for colonial consumption as early as 1643. But their experiments were not quickly replicated elsewhere: countermarked coinage was essentially a phenomenon of the last half of the eighteenth century and the first quarter of the nineteenth.

But what a varied phenomenon it was! Cut and countermarked coinage exists with round holes (St. Vincent), heart-shaped holes (Dominica), scalloped holes (Tobago), and octagonal ones (Trinidad). Coins might be wedges, cut from a Piece of Eight like pieces from a pie, issued without countermarks (Barbados), or with one (Tortola), two (Guadeloupe), or more (St. Lucia, St. Vincent). Those countermarks might range from simple designs (an unadorned letter M for Montserrat) to the relatively complex (a fancy D with a star, all within a looped border, for Dominica).

Thus far, we have been speaking of British colonial coins, but the same general range of ideas may be found elsewhere, on the coinage of Dutch Curaçao, Danish St. Croix, French Martinique, and even of Swedish St. Bartholomew. And while this coinage was most commonly issued in silver (if for no other reason than that more silver than gold was struck by the Spanish-American mints),

Mexican Piece of Eight countermarked for use in Jamaica, 1758. The new value was six shillings eight pence. Courtesy the NNC.

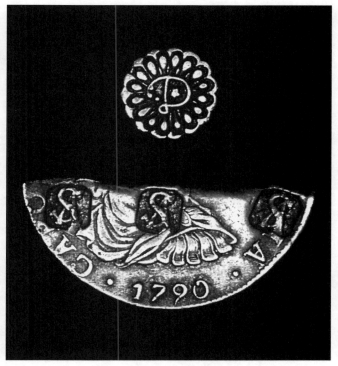

Cut coinage from Dominica (above) and St. Vincent (below), late 1790s. Courtesy the NNC.

we also find it in gold (an area where Brazilian, and not Spanish-American coinage predominates; Brazil was *the* major gold producer during much of the eighteenth century) and copper or billon (an area where anybody's coinage was fair game if it wandered into the neighborhood).

Of course, the most common form of Caribbean coinage wasn't countermarked at all: it was far easier to simply take the Piece of Eight as it was, relying on its well-known designs and its fabled metallic purity to place and retain it in trade. These unmarked dollars circulated at all times and in all places, from Cape Breton to Cape Horn. Wherever they went, they left their mark to a greater or lesser degree; never was their mark more indelible than in those areas which would one day become the United States of America.

Chapter 1

The Thirteen Colonies and their Monies

CHAPTER 1

THE THIRTEEN COLONIES AND THEIR MONIES

British colonization of the future United States began in earnest shortly after 1600, carried forward in a number of ways, by diverse peoples, from a variety of motives. In Virginia, whose first settlement was loyally named Jamestown after the reigning British monarch, economic profit was the primary motive (although the gentlemen who led the new colony soon found to their horror that the only way to make money from Virginia was to actually *work* there, to invest their own sweat in the new land rather than aping the Spanish to the south and forcing others to invest it for them). In Massachusetts, a religious motive—the desire to commune with the Deity in a particular though officially frowned-upon fashion—led to the Pilgrim settlement at inhospitable Plymouth. One of those who came there in 1620 was a quarrelsome indented servant named Edward Doty, who fought the first duel in New England. A few miles to the north, a second settlement was established some ten years later, in 1630. Unlike Plymouth, Boston was a going concern from the very beginning, perhaps because its founders were both people of conscience and people of business. The town would soon be trading in a number of places where it had no business operating—with interesting effects upon America's money.

Economic and religious motives lay behind most of the first colonization attempts, motives which were often intertwined so completely that neither original colonizers nor subsequent historians could separate them. But this simple statement should not blind us to the nature of the fabric of America's early history. The identity, color, and weave of that fabric would always be complex, would shift color and shape over time, and it still does so today.

For example, dissenting Protestants were hardly the only sects represented in the new settlements. Maryland, which was first colonized around St. Mary's City in 1634, was meant as a haven for English Catholics. Lands there were granted by King Charles to the Calverts, Catholic noblemen who had aided the monarch and thus gained his ear. Maryland retained its distinctive flavor through much of the colonial period. The nature of its founding had an interesting effect on early American money as well. Other non-Anglican peoples came over too: Jews were represented by the 1640s at the latest, while Lutherans might be found here as early as the 1630s. In both cases, other European powers held the key.

There was more than one colonizing country along the Eastern Seaboard, and the fabric did in fact contain bold colors other than British red. Swedes penetrated the future Delaware, building Port Christina (the future Wilmington—loyally named after their current monarch), in 1638, holding power there and along the adjacent rivers until 1655. They were ejected from there and adjacent settlements in New Jersey by the Dutch in 1655, but they left a permanent mark on America's history nonetheless, in the form of the humble log cabin.

Those Dutchmen were the main competitors to British colonization. Some of them were associates of the Geoctroyedische Westindische Compagnie (the G. W. C., or United West India Company), the same organization responsible for Dutch Brazil, and they were the main players in the Middle Colonies between the 1620s and the 1660s. In 1626 Peter Minuit purchased Manhattan Island from a local chieftain for trade goods valued at sixty guilders, the rough equivalent of twenty-four Pieces of Eight. While the Dutch concept of property varied signally from that of Native Americans (to whom the buying or selling of what was manifestly a commodity owned by everyone and no one merely indicated the strangeness of their new neighbors), Dutch guns, installed at a tiny fort at the toe of Manhattan Island, underscored the concept—at least until 1664, when Britons with a similar property sense swept the Dutchmen and their fort away. The British ejected them from Delaware and New Jersey that same year, but all three areas long retained an individual and determinedly non-English flavor, including a splendid, distinctly unusual tolerance for non-Christians. The Dutch left another legacy to those who would follow: they had become accustomed to trading in a Native American monetary medium called wampum, to which they were introducing their English neighbors by the end of the 1620s.

By the mid-seventeenth century, the British and their competitors were moving into areas from Maine to Virginia. Settlers looking for economic opportunity and political liberty were advancing along the Connecticut River by the early and mid-1630s. Their counterparts in search of religious toleration were settling that smallest and quirkiest of English American colonies, Rhode Island, just a few years later.

South of Virginia, colonization generally came later. South Carolina was set up as a proprietary colony, an arrangement tending to result in closer ties with the mother country than was usually the case elsewhere. Settlement here was first attempted by the Spanish in the 1520s and by the English a century and a half later. In the meantime, Huguenot refugees from France populated part of the land: the city of Charleston would be established by the English in 1680, but it would long retain a distinctly French flavor from that earlier contact. North Carolina, home of the first and failed English colonial experiment at Roanoke in the 1580s, was one of the last places to be settled. Colonists from Virginia made cautious approaches to the area around Albemarle Sound in the 1650s, but it would not be until the beginning of the eighteenth century that the colony would be placed on a permanent footing, with the founding of the towns of Edenton and Bath. The combination of coastal swamps and hostile Native Americans would long act to deter full European colonization of this area, and the population of North Carolina would long remain modest.

That left Pennsylvania and Georgia. Both were "planned" settlements—unlike many other places, these two areas of British colonization were deliberately organized and selected, brought into existence from a mixture of public and private goals. Pennsylvania was intended in part as a home for adherents of another non-Anglican religious sect facing difficulties at home, the Society of Friends, or Quakers, followers of the saintly George Fox. The Swedes and Dutch were there first, but the pious Quakers had the better of the argument: in 1681, William Penn (to whose father King Charles II of England owed a good deal of money) accepted a royal grant to a vast new domain (which was named after him—Pennsylvania, or Penn's Woods); the new colony's entrepôt was platted the following year. This was Philadelphia. From that time forward, the city, and the proprietary colony whose front door it was, shone as a beacon of hope to the persecuted, a beacon of gain to the economically discontented. One of the latter was a teen-aged printer named Benjamin Franklin, who appeared on its step in 1723. Philadelphia, America, and numismatics would shortly hear a good deal from him.

The motives for founding Georgia were no less laudable. Led by James Oglethorpe, a number of English philanthropists were interested in establishing a haven where debtors might go to get a second chance in life. They expressed their aspirations to the British Government, which was interested in setting up a buffer zone between its established colonies to the north and Spanish Florida to the south. The goals of both groups coalesced in the founding of Savannah in 1733. This, the first city in the new colony, was a planned community in the eighteenth century sense of the term. Its riverfront esplanade, right-angle streets, and many small parks could have only been devised by Englishmen of that era, and to this day Savannah retains a distinctly British flavor while Charleston, which was long its rival, still strikes us as distinctly French.

By the early years of the eighteenth century, British colonization had been under way for five generations. What had resulted was not one single, uninterrupted stretch of British red from Maine to Georgia, but a number of nuclei of varying sizes and fortunes, strung rather like beads on a string—with large spaces between one bead and another. In comparison with the Spanish colonies demographic or even with Brazil, these British lands in the New World could not be called great successes: at a time when the population of New Spain alone stood at perhaps ten million, New England was hard-pressed to come up with more than a tenth of that figure. But notability is not always commensurate with sheer numbers. These new English lands had some memorable accomplishments to their credit, accomplishments which claimed the attention of their contemporaries, the admiration of those to follow. Among their most significant feats was the creation of a monetary system. It was notable because it was essentially based on thin air.

It was created in this fashion because of the lack of an orthodox monetary alternative. Always remember that we are speaking of transplanted Europeans during the first decades of British colonization, and Europeans preferred coins in commerce whenever they could get them. To the south, in the colonies of Portugal and Spain, this preference caused little problems for new settlers. The economic development of Brazil proceeded so gradually that a need for coinage seems never to have reached a crisis point—at least, not until the middle of the colonial period. And in Spanish America, an abundance of silver and gold met the requirement with a vengeance, as we have already seen.

But what of English America? The first colonizers there found no gold, no silver, and even precious little copper, even though they devoted a good deal of effort to searching for these metals. They and their descendants might search all they pleased, but nothing much would be found for over two hundred years. In short, no metal meant no coins. Combined with two other factors, this would mean that the monetary development of the future United States would not proceed on a "normal" and preferred path.

Of the other two complicating factors, the first originated in Europe, the second in America. The European contribution to the monetary problem was a politico-economic theory of national wealth and power called Mercantilism. While parts of the theory were developed by the Spanish and Portuguese, many thinking Europeans elsewhere embraced it and added to its tenets due to the very success achieved by Iberians in the early stages of Europe's expansion overseas. Simply stated, Mercantilism viewed a colony and its mother country in a fixed, monopolistic trading relationship, in which anything of value found in the ground or grown on the land was sent home. Furthermore, anything needed by the colonists which they could not produce themselves, or were not allowed to produce (e.g., for centuries, Latin Americans were discouraged from growing grapes because of complaints from vintners in Spain), had to be sent from the mother country, in ships of the mother country, and paid for in currency of the mother country. In other words, any coins which the colonies managed to accumulate should be remitted to the metropolis in payment for goods received under the closed economic arrangement. If we apply the theory of Mercantilism to the metal-poor English colonies along the Atlantic coast, logic tells us that the British Government would hardly make an effort to export coinage to these shores when it was seeking to extract wealth from them. Also, because trading was legally circumscribed (and British colonial commerce with those lands which had the precious metals surrounded by a host of prohibitions), logic also suggests that the British colonies would remain coin-poor if the British metropolis accepted the Mercantilist idea. And this, of course, it did: hadn't Mercantilism enriched the Spanish and the Portuguese?

Thus the European factor. If New England had remained as economically marginal as La Nouvelle France, no real difficulties might have arisen—it was perfectly possible to conduct a cashless economy in the seventeenth century. But to do so, there must be two conditions: first, the economy in question must be small, and second, the population which employed it must be stable. The American contribution to the monetary crisis was a failure to meet either of these conditions.

Almost from the start, these English colonies were economic and demographic successes, wherein the monetary supply never had a chance of catching up with or surpassing the monetary demand. Far from easily sending coinage back to Britain, people here could have used every spare piece of change which Britain could send. Along with the shortage of native precious metals, this inability of supply to ever overtake demand would shape the story of American numismatics for the first two hundred and fifty years, a period longer than that of American independence. It was even more important than the influence of Mercantilism, because it continued to shape America's money long after the British and their theory had departed its shores. These factors combined would create a unique chapter in the story of numismatics: faced with perpetual lack and growing need, confronted with the very results of their success, the men and women of New England and the other colonies would replicate and create, try, reject, and redesign every monetary form ever invented anywhere else throughout the course of numismatics. But they would conduct their experiments in a matter of years rather than centuries, for their need was great, and always growing.

Their first investigations involved barter: if you don't have something, trade something else to get it. While theory tells us that anything can be swapped for anything else, logic tells us that some commodities have a better chance than others of becoming trading goods. The same criteria (durability, utility, scarcity, etc.) which I mentioned in the opening section held as true for the first colonists as they did for the Native Americans who welcomed them, but arriving Europeans soon developed a distinctive list of trading objects, goods which had preferred value to *them*, in their particular colonizing experiment.

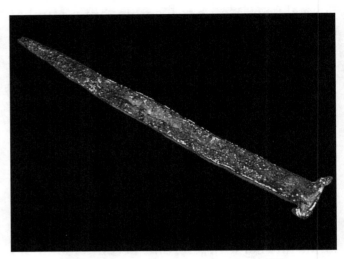

Colonial currency: a nail. Courtesy the NNC.

Their list contained shot and powder, obviously useful in their new circumstances. It also contained nails, which is odd until we stop to think about it for a moment. Nails were obviously easily quantifiable (indeed, people as widely separated as ancient Greeks and tribes in West Africa had employed thin, long pieces of iron in trade, in part because this form of money *was* so easy to measure). Nails were also durable. And they were very scarce in the beginning days of English settlement, because they had to be imported from the old country.

Nails were traded against British currency, a hundred of one size equal to six pence, a hundred of a larger size equal to ten pence, etc. To this day we still use the terms "sixpenny" and "tenpenny" to refer to nails of a particular size. So popular did this exchange medium become that in 1646, the legislature of the colony of Virginia had to pass a law to discourage the burning down of abandoned houses—people were torching them to get the nails!

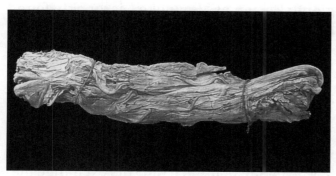

Colonial currency: tobacco. Courtesy the NNC.

Other trade goods had a more direct connection with the land. John Smith and his companions may have come to Virginia to extract instant wealth from the ground, but they failed in this attempt and nearly starved until one of their company found another, more arduous, way to coax money from the soil. In 1612, John Rolfe (who is perhaps better known as the husband of Pocahontas) put in his first crop of tobacco, and the colony was saved. Tobacco had been known in Europe since Columbus' return from his first voyage, for he had witnessed Caribbean Indians nonchalantly smoking the weed in the form of cigars—through their noses. The plant had come to Europe by the beginning of the 1560s, and by the last years of the century tobacco was set to become Europe's latest craze.

The ill-starred Sir Walter Ralegh helped create a demand for the plant, while Rolfe and his fellow gentlemen-turned-farmers helped supply it. Despite counterblasts from moralists ranging from churchmen to a King of England (James I: had he known how much revenue could be obtained from the sale of tobacco to generations of addicts he might have abated his attack!) tobacco was henceforth popular. It made grateful slaves of those who consumed it and paid the bills of those who produced it.

It was inevitable that the plant would quickly assume a monetary role. It did this within seven years of its introduction to Virginia: in 1619 the colony's first legislature granted it a monetary status, fixing its value at three shillings per pound for the best grade, half that for the lower. These generous valuations suggest how popular the commodity had become. That pioneering legislative session also legalized the importation of slaves from Africa, thus thoughtfully ensuring that those who profited from tobacco would soon enjoy the labors of others to actually grow it.

Tobacco's high value would soon descend precipitously. Bear in mind one of the primary conditions for the suitability of a commodity as money: it must be, or must be kept, in short supply. But every member of the Virginia colony soon began growing his own money to take advantage of its high value, and that value inevitably fell. By 1645 the same pound which had brought three shillings in 1619 could scarcely find a buyer at a penny and a half. By the 1680s planters were petitioning the colonial legislature to prohibit the growing of tobacco for a set time, hoping to force the price upward. The lawmakers refused, whereupon a number of irate farmers took matters into their own hands and burned innocent tobacco plants wherever they found them. This elicited a response from the legislature: those harming a tobacco plant could suffer the death penalty! Both sides eventually saw reason, but overproduction would always be a problem with this form of currency.

Its perishability was another. An ideal trading good must also be durable. But tobacco could easily dry out or rot. That being the case, producers would eventually hit upon a system of warehousing prior to shipment to England, wherein paper certificates were issued against the value of the crop, based on quantity and grade. These "tobacco notes" would eventually acquire some of the attributes of money, being exchangeable for other goods in a limited fashion. Like the bill of exchange (which was a paper certificate of indebtedness between one merchant and another, promising payment of a particular sum at a particular time), and like slightly later receipts for another popular colonial product, rice, the tobacco note pointed the direction which American money would finally take.

Colonial currency: wampum. Courtesy the NNC.

The cultivation of tobacco was taken over from Native Americans. So was the trapping of wild animals for their pelts. And this would give colonists another form of commodity money—or rather several forms. While beaver was always the most popular pelt taken, and was the yardstick against other pelts (and other goods, ranging from yards of cloth to thread, hats, shirts, and axes) were calibrated, otter skins were also popular, as were those of foxes, martins, raccoons, and even "mincks." Furs were more popular in frontier areas than elsewhere, and their usage extended from the Atlantic to the Pacific, matching and anticipating the march of European settlement itself.

And there was a final type of commodity money, one with a life of three centuries. This was wampum.

We have discussed the circulation of wampum among those who originated it, Native Americans. Among the new arrivals, the Dutch appear to have taken it up first: they would have obtained it from native tribes on Long Island, which was long a major center of wampum production. A Dutch colonial official named Isaac De Razier carried it to Plymouth Colony in 1627 (where he traded some £50 in beads for maize to get his fledgling colony through a grain shortage). From Plymouth, wampum spread across New En-

gland; known as "Roanoke," it quickly found popularity to the south as well.

Its vogue seems to have increased among new settlers and old ones. That is, the colonists happily embraced the medium as another partial solution to their chronic lack of cash—and the tribes began viewing it with increased favor as well, in part because their new neighbors seemed to take it so seriously. The growing popularity of this exchange medium led to two results which we might have predicted. It was overproduced, and its value therefore declined. And it was adulterated.

When first introduced among Europeans, wampum was tariffed at so many beads to one English penny, in much the same manner as tobacco or nails. Rates varied between colonies: in 1637 it took four white beads to equal a penny in Connecticut, while the rate in Massachusetts was fixed at six. Purple or black beads went for about twice as much as white ones, because the purple component of the shells from which these beads were made was scarcer than the white. Wampum beads were usually traded in strings of 360, called *fathoms*.

This fixed valuation began fraying in the later 1650s. Encouraged by its popularity among both peoples, Native Americans—and soon enterprising Europeans as well—expanded production. Inevitably, wampum's value descended: the colony of Massachusetts Bay revoked its legal tender status in 1661, and other colonies followed suit. The last official use of the medium among Europeans appears to have taken place in the early 1690s, but by then, other monetary expedients were being pressed into service.

If wampum were subject to overproduction, it was also subject to adulteration. This was achieved in two fashions. Counterfeit wampum was being concocted in Europe by the middle years of the seventeenth century and was sent to the New World with other trading goods. And a family of immigrants named Campbell began producing ceramic wampum later in the colonial period (for monetary service among Native Americans beyond the seaboard area), and its operation continued down to the closing years of the nineteenth century—which must be a record of sorts for counterfeit money! Earlier, during the time when wampum was in use along the seaboard, enterprising settlers discovered that white beads could be dyed purple, and the value of one's bank account thereby doubled. A number of homemade tints were devised, one of the most popular being blackberry juice. The white beads were steeped in it, then allowed to dry—and quickly spent, before the tint rubbed off or it rained. Native tribes rarely fell for the adulteration, for they had after all invented the medium in the first place. But it did gull the newcomers often enough.

That grown men were playing childish tricks on each other suggests the monetary desperation in which they found themselves. Pelts, nails, tobacco, and wampum of variable plausibility—all would have been gladly laid aside at the sight of a coin. But no metal for such a coin existed. And even if it did, it must be remitted to England, not retained in America. One locality in the new lands was about to find a way around both limitations, though. That place was the town of Boston, and what Boston did must not only rank as a benchmark in the story of numismatics, but in that of the human spirit as well.

Lightweight Bolivian Piece of Eight, 1647. Coins such as this served as the raw material for Massachusetts coinage. Courtesy the NNC.

In 1652 the colonists of Massachusetts Bay began producing crude coins bearing a fancy NE (for New England) on the obverse and the Roman numerals III, VI, or XII (for three, six, or twelve pence) on the reverse. Where did these upstarts get the raw materials? How did they imagine they could keep their products in circulation in the New World? And as far as that went, how dared they strike coinage, when everybody knew that right was vested in the Crown and nowhere else? In all three instances, the answer involved a thumbing of local noses at Mercantilism and regal pretensions in Great Britain: these colonials, some of them barely off the boat, were already beginning to think like Americans instead of transplanted Englishmen.

They got the silver from illegal trade with the sugar islands of the Caribbean. That area was still largely a Spanish lake. The good people of Boston sent down rum, timber, and grain. The good people of Hispaniola sent back sugar—and coins, mostly Pieces of Eight. These coins should be sent on to Britain, but in practice, many of them were retained in Massachusetts, especially if they were lightweight or of poor silver quality (and in fact the mint of Potosí was currently in the midst of a major scandal, venal minters having adulterated the silver coinage there).

But the acquisition of silver, even its elaboration into an American coinage, would be of minor difficulty compared with keeping the coinage there once it had been minted. Was there a way of making it unattractive to Britons, while ensuring its appeal to Americans?

Indeed there was, and here is where Yankee ingenuity shone forth. An unsung genius (presumably someone connected with the fiscal arm of the colonial government) had an idea. If local minters were to deliberately make their new coins lightweight in British terms, while still expressing their denominations in British currency, they could simultaneously achieve both goals. No London merchant would touch the coins, for he would

Willow Tree coinage, struck between 1653 and 1660, but always dated 1652.

Oak Tree coinage, struck between 1660 and 1667, but always dated 1652 — with one exception.

Pine Tree coinage, struck between 1667 and 1682, but always dated 1652.

have to go to the trouble of melting them down and selling them as bullion. But the Boston merchant would embrace them, for they would form part of a closed monetary system based on familiar coins, the threepences, sixpences, and shillings of the mother country.

It was done: in late May 1652, enabling legislation for the new coinage was passed, and a small mint was set up on the property of John Hull, a local silversmith. He and his partner Robert Saunderson enlisted the services of a Saugus ironmaster for tools and dies, and work got under way.

Their first coins were produced between June and October 1652: they were members of the NE series, of excessive rarity today, whose minting was stopped when it was realized that the tiny devices (produced by small punches rather than complete dies) were easy targets for the clipper and the forger. They were followed by pieces of a more elaborate design, named after the type of tree occupying the central space on their obverses. And all of them were about a fifth lighter than they should be, in comparison with British money.

We call the earliest series the Willow Tree pieces. They were made in tiny numbers between 1653 and 1660, during a time when Hull and Saunderson were just begin-ning to master their craft. The pieces demonstrate that they still had much to learn: they are double- and treble-struck, very rarely show all of the designs on either side, and we call them Willow Trees because the tree on their obverses resembles a willow slightly more than it does anything else! The Willow Trees were followed by Oak Tree shillings and subdivisions (including a tiny twopence, struck for the first and last time). Then came the Pine Tree coins. The Pine Tree shilling is perhaps the most common of our early colonial issues (although none of these first coins has survived in anything more than minute quantities); it is also among the most famous of all American coins, and it will repay a closer look.

On the obverse is what is unmistakably a pine tree; it may be an oblique reference to one of New England's few viable exports at that time, timber for masts for the Royal Navy. Around the tree is the name of the colony, rendered as MASATHVSETS (a spelling which supposedly mimicked the sound of the original Native American name for the region). On the reverse, the remainder of the mint name is spelled out, along with the denomination (XII, for twelve pence or one shilling) and the date.

It is this date which suggests the final element of ingenuity surrounding Massa-

Oak Tree twopence, dated 1662.

chusetts silver coinage. With one exception, it is always rendered as 1652. (The exception is the Oak Tree twopence, dated 1662.) Why that particular date? There are two possible answers. The mint actually was founded in 1652, and perhaps this coin was the first American commemorative. But the second possibility is more likely: the coins were deliberately and consistently dated 1652 to evade British law.

Under that law, the King enjoyed sole right of coinage. But in 1652, there was no King: Royal Charles' head had been separated from his body some three years previously, and Cromwell's Commonwealth of England ruled in royalty's place. Surely regicides would hardly look askance at a Massachusetts coinage, for it could be represented as issuing from the same lofty motives as their own.

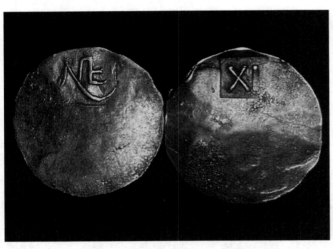

New England shillings, 1652. Courtesy the NNC.

In 1660 the English monarchy was restored. Now there was an even greater reason to retain the 1652 date on the coinage: if a suspicious Briton commented on the odd-looking coin with a tree on one side, an American could answer, "Oh, no, that's not a recent coin. Look at the date; we'd *never* presume to do the King's business for him." The new King, Charles II, saw through the ruse, and if he required proof, the diminutive twopence would have given it. (The fact that this coin alone bore a different date may be explained by the fact that it was so tiny and issued in such modest quantities that it was unlikely that British officialdom would ever come in contact with it.) But King Charles had more important matters on his mind, and he left the upstart coinage alone for the first two decades of his reign. During those years, the Oak Tree pieces were struck (down to 1667), as well as two issues of Pine Tree coins (between 1667 and 1674, and 1675 and 1682: the latter can be distinguished by their somewhat dumpy appearance and were probably made on a screw press rather than on the rocker or sway press which Hull and Saunderson had earlier employed).

Those gentlemen's contract with the Massachusetts General Court expired in 1682, and there seems to have been no talk about a renewal of the agreement. The tiny mint appears to have been working full-bore for the last two years of the contract (as colonial authorities began receiving indications that the Crown was finally about to resume its prerogatives and accordingly hurried their local coiners along). The Crown did reassert its monopoly over the coinage, and a new King, James II, was soon asserting much more than that. James sent over Sir Edmund Andros as the new governor of a centralized, dictatorial administration over all New England. Andros had instructions to bring the region to heel, which might conceivably have included a forced resumption of its earlier use of barter. James was ousted in 1688 and Sir Edmund in 1689, but the prohibition against a local coinage remained in force. And by that time, there would have been no one left to manufacture it: John Hull died in 1683 and Robert Saunderson was in his early eighties. The Massachusetts coinage was never resumed, but this colony was about to make another and even greater contribution to our story.

While Massachusetts was producing its own coinage, others were coping as best they could. A second entity had coinage produced *for* it. This was Maryland, recipient of one of the most enigmatic of all colonial issues. We know why the coinage was made: the Calvert

Maryland shillings, 1658–59. Courtesy the NNC.

family wished to provide convenient money for its co-religionists in Maryland, the circulation of tobacco having become difficult there as elsewhere. We know why the coinage was allowed: Cecil Calvert, second Lord Baltimore, had been granted the right to coin and decided to exercise it in the uncertain days of the Commonwealth. And we even know when it was minted (during the winter of 1658–59), although none of it is dated. But we have no idea by whom it was struck. The members of the series (silver shillings, sixpences, fourpences or groats, threepences, and a "denarium" or copper penny, of which just five are known) are well-struck, and it is commonly suggested that they were made at the Tower of London, along with regular British coinage. But they are far superior to most coinage of the period, and one is a bit hard put to accept the idea that the Cromwells would have allowed pieces with such reminders of nobility to be made at the Tower mint—unless they were the rulers being so honored.

Its case soon becomes even less plausible. During the second half of 1659, one Richard Pight, a clerk at the mint (who happened to hold a commission as informer on counterfeiters) informed on Cecil Calvert, who was arrested on October 4. He was hauled into court the following day, constrained to ex-

plain his coinage. He evidently did a good job, for he lived on until 1675, when a penalty of death would have been a real possibility. All of this suggests a coiner other than the Tower of London, unless one of the Lord Protector's hands was unaware of the activities of the other.

I suggest Ireland as a possible site of the Calvert mint. The fabric of these pieces does not suggest the Tower Mint to me, and a Catholic island would have been a logical and sympathetic place to coin for a Catholic duke. But we may never know for certain, and the mystery still remains for the present.

Ireland is linked to a second series which circulated in the early colonies, although that link is anything but direct. In 1681, a Quaker named Mark Newbie (or Newby) came to America with a number of the faithful. The group wintered at Salem, New Jersey, but in the spring of 1682, it sailed up Newton Creek and finally came to rest in the vicinity of the modern city of Camden. Mark Newbie died there later that year, and his story thus came to an end, except for one thing: reasoning that his fellow colonists would be short of small change, he had carried along a cask containing £30 worth of coppers to distribute upon his arrival. These pieces, farthings and halfpennies, are named after him, called Newbie coppers. They are also known as St. Patrick coppers, for that saint adorns their reverses. And that brings us back to Ireland.

The coppers may not have been struck there—they at least had an English origin, perhaps the Tower, perhaps another mint or mints—but they were struck for Irish consumption. They were originally intended to pay Charles I's Catholic troops, engaged in fighting Cromwell's people in the Ulster Rebellion. The pieces were made sometime in

Mark Newbie's farthing. Courtesy the NNC.

1641 or 1642, and the monarch who adorns their obverses bears a suspicious resemblance to the monarch who had ordered them struck. And the obverse Latin motto, FLOREAT REX, may the King flourish, can only refer to the beleaguered King Charles.

That monarch was defeated, then beheaded, and it became impolitic to use this issue in trade. With the Restoration of 1660, it appeared in commerce once more, both in Ireland and on the Isle of Man. But it had been demonetized in both places by the end of the 1670s. Then Mark Newbie came across these pieces at the beginning of the 1680s and gave them a new lease on life.

They are handsome, their good appearance being augmented by a bit of yellow metal (brass, meant to resemble gold), which was apparently splashed onto the copper during the minting process and so positioned that it

would appear to be giving the King a golden crown. This care suggests a limited mintage, a suggestion belied by the known number of die combinations, over 120 for the farthings alone. It has been suggested that Nicholas Briot was responsible for these pieces. If so, they may have been produced on his roller press. Briot made several attempts to get this apparatus accepted at the Tower Mint and elsewhere without major success. His technology featured a process which struck pieces first in a strip, cutting them into coins later; this technology would indeed have made it slightly easier to position the brass splasher in its correct place. But it has by no means been established that the St. Patricks were created by the roller method: as with so many of the other early colonial issues, we know much less about these pieces than we would like.

The same may be said for a curious issue featuring an elephant on its obverse, intended for British settlements in the Carolinas. We know that much because the reverse of this copper halfpenny token says GOD: PRESERVE: CAROLINA: AND THE: LORDS: PROPRIETORS. It is clearly related to another, rarer issue with a reference to the northern colonies (whose reverse inscription reads GOD: PRESERVE: NEW: ENGLAND). Both pieces are dated 1694, and both pieces are connected to a third—and here is where our mystery begins.

This third token has the arms of London, along with the legend GOD: PRESERVE: LONDON, but no date. Was this token struck prior to the others? Many believe it was, the reverse legend perhaps referring to the plague and Great Fire which beset the English capital in 1665–1666. Others believe that the London token was struck at the same time as the two others, in the mid-1690s, although they are unable to explain the legend in that case.

And what about that elephant? It has been persuasively argued that the beast was put on the obverse by order of the Royal African Company, which had gotten the copper for the issue from West Africa. Certainly golden guineas from the reign of Charles II and his immediate successors bore a tiny elephant to suggest the origins of the metal they contained. But why would the African Company go all the way to the Fever Coast to obtain a metal which was easily available in nearby Cornwall? And why would the Royal African Company be striking tokens for South Carolina and New England? And who struck the tokens, and where? Clearly, we know far too little about this, one of the last seventeenth century British issues with an American relationship.

We know a bit more about another piece, a fleeting reminder of the attempt by James II to achieve a close control over the already-fractious inhabitants of British North America. In the summer of 1688, a handsome coin was authorized by a Royal Patent, struck during the final weeks of James' reign. The new issue would be struck from tin, a most unstable coining material if used alone, but a sop to the miners of tin-rich Cornwall. The coins, bearing an equestrian portrait of the King (and one which would shortly be replicated on an emergency issue struck by the ousted monarch in Ireland), were shipped across the Atlantic, and many of them were moldering even before they reached port. In the inhospitable climes of the New World, they deteriorated still more rapidly. Today an unblemished piece is a major rarity.

We know why these pieces were made, we know who designed them (the artist John Croker), and where they were struck (at the Royal Mint, in the Tower of London), but we are somewhat confused as to their value. The pieces bear the legend VAL. 24. PART. REAL. (value 1/24 real), suggesting they were to be tied in with a Spanish or Spanish-American monetary system rather than a British or British-American one.

But this denomination cannot be equated with anything in common use in Spain, Great Britain, or their colonies. Pieces of a similar size were struck at the Tower by James II and circulated as halfpence, and generations of collectors have assumed that these American coins had the same value, regardless of denomination. But it *would* be satisfying to know what James and his coiners intended.

With James' successors, the story of America's money would take an essential new path, one it would follow for the next two centuries. The new monarchs (William III and Queen Mary, whose claims may have been debatable but whose hearts were unquestionably Protestant) promptly became involved in a war with the Catholic French in Canada. This struggle for control of North America would persist through most of the ensuing three-quarters of a century, and it would eventually leave the English victorious, even as the seeds were being planted for their most resounding defeat.

For us, the essential fact is this: English colonists were expected to do their bit for a war effort which was being waged at least partly for their benefit. The first time this occurred was in 1690 when Britain and France had come to blows during the previous year, and Massachusetts was now asked to pay expenses for a military action against the French in Canada. The order put the colony in a quandary, for there was a scarcity of cash to meet the request. The late silver coinage had been disallowed, any other specie in the area still left the colony as soon as it entered it, and King William's people would hardly accept payment in wampum or furs. What to do?

Someone in the colonial government hit upon an interesting idea: why not issue official paper certificates to hire the troops and purchase the supplies? This scheme would work because the colony and its citizens knew that they would be reimbursed by the Crown at the end of the war. But because that was the case, someone else carried the scheme one further, crucial step: because reimbursement had been promised and everyone knew it, and because the paper would therefore circulate as readily as coinage, *why not leave it in circulation rather than redeem it at the end of the war*? Everyone would know that it *could* be exchanged for specie if absolutely necessary—and so it could continue to circulate at par, in the process augmenting cash in a cash-strapped economy.

It was done. In 1690–91, two issues with an aggregate face value of £40,000 were printed and circulated. The notes were receivable by the colonial treasurer in payment of taxes at a five percent premium, which was another way of ensuring their popularity and use. The paper money practice soon spread elsewhere (at first to pay for wars, later for many other purposes), and a new chapter in the global story of numismatics was under way.

Massachusetts, two shillings six pence (illegally raised to twenty shillings), 1690–91. Courtesy the NNC.

Americans were by no means the first people to devise and employ paper money. The Chinese had been sporadically issuing notes since the Sung period, and perhaps as early as the T'ang (618-907 A.D.). They were still doing so late in the thirteenth century when a traveler named Marco Polo saw the practice and reported it back to Europe. But Europeans would not take up paper just yet: their economies were growing, but they were by no means large enough or global enough to require a cheap and safe substitute for coin. Still, goldsmiths' notes and bills of exchange kept the concept alive through the ending of the Middle Ages, and the beginning of the Renaissance.

When paper finally came to Europe, it first did so through the medium of the private, note-issuing bank. The first was the Stockholms Banco, chartered in 1661, defunct by 1666. The Bank of England followed in 1694, the Bank of Scotland shortly thereafter, and by the middle years of the eighteenth century, the private bank which circulated its own money was a prominent feature of the European economic landscape.

But the *public* note-issuing bank was something else again, and here is where Americans entered the picture. They were the first people in the Western world to circulate state-issued and -supported currency, and they would use it more devotedly and more consistently than any other people down to 1914. They had little choice if they were to keep their economies alive and growing.

Here is another important attribute of America's early paper money, one which it would carry for most of the next two hundred fifty years. While it started out as a war measure (and most of the first issues of the individual colonies were indeed defense-connected in one way or another), it was soon recognized for what it was and for what it might be: the greatest single economic spur which ever came our way.

Georgia, one pound, 1769 (proceeds of which went to rebuild the Tybee Island lighthouse). Courtesy the NNC.

Paper could be used to provide local economies with the capital necessary for their development. The most common method of issuing such notes was through complicated schemes involving public loan banks. A colony's legislature would designate a Loan Office, staffing it with Commissioners who made loans of non-interest bearing paper money to selected individuals, with real estate or silver plate put up as security against the loans. These debtors paid interest on the loans they had received (even though the notes loaned them did not pay a premium); such interest paid the salaries of the Commissioners, and whatever was left over could be used for other public expenses. Under these schemes and under much simpler arrangements involving the issue of Bills of Credit, public expenditures for matters deemed in the public interest, from the building of a courthouse or a jail, to a new lighthouse for Tybee Island off Savannah, to the relief of the poor of Philadelphia, all got taken care of, and an ever-expanding economy received its lifeblood into the bargain.

Paper was scarcely an unmixed blessing. Some of the colonies issued more notes than they had the ability or the intention of redeeming, to the chagrin of their and other colonies' wealthier citizens and to the annoyance of the King and his Ministers. The latter made periodic attempts to restrain the more exuberant of the issuers, passing successive Acts of Parliament whose constant repetition suggests their ineffectiveness. But the fact that some colonies issued more paper with less backing than others suggests a rather curious fact about money in early America: there was not one currency system but thirteen, all of which fluctuated against each other and against specie. The chaotic currency system must have made life miserable for colonial bookkeepers, but it was obviously better than no currency system at all.

Another of paper's attributes posed a threat to everyone in the community: under current technological conditions, early paper currency was very easy to counterfeit or adulterate.

There were only two practical methods of production available to the eighteenth-century printer. He could print his colony's notes from an engraved metal plate on a flatbed press, wherein the design cut into the inked plate could be transferred onto paper as a raised, colored line, or he could create money on an ordinary printing press, pressing inked lead type set into a printer's chase downward onto a piece of paper, leaving behind an impression of the type. Neither method was perfect, nor was either free of problems. The engraved method produced an admirably fine line, one very difficult to replicate on the outside. But because the plates from which it was done were made of copper (for no one had yet devised a way of engraving on steel), and because copper was soft, those plates were only good for a limited number of "pulls" before retouching or reengraving became necessary. When this was done, the utter consistency which lies at the heart of any good security printing system was lost.

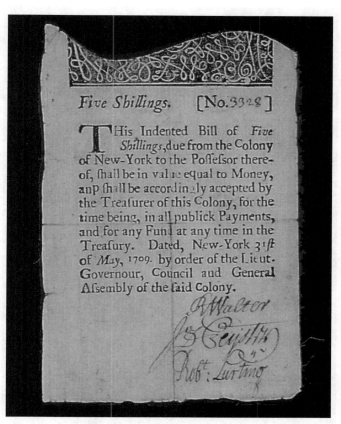

New York, five shillings, 1709; note the indentation along the top margin. Courtesy the NNC.

The typeset method allowed a more generous number of prints, but those prints were far easier to mimic illegally. Indeed, in the early years of America's paper money, virtually *any* crooked country printer could make a plausible counterfeit of any typeset note—and a good many of them did so.

The colonies knew that their products were vulnerable, and they did what they could. They employed the best artists they could find to engrave copper plates. There is an interesting connection between American paper money and American silversmith-engravers from the beginning through the end of the eighteenth century and even beyond. Artists ranging from John Coney to Paul Revere and eventually Jacob Perkins adorned our engraved notes with fancy borders and vignettes of varying competence, all in an effort to render them safer.

Early issuers also used the indenture. Here, a variably wavy line was cut between a numbered note and its stub in a book kept at the governmental seat. To redeem the note in cash, the tender had to make an exact physical fit between his note and the stub with the same number, which was usually difficult after a note had enjoyed even limited circulation.

As time went on, it became apparent that the typeset method must predominate, because only it could keep pace with the steady economic growth which paper money was helping to inspire. But it must somehow be made safer, more difficult to replicate on the outside. Colonial printers adopted fancy engraved border and letter cuts, which they added to their batteries of type. They experimented with paper and inks. Most of their names have long since been forgotten, but we know one of them very well. He is Benjamin Franklin, whom we last met at the gates of Philadelphia. His story and that of America's early currency are virtually syn-

Pennsylvania note featuring one of Benjamin Franklin's nature prints, 1739. Courtesy Joseph Lasser.

onymous although we rarely think of him in this context.

Franklin had previous experience as a printer in Massachusetts and London. In 1728 he established his own printery in Philadelphia, and by 1731 had been given his first contract to print paper money, for the colony of Pennsylvania. The firm which he founded would be a leader for the next half century, printing notes for his home colony, the colonies of Delaware and New Jersey, and finally for an entire country, the United States of America.

But the latter was far in the future, and Franklin's early experiments in security printing gave no hint as to what was in store. He experimented with indentures and fancy engraved border cuts, but so did everyone else. He tinkered with special paper, but that was done elsewhere as well. And he was sometimes too clever by half. In 1739, he printed the first of several issues for his adopted home in which the colony's name was deliberately misspelled. Franklin reasoned that, if he spelled Pennsylvania "Pensilvania" or an equally incorrect variant, forgers would assume that *his* note was a counterfeit and correctly spell the colony's name on their own products. But the counterfeiters saw through his innocent foolery, and every time he tampered with the name of Pennsylvania, they loyally matched him, note for note.

Out of Franklin's delvings into the mysteries of paper money came one expedient which actually worked: the nature print. The same 1739 notes whose obverses misspelled the colony's name featured reverses upon which there appeared what looked like a delicate engraving of leaves. But this was no engraving: Franklin had devised a way of taking real leaves, making a thin, positive lead cast from them, then nailing the cast into a printer's chase along with normal type.

Suddenly the advantages of the engraved and typeset printing methods came together, fineness of line married to the capability of mass production. The lead plate, or cliché, which Franklin employed could be used and reused for thousands of impressions (and even carried over and recycled to much later issues), because the positive cast was not subject to the same sorts of abrasion as was the negative relief of an engraved line on a copper plate. Franklin's new invention proved a godsend to his own printery and to others, with whom he shared his secret on a zealously controlled basis. But it proved a greater godsend to the average citizen, who could henceforth be a good deal more comfortable about the money he carried in his pocket. Forgers never caught on to Franklin's methodology, and indeed, it would not be until the 1960s that a researcher named Eric P. Newman would discover what Franklin had done, and how. With the nature print, the American colonial note achieved its zenith of artistry and security.

The year 1750 is a good time to pause for a moment, to review the nature of America's money during the best years of the colonial period. As I have said, paper lay at its heart: by that year, twelve of the thirteen colonies either had issued paper or were currently doing so, and the thirteenth, Virginia, would join the parade in 1755. But paper was only the most prominent of non-commodity elements (and we do well to remember that an amazing amount of barter still went on, and not all of it in the back country). What were some of the others?

There was coinage, of course—when it could be had. Great Britain occasionally sent over specie, payment for American participation in its ongoing saga with the French. A large number of halfpennies and farthings arrived on these shores in that very manner in 1749, part of a remittance to Massachusetts for that colony's recent expedition which had captured Cape Breton from the French. Much of the rest of the remittance was made up of silver coin, which likely flowed back to England in short order. But the coppers did stay in America.

The colonists used English money whenever they could find it, but with two exceptions. Back in 1722, William Wood had received two contracts from King George I to strike base-metal money for Ireland, and for the English colonies in America. Wood had to pay a £10,000 bribe to the King's mistress, the Duchess of Kendal, to obtain that lady's help in getting the contract past her paramour; this bribe and others meant that if Wood were to make a profit from his contracts (which was of course why he had solicited them in the first place), anything he put into circulation in Ireland or America would have to be distinctly overvalued.

Wood set to work. He enlisted the services of a talented designer (perhaps John Croker, but historians are uncertain), and set up mints in various places in London and possibly Bristol. His coins were handsome: the Irish ones featured a seated figure of Hibernia, the American ones a splendid open rose; their common obverse was a right-facing portrait of the King. They were well-struck in a handsome alloy which Wood had invented, which he called Bath metal. The alloy consisted of three-quarters copper, slightly less than one-quarter zinc, and a tiny amount of silver (not nearly enough to make the coins struck from it circulate at their stipulated value). The Irish pieces were summarily rejected as soon as they arrived, refused from a combination of outraged nationalism and anger over their short weight. The great satirist Jonathan Swift led the charge, with his bitter series of Drapier's Letters, a smear campaign against William Wood and those who had hired him. Some of the "Hibernia" pieces were later foisted on the colonies, where they met a somewhat better reception than did Wood's coins specifically struck for American consumption.

The latter consisted of twopenny, penny, and halfpenny pieces, called the "Rosa Americana" coinage from their reverse legend and type. These pieces were less than half the weight they should have been. But more to the point, the Crown had not bothered to consult local assemblies before putting shipping the coins to New England and New York. Colonials refused to accept them, and one legislature issued emergency parchment money for one, two, and three pence even *before*

Wood's coinage arrived. This was Massachusetts, and its angry reaction (and that of its fellows) in this minor instance augured much trouble to come. The Rosa Americana coinage was never effectively put into circulation in the North (although it did enter commerce in the South somewhat later). Its poor reception persuaded Wood to suspend production early in 1724.

The colonials would use ordinary English money without demur, but they would use anyone else's as well. While the theory of Mercantilism would have preferred that any coinage in circulation here be British, practice found Americans trading all over the world, bringing back foreign coinage as they did so. Provided the coinage was of good gold or silver, it would circulate in the colonies by weight, and elaborate tables were prepared and published, enabling businessmen to calculate what a Portuguese gold "johannes" or "joe" ought to weigh, and how much it was worth against other people's money (it weighed about an ounce, and it passed for £5.15. in local money in Pennsylvania in 1751). While Americans would use anything—and frequently did, from silver French *écus* to Turkish golden *zeri mahbubs*—they were coming to prefer one particular foreign coin over others, and they were coming to prefer it over anything British as well. This was the Piece of Eight.

By now, they knew it as the "Mexican dollar" (because most of those coming their way originated at the busy mint at Mexico City) or the "Spanish milled dollar" (because Spain had introduced coining machinery to the Americas by this time, using it to strike the Piece of Eight). The coins it struck and Americans used were now indistinguishable from other eighteenth-century issues, save for one thing, their marvelous, evocative designs.

The obverse of the new Piece of Eight featured a splendid Baroque crowned shield, along with the name and titles of the King of Spain, but it is the reverse which claims our attention. There, the Pillars of Hercules (which had been appearing on Spanish-

Lima, Piece of Eight or eight reales, 1753. Courtesy the NNC

American coins since the 1530s, proclamation of the New World origins of the silver they contained) now flanked two globes, rendered in astonishing detail, with waves of the sea beneath. Around the design appeared the motto VTRAQUE VNUM ("both worlds are one"). And around the two pillars were placed two ribbons with a second motto, PLUS VLTRA ("more [lands] beyond"). It has been suggested that the dollar sign ($) was inspired by the right-hand ribbon. It has also been suggested that the sign originally started out as a "P" with an "s" on its upstroke, an abbreviation for "peso," as the Piece of Eight was also known. Either explanation hints at the importance of this coin to the ongoing story of American numismatics.

Here and there, people were now beginning to reckon their money in terms of Mexican dollars instead of sterling. We should not be surprised: the American colonists had been using the Piece of Eight since the very beginning, and they were now more familiar with it than with several members of the British system, including that nation's closest equivalent, the "crown." We know of the change from one system to another by the fact that various colonies begin printing paper money denominated in dollars rather than pounds. Massachusetts led the way in

this very year of 1750, its notes backed by a deposit of Pieces of Eight it had recently received. Other colonies would eventually follow—in part because the denomination would soon have a new appeal, that of nationalism.

In addition to foreign coins, to paper money, to "country pay" or barter, a few other odds and ends made up America's money at mid-century. There were several issues of domestic tokens, one in Virginia, another in Connecticut, and a third in Pennsylvania.

The Virginia issue is known from precisely two specimens, brass shilling tokens from the town of Gloucester dated 1714. We know nothing about the reasons for the issue, which seems to have been the idea of two local landowners, Christopher Righault and Samuel Dawson.

Higley tokens, 1737. Courtesy the NNC.

We know a bit more about the second issue, from Granby, Connecticut. In 1737 an enterprising owner of a copper mine in the region issued threepenny tokens denominated THE VALUE OF THREE PENCE. When his neighbors complained that his tokens were overvalued, he changed his obverse legend to VALUE ME AS YOU PLEASE, but still retained the III for three pence! The tokens' maker was Samuel Higley. He perished en route to England with a shipload of copper in May 1737, but his brother John appears to have taken over the mint, striking undated pieces and a few dated 1739. We have no idea of the original extent of the Higley issues, but eight obverse dies and five reverses are known. Because most show no signs of breakage, the mint's output could have been fairly extensive. Yet its tokens remain excessively rare today, for Higley's copper was so pure that it was frequently recycled into other uses.

The Pennsylvania issue came about in 1766, a product of the furor over the Stamp Act. The maker was James Smither, a British gunsmith who had just emigrated to Philadelphia, and he poured all of the anger and frustration felt by the colonials into his "halfpennies" and "farthings," which may have begun as commemorative medalets but which ended as part of the monetary supply. The portrait on the obverse is of William Pitt the Elder, one of the voices of reason on the British side during the Stamp Act crisis. His more famous son would eventually become Prime Minister in the 1780s, just in time to deal with an infant United States, created in part by those very policies of coercion which the father had deplored.

Added to these American tokens was an import, which began with one message and ended with another. In 1760, an Irish button maker named Roche struck halfpenny and farthing-size copper tokens with the words VOCE POPULI surrounding the head on the obverse, and the word HIBERNIA surrounding a representation of Ireland on the reverse. Mr. Roche probably intended the obverse to remind Dubliners of the deposed Catholic Stuart regime or the virtues of home rule, for the portrait has been identified with the two Jacobite Pretenders, while the legend is Latin for "by the voice of the people." But Roche's tokens were eventually shipped to America in large numbers, and colonists there embraced them because their obverse sentiment now seemed appropriate to their own struggles against Mad King George.

Regardless of odds and ends, the primary circulating medium in America was now paper money. Americans had used it to pay for wars on behalf of England, and they were about to use it to fight a war *against* England. And when they did so, that previously trustworthy medium would betray their confidence.

Pitt tokens, 1766. Courtesy the NNC.

CHAPTER 2

TIMES THAT TRY MEN'S SOULS: THE WAR FOR INDEPENDENCE AND ITS AFTERMATH

CHAPTER 2

TIMES THAT TRY MEN'S SOULS: THE WAR FOR INDEPENDENCE AND ITS AFTERMATH

Of all of the world's wars for national sovereignty, that which created the United States of America was among the most confusing and complex. It had many of the attributes of a *civil* war, because neighbor fought neighbor, fallings-out came to blows, and old scores got settled. The war was confusing as to who made up which side, and why. There was a prominent antiwar party in London, just as there was in Philadelphia, even Boston. It has been observed that a third of the American people were ardent patriots, another third remained stubbornly loyal to the mother country, while the final third had no opinion and scrambled to get out of the way of the other two. This observation grossly oversimplifies matters, but there is a grain of truth to it all the same.

The war was generally more popular in New England than it was in the South—but the new nation's greatest general was a Virginian. And the war was fought to free a people. But which one? Certainly not Native Americans, certainly not African Americans: the future status of these two groups occasioned sincere soul-searching, but it was finally agreed that they would occupy no places at the victory table to be spread once the war was won. And certainly not women—although they might partake of the banquet as guests of their husbands. Indeed, this was a most confusing war...

At bottom, we do not even know when the complaining, which is the perennial practice and right of any colonial people, achieved critical mass, reached a point which might finally yield a bid for independence. We think we know when it began to accelerate: after the final victory against the French in 1763, when Britons sought to enlist American resources to help pay for the war, and Britons

and Americans fell to quarreling over the spoils the war had won. In this way of thinking, the opening salvo was the Proclamation Act of 1763, wherein a young king George III drew a line from one end of the Appalachian Chain to the other and forbade settlers to cross it. Americans were angered (and worthies like Daniel Boone were soon ignoring the line anyway), but the crisis over the Sugar Act (1764) and the much greater furor over the Stamp Act (1765), both of which were seen as revenue-raising measures by Britons, intolerable affronts by Americans, kept the pot at a boil.

All of this is true enough, but it still does not tell us *when* the mutual estrangement really began. And to find that out, we would have to go back to the very beginning. The earliest settlers found that English ways of doing things did not always work in an American setting: they discovered that makeshift, local expedients might actually serve better than orthodox, imported ones, and when they complacently told their cousins of their discoveries, their cousins branded them hayseeds and hicks.

We have seen this sort of mentality at work in American numismatics, and indeed money is one of the best windows into what was going on, views into a slow process by which transplanted Englishmen were becoming Americans. We have seen it with the Pine Tree shilling, and we have especially seen it with paper money. Give such a people one and one-half centuries in which to evolve in new directions, and there is virtually no chance that they will *not* strike out on their own at one point or another.

But they would still do so with mixed feelings when the time finally came. The estrangement reached its flash point in the

New Jersey, six pounds, 1776 (detail of the face). Courtesy the NNC.

New Jersey, six pounds, 1776 (face). Courtesy the NNC.

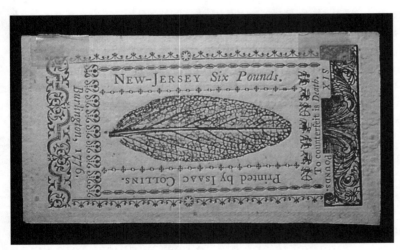

New Jersey, six pounds, 1776 (back). Courtesy the NNC.

spring of 1775, when royalist governor Thomas Gage of Massachusetts sent British regulars to Concord to seize military supplies stored there by the Americans. Alerted by Paul Revere and William Dawes (Revere would go on to many different activities, including engraving Massachusetts and New Hampshire currency, but Dawes actually got through with the message) Americans assembled on the morning of April 19 on Lexington Green and fired the "shot heard round the world." But not all of their fellow colonists agreed with their stance, nor did all Britons agree with that of the Redcoats who opposed them. On both sides of the Atlantic, war fever would take some time to build up, clarify, and capture the popular imagination. And it would never monopolize thinking in either place.

The mixed messages sent and received during this first year or so of the conflict are admirably reflected on one of the last colonial notes, a New Jersey £6 issue of March 25, 1776. We may view this piece of paper on several levels. It is aesthetically pleasing with its combination of fine engraving and precise typesetting. It is also an excellent example of the most advanced American security printing practices then available, with fancy type and an elaborate vignette of the arms of King George on the face and one of Franklin's nature prints on the back. But let us go deeper and see what else this note may teach us.

It ostensibly proclaimed loyalty to a King, but it was actually a product of local authorities who were in revolt against that very monarch. Those same authorities would soon be rejecting the sterling denomination as unpatriotic, and a new *state* of New Jersey would shortly be issuing paper money whose values would be expressed in terms of dollars.

And this currency tells us still more. One of the signers of the issue was John Hart, who would soon be affixing his signature to another, somewhat more important document, the Declaration of Independence. And finally, back to those borders on the face. If we look very closely at the one on the left, we can barely make out the letters of the name RITTENHOUSE (David Rittenhouse, who engraved the cut, eventually became the first director of the United States Mint). And so this note faces both ways and suggests divided loyalties. But it also suggests something else: this was how Americans would pay for their war.

They would have to, especially at the beginning. While military aid might in time be forthcoming from Britain's enemies France and Spain—and golden *onzas* and silvery *écus* come to America along with the soldiers and arms—the insurgents would first have to prove that their unaided cause was a going concern and had a chance of defeating England (or was at least capable of holding on until that country gave way). Americans in fact were experiencing the first law of credit: you can only get it if you can prove you don't need it. This cautious attitude on the part of

Britain's former and potential enemies meant that American money would have to pay for an American war—at least for the present, and perhaps for good. As I have already suggested, the form that money would take must be paper, for there was really no other possibility.

This was all well and good, but Americans might have countered with two observations. They had been able to pay for previous wars through the issue of paper, so why not this one? And if the war were short, paper would serve to finance it well enough. There were two unanswerable responses which would dash these hopes.

The first should have been obvious even in 1775: the reason why paper money had worked for prosecuting earlier campaigns was that Great Britain had directly or indirectly stood behind the currency being issued. The mother country was scarcely likely to do so in this case unless Americans succeeded in invading, defeating, and occupying it, extracting such payment by force. Not even the most ardent patriot could have expected this scenario to take place.

The second was becoming obvious by the end of 1776. Another reason why paper money had worked as a war measure was that earlier American participation in wars had been limited and short-lived. But this war would be different: it would go on year after year and would involve enemy occupation of many of the most productive portions of the upstart nation, including several of its largest cities. What Americans needed was a short, victorious war, but what they would get was a long, inconclusive one. Their paper money would faithfully reflect their dawning realization that there was a wide and growing gap between necessity and reality.

The insurgents did well enough for the first year or two: they had caught the British by surprise and had soon taken most of New England, which would remain their strongest base through the remainder of the conflict. But they failed in a bid to bring the blessings of liberty to the remainder of British North America, and despite the urgings of Benjamin Franklin and other leaders, Canada would remain in British hands.

And the tide elsewhere began to move against them. They lost New York City in 1776, their General Washington being soundly defeated at the battle of Long Island that August. And the same British adversary, Sir William Howe, took the national capital of Philadelphia a year later. A striking victory at Saratoga (in October 1777) would eventually mean a favorable turning for the war, because it would embolden France and Spain to finally enter the conflict on America's behalf. But it produced little of concrete benefit just now, and Washington had his hands full simply keeping his tiny army in being during the miserable months spent at Valley Forge in the winter of 1777–78.

America's money reflected all of this. In the spring of 1775, the colonies (or states, as they soon began calling themselves) began the issue of paper currency to pay for their portions of the fighting. So did a new, ad hoc national government, whose modest, tempo-rary powers would eventually be made law under the Articles of Confederation. This central government issued what it called Continental Currency: Benjamin Franklin's old firm (he had taken on a partner named Hall before selling out entirely, and Hall had engaged a partner of his own named Sellers) printed the notes, which were denominated in terms of "Spanish milled dollars."

Continental Currency may be examined from a number of directions. It bore allegorical vignettes with Latin mottos, suggested by Benjamin Franklin himself. It came in odd denominations, eventually ranging from one-sixth of a dollar to eighty-five dollars. This spread makes sense if we remember that, in an economy essentially paper-powered, odd denominations would be necessary for making change; we shall see the phenomenon in later American paper money too.

The fractional notes printed under the resolution of February 17, 1776, deserve a particularly close scrutiny. They featured obverse and reverse graphics suggested by

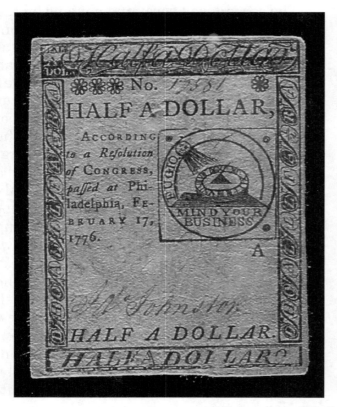

Continental Congress, half dollar note, 1776. Courtesy the NNC.

Franklin and cut by a New Jersey engraver named Elisha Gallaudet. Their sundial with its motto is pure Franklin, as are their linked rings, but they are most interesting because of what happened next.

The Continental Congress had hopes of issuing a coinage as symbol of its sovereignty, as a bolster to local morale, and as a backing for Continental Currency. When it came time to print the fifth issue of national paper (under the resolution of July 22, 1776), the dollar note was deliberately omitted, because Congress had a replacement for it in mind—a Continental dollar coin, struck from silver provided by the French. The coin was authorized, and Elisha Gallaudet was set to preparing dies for the new issue. He used the motifs, the sundial and the linked rings, from his earlier fractional currency.

The national government had no mint at this time, so Gallaudet set up his own facility, either in his hometown or in nearby Philadelphia. He made a few patterns in silver, a few more in brass, and more still in pewter (the latter alloy looked enough like silver to give a good idea of the appearance of the future coinage, but was at the same time soft enough not to damage his dies). Then the project ground to a halt. No French silver was forthcoming, and it soon became impractical to issue a dollar coin in any metal.

Some final observations about Continental Currency may be made. The currency was issued in a number of places, reflecting the shifting fortunes of the patriot cause. While the first and last series were from Philadelphia, the original site of the national government, one in 1777 was circulated from Baltimore, while another in 1778 came from York, Pennsylvania—places to which the government had been forced to flee ahead of British troops. The York issue is particularly interesting, because it leads us to a major problem with Continental Currency: it was extensively counterfeited. It was forged by Americans, and there was nothing particularly new about that. But it was also forged by Britons, and by Britons acting in an official capacity. And that *was* new.

In 1777–78, the forces of King George still occupied New York City—and indeed would remain there for another five years. Someone hit on a novel idea: why not hurt the patriot war effort by sending counterfeit currency into its economic bloodstream? The idea looked promising, and it was soon put into practice.

Genuine Continental Currency (above) and British counterfeit (below). Courtesy the NNC.

A sloop was anchored in New York Harbor with a printery on board. Counterfeit Continental Currency was created, signed, and dispersed. Anybody wanting it could row over to the sloop and carry it off for a nominal sum, and it could also be procured in the city from a shadowy gentleman calling himself "Q.E.D." The forgeries were fairly deceptive (Franklin's nature print remained as the sole practical defense; the Britons tried to duplicate its appearance with engraving but never quite succeeded), and the national government was sufficiently worried about them to introduce bicolor (red and black) printing in 1779. But by then, its notes were hardly worth counterfeiting anyway; nor were those of the states.

Under prevalent political theory, those states were as fully sovereign as the nation itself. As the issue of money has always been viewed and jealously guarded as an exposition of sovereignty, the states could and did issue their own paper money. Their notes fared no better than those of the central government. In both cases, an inflationary spiral was under way by the early autumn of 1777, as a military stalemate seemed to be coming into existence. While British armies could not finally defeat General Washington, he could not finally defeat them either. The war gobbled up ever-increasing numbers of men and ever-larger quantities of matériel, and the only way of paying for everything was to resort to the printing press.

If we assume that at the time of the first issue of federal and state paper in the spring of 1775 one dollar in national or North Carolina paper could purchase one Mexican Piece of Eight, we see matters as they were for the first twenty months of the war. By the beginning of 1777, Continental Currency is still standing firm, but that of several states is now slipping: it now takes $1.50 in Maryland or Virginia notes to purchase that same dollar coin.

But the autumn of that same year is the crucial point: by October, issues of the states range from a ratio of 1.09:1 to 3:1, and the value of Continental Currency has now descended as well, down to 1.10:1. This is worrisome, but hardly fatal if it stops there.

But it does not stop there. By March 1779, even though French and Spanish aid is coming in, and even though the British are now permanently out of Philadelphia and the Americans are permanently in much new land in the Northwest, state and federal currency alike has slipped to around ten-to-one against the Piece of Eight. By now, the Continental Congress is printing the new, safer bicolor notes, but it is increasingly unable to persuade anyone to accept them. The states have no better fortune with their issues, and paper continues to slide. By April 1780, the ratio of Continental Currency to the Spanish Dollar is forty-to-one, and the national government has decided not to issue any more.

This is just as well, because by that time, it has circulated nearly a quarter-billion dollars' worth of paper. The states which continue to print money (and most do: what other choice have they?) see it fall to a hundredth, and finally a thousandth, of its stated specie value. By then, they have printed as much money as the federal government, meaning that there is enough paper in circulation to purchase every house, factory, and farm in the new republic several times over—if there were anyone foolish enough to take this currency at face value.

We must tell of the fate of all these state notes, along with their federal cousins, but let us examine them for a moment before we do so. They will repay our scrutiny.

Both state and federal currency provide constant reminders of a major fact of early American life: in a new nation with a population of barely three million (and only a fraction of that actively favoring independence), a remarkable amount of doubling in brass was bound to take place, in money as everywhere else. We have seen earlier instances of the phenomenon. John Hull was a silversmith, but he was also Massachusetts' first moneyer. Benjamin Franklin was a printer of newspapers and books, but he was also a printer of paper, and a scientist, philosopher, etc. The Revolutionary period acted as a forcing ground for this sort of activity, positively coercing people with a mastery of one area to try their luck in another. Nathaniel Hurd and Paul Revere of Massachusetts had been silversmiths and now became currency engravers. So did Gabriel Lewyn and Thomas Sparrow of Maryland. And a Carolina artist named Thomas Coram, who was not making much money on canvas, would turn to copper plates and make a good deal more, for a state rather than for himself.

Such artisans did their bit for the war effort. And in a neat sharing of labor, many people better known in a military capacity signed some of the state and national notes their artist friends were creating. For instance, Anthony Morris, Jr. signed Continental Currency in 1775 and 1776, but he is more famous as a soldier (he finally died at the battle of Princeton in 1777); Tench Tilghman signed an issue of Continental Currency in 1776, but history knows him better as General Washington's aide-de-camp, where he served in virtually every military action down to the end of the war; and a gentleman named Daniel Roberdeau (who signed Pennsylvania currency shortly before the Revolutionary War) performed essential work in a host of defense-related occupations ranging from outfitting privateers to working a lead mine on behalf of the national cause.

Other signers of insurgent currency found autographic fame in other areas. We have mentioned John Hart, signer of the Declaration of Independence, who affixed his name to 1776 notes for New Jersey. He was joined by other signers of that historic document, such as William Ellery, who signed 1776 notes for Rhode Island; Lyman Hall, who signed money for Georgia in 1782; James Wilson, who signed Continental Currency issues in 1778 and 1779; and a host of other worthies, framers of the Articles of Confederation, the United States Constitution (two Pinckneys, for example, both of whom had left earlier marks on the paper money of South Carolina), and even a few graying veterans of the Stamp Act Congress of 1765. The fact that these gentlemen signed these notes should not be taken lightly: they stood behind them, had pledged their lives, fortunes, and their sacred honor to the defense and the success of the new states and new nation which had printed this money.

In a crisis, money can serve functions beyond the purely economic. One is the molding of public opinion, the fostering of popular support for a war effort. Paper is a logical medium for such a function, because its large, rectangular format affords ample space for expression of ideas on a familiar canvas. These ideas may be simple and bold, and they may even be sequential and fairly involved. Americans would use their paper money to display and inculcate both types of idea.

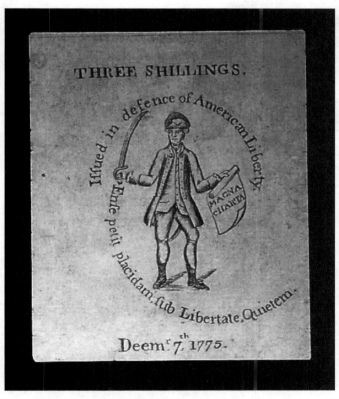

Massachusetts, three shillings, 1775.
Courtesy Joseph Lasser.

Massachusetts, thirty shillings, 1776.
Courtesy Joseph Lasser.

One of the earliest and simplest attempts to sway public sentiment was undertaken by Paul Revere, who created a series of notes for Massachusetts in 1775 and 1776. Collectors call them the "sword in hand" money because of the armed insurgent on the backs. Revere would use this figure to reflect and foster the hardening of colonial sentiment in favor of independence.

Look closely at the scroll carried by the first patriot on a 1775 note. It says MAGNA CHARTA: this soldier is fighting to defend the rights of all free-born Englishmen, including those in the British colonies, rights enshrined in the thirteenth-century docu-ment. Now look at the scroll carried by his counterpart of 1776. It uncompromisingly calls for INDEPENDANCE: everything had changed between the first and second issue of these notes.

As I mentioned, Continental Currency employed inspiratory designs suggested by Benjamin Franklin. The vignettes were dignified, stressing themes of unity and perseverance—and it helped if you knew Latin, because their mottoes were rendered in that language. Notes of the states might spout Latin inscriptions as well, as did those of South Carolina. Thomas Coram created a marvelous series there in 1779 with Latin

South Carolina, seventy dollars, 1779. Courtesy the NNC.

Georgia, twenty dollars, 1778. Courtesy the NNC.

mottoes on the faces and allegorical images on the backs. One of Coram's ideas featured an American eagle assiduously plucking at the liver of a chained British Prometheus, which is perhaps the earliest association of the eagle with the new nation.

State notes more commonly used English to express and foster insurgent sentiments, and their images tended to be more obvious, more vibrantly nationalistic. Thus, the coiled rattlesnake on a 1778 Georgia note would be perfectly explicit even if you didn't read Latin—or English. Interestingly, the Latin motto surrounding this particular vignette was borrowed from Scotland. You can see the words NEMO ME IMPUNE LACESSET on the edges of Scottish sovereigns to this day.

North Carolina restrained itself to small, inspiratory slogans in fancy boxes at the lower-left of its notes of 1778, 1779, and 1780—but what slogans! A 1778 five-dollar bill sees the war as A LESSON TO ARBITRARY KINGS AND WICKED MINISTERS, while a 1780 fifty-dollar bill reminds Britons of PERSECUTION THE RUIN OF EMPIRES. But a twenty-dollar bill of the previous year would have settled for PEACE ON HONOURABLE TERMS—and so would have those who printed and vainly attempted to spend it before it lost its value.

So far, the slogans revolved around relative simplicity, but some of the propaganda was fairly elaborate. The prize in this category must certainly go to Thomas Sparrow,

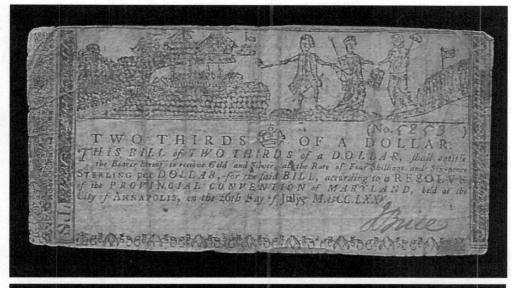

Maryland, two-thirds dollar, 1775; patriotic sentiments as presented by Thomas Sparrow. Courtesy the NNC.

New Hampshire copper pattern, 1776. Courtesy the NNC.

an Annapolis silversmith who had engraved border cuts for Maryland currency before the war, but who outdid himself on woodcuts for its first insurgent issues of 1775. Sparrow used the storytelling possibilities of the note in the most advantageous way. What resulted was at least as much political cartoon as currency. On the face, from left to right, we see a British fleet attacking an American city (Baltimore?), while George III does his bit, attempting to set fire to it. At the same time, this agile monarch is trampling on a scroll labeled M[agna] CHARTA. Next we see Britannia receiving a petition from America, a scroll labeled CONG PETI (a petition from the Continental Congress [Sparrow had to abbreviate a good deal of what he wanted to say]). Meanwhile America defiantly tramples on another scroll marked SLAVERY, while it also raises a Liberty cap before advancing patriot troops carrying the flag of Liberty (shortened to LIB on the cut). The right-hand border carries a Latin inscription (PRO ARIS ET FOCIS, for altars and the hearth), while the left-hand border carries AN APPEAL TO HEAVEN. Sparrow placed his initials at the left bottom on the face, for he was quite proud of his effort.

His back was somewhat more restrained and reconciliatory. Here, Britannia and America are shown clasping hands with an olive branch of peace between them. A lower inscription reminds the viewer that PAX TRIUMPHIS POTIOR, peace is preferable to victory. The artist adds his own name to the back, plus another LIBERTY at top-right, just to make sure. Notes ranging from two-thirds of a dollar to sixteen dollars were issued and circulated with these designs.

Did Sparrow's efforts pay off? Did his artistry and that of his fellow silversmiths mold and harden public opinion in favor of independence? It is likely that they helped form the mental pictures through which Americans visualized this new political status, but it is unlikely that they contributed much to its creation. We might say that the very act of accepting insurgent paper suggested at least a tacit agreement with the independence idea. In any case, even the most patriotic would have been far more concerned with the value retained by their money than the sentiments it espoused. And that, as we have seen, posed a problem.

So great was this problem that Congress and the states finally decided to do something about it. By a resolution passed on March 18, 1780, a new issue of paper was authorized, but it was one with a difference. This issue would consist of bills circulated by the states, exchangeable for Continental Currency at forty-to-one, the same value ratio as the Continental notes now had against the Piece of Eight or Mexican dollar. The states of Maryland, Massachusetts, New Hampshire, New Jersey, New York, Pennsylvania, Rhode Island, and Virginia participated in the scheme; the other states were either unwilling or unable to do so or were still occupied by British troops. In this way, over $111,000,000 in Continental Currency was removed from circulation, and a goodly amount of state paper was also lured in by the same law and destroyed.

In time, much of the remaining federal and state paper of the Revolutionary era was presented and redeemed for federal bonds under the funding schemes of Alexander Hamilton and other Federalists. And some of the state issues at least stayed in circulation for some years, rendering continued if suspect service on the local economic scene. Other notes crept into cupboards and jars, awaiting a redemption that never took place. And a new phrase crept into American English usage: "not worth a Continental," meaning worthless and useless. Americans had been badly mauled by their previously trustworthy paper currency, and on the national level at least they would not soon forget the experience.

Their war finally ended, despite the collapse of the medium they had chosen to pay for it. Hoping to reverse the trend symbolized by the surrender of Philadelphia and the loss of the west, Great Britain struck south, capturing the capitals of Georgia and South Carolina (whereupon the artist Thomas Coram rethought his sentiments and signed an oath of allegiance). Troops under Lord Cornwallis then swung north, hoping to roll up the American war effort before France and Spain could make a difference. But a supporting Loyalist force was defeated by patriot frontiersmen at Kings Mountain, South Carolina (October 7, 1780), and Cornwallis eventually found himself bottled up on a tongue of land between the York River and the James, with American General Washington approaching from land and French Admiral de Grasse from the sea. A siege resulted at Yorktown, and when Cornwallis surrendered his forces on October 19, 1781, the war was effectively over (although it would take two years of the canniest American diplomatic efforts to win the peace, with the Treaty of Paris of 1783). The timing of the Cornwallis debacle could not have been more fortunate: had the war gone on for another year or even a few months, it is more than possible that Americans would have concluded that it was simply not worth the struggle. Furthermore, the collapse of their currency might have served as an apt symbol of a much greater failure.

Perhaps we should not read more into that collapse than did those who experienced it. What would it have meant to them? That would depend upon whom we might have asked. For the seacoast merchant of the middle or southern regions, the inflation might have signaled ruin. To his colleague in New England, it might have signaled ruin as well, but this businessman might have observed that a weak currency was, after all, a small price to pay for the blessings of liberty, and modest indeed in comparison with what others had paid with Washington at Valley Forge. To a backcountry farmer, the depreciation might have seemed a godsend: now he could easily get out of debt, pay for feed and seed, and keep his business going and growing. And for the farmer who lived still further back in the hills, the problems with paper might not have meant much at all, for he and his were self-sufficient and well beyond the reach of any fiscal system, even a tainted one. As with many questions, the answer to this one depends on whom you ask.

After Yorktown, Americans were granted an opportunity they had never had before and would never enjoy again. They had defeated an enemy and were therefore free to reject its monetary system as well, and because their own, makeshift monetary system had buckled, they were enabled and forced to reject it too. What would they seek to erect

Massachusetts cent, 1788.

in the places of these failed and rejected precursors? Would it work any better?

While groping toward a new arrangement, Americans continued to rely on old expedients partly out of habit and partly as a stalling measure which would buy them time. But they added some new ingredients to the mixture and removed old ones at will. The resulting situation was more stew than unified monetary system, but it served them after a fashion through the "critical period of American history," the years of the 1780s.

They kept some kinds of paper money, but not all. States continued to print paper notes (now usually expressed in dollar denominations, though not always). The large amounts of specie, Spanish Pieces of Eight and French écus, which had come in during the final stages of the war, enabled states to back some of their notes with promises of cash payment—although this hard money soon disappeared and the states still continued to print. Georgia, New Jersey, New York, North Carolina, Pennsylvania, Rhode Island, and South Carolina all circulated currency after Yorktown, and Rhode Island's issues of 1786 are among the most common of all eighteenth-century notes. They and most of the other issues continued to be type-set, although Franklin's nature print had now dropped out of use. Perhaps it reminded people of Continental Currency.

The states could issue such paper because they were sovereign entities. Several of them also espoused a coinage of sorts. The only one to set up its own mint was Massachusetts. It had made a previous attempt to coin back in 1776, as had its neighbor New Hampshire, but the exigencies of war and a shortage of copper had stopped both projects in the very beginning of the pattern stage. Now Massachusetts made a second, successful attempt, and its coppers made numismatic history: they were the first American coins to bear the denominations "cent" and "half cent." Some of the later dies for the series were cut by a young silversmith named Jacob Perkins, who would soon go on to greater things. The Bay State's coins were handsome, and they contained a generous amount of copper.

Other states allowed private mints to produce their coinage, which resulted in generally lighter pieces and less artistic imagery. Connecticut is a prime example. Between late 1785 and early 1789, several firms (the leaders being the Company for Coining Coppers and Jarvis & Company, both of New Haven) struck more than 340 varieties of

Connecticut copper, 1787.

halfpenny-size coppers. They bear dates of 1785 through 1788, and all feature a man's mailed bust on the obverse (with the legend AUCTORI: CONNEC: [by the authority of the state of Connecticut]) and a seated figure on the reverse, along with the legend INDE: ET. LIB: or a slight variant (independence and liberty) and the date below. If these coppers remind us of earlier British halfpennies, that was deliberate on the part of the coiners, one of which was also busy making straight counterfeit *British* halfpennies with the same general designs. This was Machin's Mills, of Newburgh, New York.

That firm was also involved in coinage for New York, although the state never got around to formally authorizing a coinage. No matter: Machin's Mills and others would coin for it anyway, their designs sometimes resembling English halfpennies, and at other times incorporating elements from the state's coat of arms. Out of this welter of unacknowledged copper would come a gold coin, the Brasher doubloon, one of the most famous coins in American history.

Ephraim Brasher and John Bailey were New York metalworkers who struck coppers on a speculative basis. It has been suggested that the Brasher doubloons were patterns for a new copper coinage, struck in gold by way of a *douceur* or bribe to state legislators to secure the contract. If so, the ploy failed, but precisely seven doubloons with one design and an eighth and ninth with another have survived.

The combined total of the various New York coppers was minuscule in comparison with that of neighboring states Connecticut and New Jersey. The latter also contracted for its money, and the result was a heavy mintage struck at Rahway Mills, Elizabeth, Morristown, New York City, possibly on Staten Island, and definitely in Newburgh, New York, where the enterprising Thomas Machin of Machin's Mills once more proclaimed his numismatic presence. These coins bear dates of 1786, 1787, and 1788, although they appear to have been struck into 1789 and deliberately back-dated. They too made numismatic history: they were the first circulating American coins to bear the national shield, seen on many later, federal issues, and the motto E PLURIBUS UNUM (out of many, one), seen on virtually all later federal issues.

Brasher doubloon, 1787.

Virginia halfpenny, 1773.
Courtesy the NNC.

Vermont Republic, five shillings, 1781. Courtesy the NNC.

None of the other states circulated its own coinage, although one of them, Virginia, saw the circulation of copper halfpence it had had struck for it during the last days of the colonial period. Virginia's charter of 1609 had given it the right to strike its own coins—the only one of the thirteen colonies to enjoy this privilege. It had never set up its own mint due to lack of metal, but its Assembly authorized the Tower to strike a copper coinage for it in May 1773. Some five tons' worth of coins were accordingly prepared and sent across the Atlantic.

But by the time they arrived in Virginia the first stirrings of the American Revolution were taking place. A timorous colonial treasurer refused to put the coins in circulation without explicit permission from London, and by the time it finally arrived, the imminence of armed conflict was removing all coinage from circulation. Most of those Virginia halfpennies which got into trade were soon pulled out, hoarded for the duration of the war. After Yorktown, however, many did go into trade, where they passed from hand to hand in company with counterfeit and genuine British and Irish halfpence and the sponsored and unsponsored issues of several states—and of an adjacent, independent country.

This last was Vermont. The area was one of the last to be colonized, the first permanent European settlement there only being organized in 1724. Vermont had sided with the Revolution, but it had also become involved in an acrimonious land dispute with its giant neighbor New York. Until that dispute was settled, it would remain resolutely out of the Union.

The Vermont Republic produced both notes and coins. The notes were issued from Windsor in 1781, and they are of great rarity. They are most interesting, however, for their political sentiment, expressed in a tiny vignette at left-center. Within a circular legend stating that VERMONT CALLS FOR JUSTICE (a reference to the land dispute), we see a circular arrangement of thirteen linked rings—and a fourteenth, which stands defiantly out of the circle. The idea of the fourteenth, outsider entity would eventually be repeated in a different way (a star) in a different medium (a copper coin).

On June 15, 1785, the Vermont legislature granted Reuben Harmon, Jr. the right to strike its copper coinage. Harmon lived in the hamlet of Rupert, in Bennington County, and here he set up his mint, with Col. William Coley of New York as his diemaker. Coley incorporated the idea of the fourteenth

Vermont Republic copper, 1785.

entity into the reverse design of his coppers: here was an all-seeing eye (adapted from a contemporaneous British import, the Constellatio Nova copper), with only thirteen stars and thirteen rays. The fourteenth star would be Vermont, and the region's aspirations of becoming a part of the new United States (as soon as those New Yorkers saw matters its way) formed the basis of the reverse legend: STELLA. QUARTA. DECIMA., the fourteenth star.

This reverse was close enough to those on the well-known Constellatio Nova coppers to encourage acceptance, but the obverse Coley chose (or had chosen for him by the lawmakers) was a completely unfamiliar departure. We see a sun peeking over mountains and trees, with a plow below, and the date. This design was among the most evocative of that or any other period of American numismatics. The name of the issuing authority forms the remainder of the obverse legend: VERMONTS. RES. PUBLICA., VERMONTIS. RES. PUBLICA., or VERMONTENSIUM. RES. PUBLICA.—all signifying Vermont Republic, all differing because no one knew the Latin for Vermont! These marvelous coins were struck between October 1785 and September 1786.

Harmon then petitioned the legislature for permission to change their designs, perhaps because of local resistance to that obverse landscape. Permission was granted, and from then until the end of the coinage in mid-1789, Harmon and other coiners, including the ubiquitous Thomas Machin, struck coppers with a male head on the obverse, a seated female on the reverse. These coins looked, and were intended to look, like the old, familiar halfpennies of colonial days. The later issues were greater successes in the marketplace, but the earlier ones are held in higher esteem by collectors.

Thus far, we have been talking about copper coinages, and with good reason: the great majority of coinages proposed and circulated during those years *were* copper—in part because of a scarcity of silver and gold. But there was one silver issue which managed to get into circulation and a second which barely got into the pattern stage.

The first of these came from Annapolis, Maryland, the product of two silversmiths. The person who actually struck the coinage was an Annapolis resident, John Chalmers, a silversmith working in the state capital, who was a onetime recruiting officer for the Continental Army, a sometime Methodist

New Jersey copper, 1786–1788.

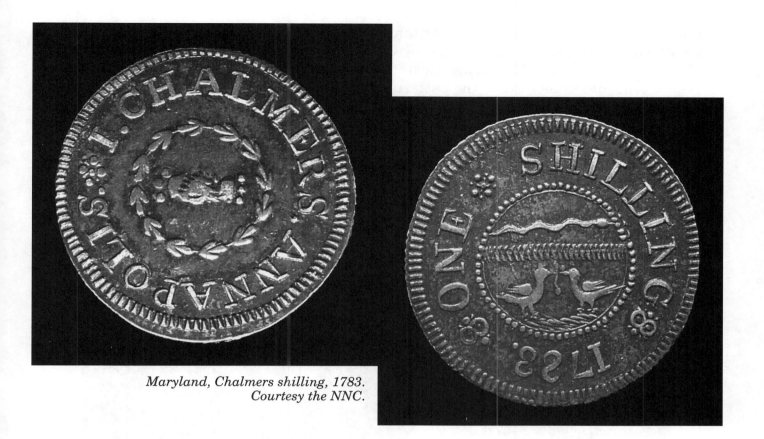

Maryland, Chalmers shilling, 1783.
Courtesy the NNC.

preacher, and a later sheriff of Baltimore. The man who designed the coinage and engraved its dies was a gentleman from Baltimore whom we met earlier, Thomas Sparrow.

With Sparrow in charge, we might expect this coinage to be loaded with messages—and it was. The most common member of the Chalmers series was the shilling, whose obverse bore clasped hands, an age-old symbol of amity. But we must examine the reverse to see what Sparrow really had in mind. For if we view the obverse as symbolizing friendship, the reverse depicts the danger which can follow when friends have a falling-out. Here are two birds (sparrows?) squabbling over a worm, oblivious to a serpent which may attack them at any time. Sparrow's message is clear enough, in the light of current politics: if the states continue to war with each other (as they were indeed doing during the period of the Confederation, even assessing import taxes on each others' products), a greater enemy may destroy them. Some have thought that Sparrow was referring to the

specter of a stronger federal government (and these nonsensical interstate rivalries were indeed driving much sentiment in that direction), but he might equally have meant extra-continental forces, such as Great Britain. Chalmers' shillings, sixpences, and threepences were made in 1783, the same year that a more ambitious, federal coinage was under discussion. This second coinage was proposed by Robert Morris, Superintendent of Finance under the Confederation.

Had it been implemented, it would have meant a complete new direction for American numismatics, for Morris was advocating a completely new coinage. It would be fully decimal, with pieces ranging from five to one thousand units, the latter a silver coin weighing about two-thirds as much as the Mexican dollar. Morris commandeered a few machines and minters, and a handful of patterns were struck in Philadelphia. Their simple designs featured an all-seeing eye for the obverse, surrounded by thirteen rays and stars, with the legend CONSTELLATIO NOVA, a new constellation (in the firmament of nations). The reverse bore the value within a wreath, with the date and the motto LIBERTAS. JUSTITIA. (liberty [and] justice).

These coins never got beyond the pattern stage, because their coiners never secured enough silver for more than a few trial pieces. But they did inspire an assistant to secure another coinage, from another source.

This assistant's name was Gouverneur Morris, whom generations of irate historians have confused with Robert, who was unrelated to him. Their confusion has been compounded by the fact that Gouverneur, and not Robert, came up with the original idea for the new federal coinage, a concept which his namesake attempted and failed to carry into execution. With the failure of the scheme, Gouverneur Morris went to England, and he eventually turned up in Birmingham, then the center of the British metalworking industry. There he found a coiner with time on his hands named George Wyon, whom he persuaded to strike undenominated coppers very similar to the ill-fated Philadelphia patterns. Wyon's coppers found a ready circulation in the United

Nova Constellatio pattern.

Confederatio copper pattern, 1785. Courtesy the NNC.

States, for their copper was good and their designs patriotic. British pieces were dated 1783 and 1785, although all were apparently struck in 1785–86. They are reasonably common, and they inspired two American counterfeits, both exceedingly rare.

The Constellatio Nova coppers were hardly the only halfpenny-size imports at this time. When Thomas Jefferson prepared his "Propositions Respecting the Coinage of Gold, Silver, and Copper" (May 13, 1785), which he wrote while serving as Minister to the court of King Louis XVI, the statesman recommended a new decimal coinage system, based on an old coin, the Spanish or Mexican dollar. The dollar would be divided into hundredths, and someone in Congress suggested the name "decad" for the large copper piece which would sit at the bottom of the new monetary arrangement. The name of the coin would eventually be changed to cent, but George Wyon was asked to produce patterns in line with Congress's current idea.

What resulted was perhaps the most iconographically-loaded coin in early American history—struck by an Englishman. On the obverse, the goddess Diana leans against an altar, trampling a crown. On the altar is a helmet, closely and deliberately resembling a liberty cap. The choice of Diana with her bow and arrow was intentional for she was the patroness of hunters, and only free men can bear the arms necessary to hunt their dinners. Around her, we see the legend, AMERICA INIMICA TYRANNIS—America, enemy of tyrants. Combined with the liberty cap and the trampled crown, Wyon's message could hardly be more obvious. The reverse returns to an earlier design idea, unity, and the word CONFEDERATIO may be taken to refer either to the current form of government or to the ideal of amity and mutual support, underscored by the close and deliberate arrangement of the stars. Wyon created two different reverses, and his dies for these patterns were muled with those for

"Georgius Triumpho" copper, 1783. Courtesy the NNC.

the Constellatio Nova coinage and several other patterns.

There was another message-bearing copper coin of the period, one with which George Wyon had no connection. This was the "Georgius Triumpho" copper of 1783. The obverse head was probably intended to represent General Washington. If this is so, this piece was the earliest in a series of Washington-related copper coins, patterns, tokens, and medalets, struck in England and America all the way down to the early 1820s.

The reverse introduces us to the subtleties of the eighteenth-century mind. The legend is obvious enough: we have seen something like it on Roche's Dublin coppers. But the design requires closer scrutiny before it yields its secrets. The female presumably represents liberty and independence. But she is enclosed in a framework with thirteen vertical bars, and there are four fleur-de-lis at the corners of the frame. The complete image probably means that American freedom is protected and secured through joint action of the states (the thirteen bars), supported on all sides by aid from the French monarchy (the four fleur-de-lis).

A slightly later American piece probably pokes fun at the General. This is the "Ugly Head" or "Washington the Great" copper of 1784, of which just four are known. This coin, too, uses symbolism: the old linked rings motif of the Continental Congress.

Those rings would make a final appearance on American prefederal coinage. By 1787, the nation's small change was composed of a confusing mixture of state coppers, British and Irish halfpennies, Morris' Constellatio Nova and other British speculative pieces, such as an undated copper with USA on the obverse, thirteen bars on the reverse—and large numbers of counterfeits

*Fugio or Franklin copper, 1787.
Courtesy the NNC.*

manufactured on both sides of the Atlantic. Congress became convinced that a standard must be issued under its aegis, a full-weight coin of good copper, against which everyone else's issues might be judged.

Not possessing a mint of its own, it had to contract for the coins along with everyone else. It picked a Connecticut coiner named James Jarvis to do the work, and it chose the designs, Franklin's old sundial/linked rings concept, seen earlier on fractional notes and the Continental Dollar of 1776.

Jarvis had been recommended by his friend William Duer, to whom he had paid a bribe of $10,000 for the contract. Jarvis was willing to pay that much for the contract because he expected to make a hefty profit from the coinage: there would be a goodly difference between what it cost him to strike the pieces and how much he would receive for them. The obliging Colonel also helped him on his way, for he gave Jarvis over seventy thousand pounds of federally-owned copper with which to begin work. This was a small fraction of what his contract called for, however, and Jarvis went to Europe in search of more metal, preferably in the form of blanks, which would have reduced his work to striking alone. He failed in his attempt, his somewhat shady reputation making such industrialists as Matthew Boulton (upon whose doorstep Jarvis appeared early in the spring of 1788) wary of dealing with him. He finally returned home without his copper.

Meanwhile, Jarvis' coining cronies had gotten the federal copper, and they were busily using it to coin Connecticut coppers! Chief among the miscreants were Samuel Broome and Abel Buell. Broome was Jarvis' father-in-law. Buell was a convicted forger, and had the cropped ear to prove it. These worthies struck coinage for Connecticut instead of the Republic because Connecticut's coppers were lighter-weight (indeed, they were one of the issues upon which the new federal coin was supposed to exert a positive influence); both eventually fled the country, as did Jarvis himself.

To minimize federal suspicion, the Connecticut coiners did strike some "Fugio" coppers on the federal pattern (their name comes from the obverse legend, the Latin for "I fly," referring to time on the sundial; they are also known as "Franklin cents"). Slightly under four hundred thousand pieces were shipped to the Treasurer of the United States on May 21, 1788. But the coins proved unpopular with the government (they were slightly under their legal weight, hence useless if the federal government were serious about its reform) and with the people (who by this time were unfamiliar with the design). Very few went into circulation. Jarvis went back to Europe, where we last find him and his brother Samuel attempting to interest a skeptical Matthew Boulton in a steam-powered Parisian flour mill in the first days of the French Revolution.

The federal government eventually sold what was left of the Fugio coins to a contractor with the unlikely name of Royal Flint. Flint was a friend of Col. Duer, and so we have come full circle. Flint went bankrupt before he could pay the government and was hauled off to jail. Duer joined him there a few years later: the Fugio story has no heroes.

But it did serve to neatly symbolize what a growing number of people were saying: the government which had sponsored them must be strengthened, either reformed or scrapped altogether in favor of a more plausible, dignified, centralized polity which would be taken seriously at home and abroad. The current central government could not tax (an attempt to give it that power, the proposed Impost of 1783, fell to the ground when a single state voted against it). It could not keep the peace (as evidenced by its poor handling of Shays' Rebellion of 1786–87, wherein a group of Massachusetts debtor farmers made things uncomfortable for their landlords and creditors, while the federal government looked on). It was incapable of being taken seriously by Europeans, as Britons moved against its newly-won territories in the Northwest, and Spaniards and others snubbed its diplomats in Europe. And the final proof of its incompetence was neatly symbolized by those despised Fugio coppers.

A gathering was held at Annapolis in September 1786 to strengthen the Articles of Confederation. Few states bothered to send delegations, and the meeting broke up without concrete result—except for a promise to hold a second convention at Philadelphia the following spring. Then Daniel Shays and his disaffected farmers swung into action, terrorizing parts of Massachusetts until dispersed by state militiamen early in 1787. Shays' Rebellion turned the tide. It sent a shiver of horror through every merchant and creditor in the Republic, for if debtors could revolt in western Massachusetts, they could make trouble anywhere. That spring meeting at Philadelphia would be well attended indeed: out of its deliberations would come a new government, and a new chapter in the story of American numismatics. Most importantly, it would set down for the ages who could make money—and who could not.

CHAPTER 3

'HARD MONEY' AND THE
YOUNG REPUBLIC, 1789–1830

CHAPTER 3

'HARD MONEY' AND THE YOUNG REPUBLIC, 1789–1830

The fifty-six delegates who came to Philadelphia in May 1787 were entrusted with debating and enacting improvements to the Articles of Confederation—most notably, granting them the power of direct taxation. But discontent was on the rise by the time of the first deliberations, and a group of young conservative businessmen and lawyers would channel it into more thoroughgoing political change. Their leader was Alexander Hamilton. Together with James Madison, John Jay, and a few others, Hamilton would take the country in a new direction. He and his fellows would attempt to do the same with its money, but with less success.

The hand of this group of "Federalist" debaters was first seen in the decision to scrap the old constitutional edifice instead of tinkering with it. In a sense, this was the most important victory of all for the Hamilton group, for it could not have done its work, could not have taken the government and the nation in the direction it wished to carry them, within the framework of the old document. What the Federalists did would be new indeed, but it would be presented to the voters who must ratify it as a return to hallowed practices, a welcome redress of prior grievances, which is how all American reformers must shape their ideas if they wish to see them enacted into law.

With the exception of a very few people like Luther Martin of Maryland (who wished to leave the bulk of political power where it currently resided) the delegates to this convention agreed on a shift of the balance of authority from the states to the national government. They wanted the change from a variety of motives. They desired the new nation to be taken seriously by the other members of the constellation of independent states.

They saw no means by which this might be accomplished if the current balance between state and national authority in America were to remain where it was—and they were probably correct. They wished their new country to be able to defend itself, its territories, its citizenry, and the possessions of that citizenry not only from external threat but also from internal danger. Here, Shays' Rebellion probably did more to effect change than all the brilliant words contained in the *Federalist Papers*: all of the closely-reasoned prose in the world would have availed nothing if the pocketbooks of those who read it were being fattened under the old system. But they were not. The Articles of Confederation, with its strong states which seemed to be increasingly favoring debtor farmers, were simply bad for business.

Joined to this was a certain snobbery on the part of Alexander Hamilton and many of his fellow delegates. Few would have gone quite as far as Gouverneur Morris, who would probably have preferred to see a King rather than a President, but it seemed undeniable that a government of the better sorts of people (or one made up of the rich, the well-born and the able, in Hamilton's revealing words) was desirable and would be easier to achieve under a new political compact than under the current one.

The members at this convention had a basic agreement on what they wanted, and they therefore managed to achieve it in the form of a written document, the Constitution of 1787. This is not to say that agreement on specific points was easily secured, for it was not. The debate over the representation granted to large states versus small virtually wrecked the proceedings until a compromise was suggested. Americans would have a bicameral national legislature, wherein large states and small would receive representatives based on equal numbers (the Senate) and unequal populations (the House of Representatives). In a less felicitous compromise, it was finally determined that African Americans would count as three-fifths of white Americans for purposes of taxation and representation in Congress.

The hands of the propertied delegates were visible throughout the document. States were expressly forbidden to interfere with contracts. The debt of the federal government was expressly recognized, payment guaranteed. The central government was authorized to put down domestic uprisings (which would have smothered Shays' Rebellion in its cradle; it would soon be used against another group of disaffected farmers, the Whisky Rebels of 1794). Federal judges were appointed for life, and while Hamilton did not secure agreement on a similar term for Senators, they would still serve terms three times longer than those of Congressmen and be elected by state legislatures rather than the people. The President would receive a relatively long term too, four years, and he would emphatically *not* be chosen by the people, but by an Electoral College.

This national conservative trend would continue into the area of money. You will recall that the uncontrolled emission of Revolutionary-era state and federal paper had threatened ruin to the mercantile classes along the Atlantic seaboard, while spelling salvation for many poor farmers in the interior. Later, the loosely-controlled printings of still more state currency (and the striking of crude state coppers of variable quality) had created continued annoyance among those whose representatives were now meeting in Philadelphia. So when they came to an discussion of what sorts of money would be allowed and be created by whom, fiscal conservatism (along with the patriotic desire that America's money be fully as impressive as the new nation and the new government now in gestation) led to a permanent change in who was responsible for money, and who was not.

The framers made their points most explicitly in two clauses of the first section of the new document. Henceforth, states could not "coin Money; emit Bills of Credit [paper money]; [or] make any Thing but gold and silver Coin a Tender in Payment of Debts" (Article I, Section 10, Paragraph 1). From now on, only the national government would have the authority to "coin Money, regulate the Value thereof, and of foreign Coin, and fix the Standard of Weights and Measures" (Article I, Section 8, Paragraph 5).

The Constitution did not say that the national government could circulate paper money.

That vagueness was deliberate: Hamilton and his fellow framers were dedicated to the idea of making the United States a "hard money" (specie-based) country if this were humanly possible. National dignity demanded as much, and so did their pocketbooks. The Constitution's silence over federal paper would, they hoped, discourage national currency in normal times, while leaving an escape hatch in abnormal ones. What they hoped and what they got would be two different things.

But the new basic accord must be ratified before its shortcomings could become manifest. The delegates to the Constitutional Convention finished their labors on September 8, 1787. There ensued more than a year's worth of furious and sincere debate, wherein the way in which people govern themselves and each other received one of the closest scrutinies in human history. The dialogue ranged from elegant counting house to log cabin, and Hamilton's Federalists had the advantage from the beginning. They were better organized and financed, and they had a plan, something to offer, whereas their opponents could merely call themselves "antifederalists" and hope that the forces of inertia would win their debate for them.

That hope was vain. Because their opponents had cleverly arranged for the new basic law to go into effect once *two-thirds* of the states had ratified it rather than *all* of them, the psychological edge was always with their

Federalist adversaries. The tiny state of Delaware was first to swing into position behind the new compact (December 7, 1787). Within a month or so, Delaware was joined by Pennsylvania, New Jersey, Georgia, and Connecticut. The ninth and crucial state, New Hampshire, ratified the Constitution on June 21, 1788. Now the new Union was a going concern regardless of what else happened. But North Carolina waited until November 1789 to ratify the Constitution, for the voice of rural dissent was strong there, and had been for twenty years. And Rhode Island, defiant to the last, refused to admit defeat until late May 1790.

But governments can function without unanimity, and this one was busily organizing itself even as the debate continued. George Washington was elected first President by acclamation (who else could it possibly be?), and in April 1789, he and his new administration got down to business in rented rooms in New York City.

Among their earliest concerns were finance and money. Alexander Hamilton had persuasively argued that the new government must be a paragon of fiscal probity from the outset. He saw a number of ways of earning and ensuring this type of respect, and much of his thinking had been incorporated into the Constitution. Article VI of that document was sheer genius on the part of the young financier and his adherents: it recognized the debts of the former government under the Articles of Confederation, and it assumed those debts and those incurred by the states during the Confederation period. It thereby agreed to redeem both Continental Currency and that paper currency issued by the states during the Revolutionary War. This article did *not* specify payment in full, and the amount actually received, in the guise of long-term bonds, was not unduly generous. But the agreement to pay *anything* on notes already widely given up for worthless was a brilliant stroke. Not only would it establish the new government in favorable contrast to the old, but more importantly, it would also

cause an inevitable shifting of loyalty on the part of the business community (which held most of the depreciated paper) away from the locality, and toward the new national polity. Several of Hamilton's other policies (he became the first Secretary of the Treasury under the new administration) tended in the same direction, including his funding of the national and foreign debts at par (1790), his suggestions as to a federal excise tax (on whiskey, enacted in 1791, which precipitated the Whiskey Rebellion of 1794, wherein the power of the new government could be demonstrated in the quelling of irate Pennsylvanian farmers), and his efforts to create the first Bank of the United States (also set up in 1791, to run with a twenty-year charter; the bank was intended to serve business, and four-fifths of its stock was in private hands). And then there was the coinage.

Because Hamilton and his colleagues distrusted paper (and because they were sincerely interested in underscoring the majesty and sovereignty of their new country and creation), they would have to do something about the coinage, and in fairly short order. The quality of America's money had definitely *not* improved since the adoption of the new form of government. Indeed it had worsened, as state issues came to a halt in the spring of 1789 and a copper panic the following July reduced the purchasing power of all copper coinage by three-quarters, driving good coins and bad from circulation. A number of public and private groups and merchants took up the slack on the local level, and issues of small change notes began appearing in commerce that summer. Many of them remained in circulation for years due to a shortage of metallic alternatives, and surviving specimens are almost always encountered well-worn. Issues are known from Connecticut, New Jersey, New York, Pennsylvania, and South Carolina; they were the products of individuals and organizations ranging from ferrymen to Dutch Reformed churches. The bills are almost always denominated in pence, al-

Bank of North America, three pence or three-ninetieths of a dollar, 1789. Courtesy the NNC.

though those of the Bank of North America also proclaimed that they were worth one-ninetieth or three-ninetieths of a dollar, an attempt to express their value according to an old system, even as their issuers were moving toward a new. This particular issue was printed on paper furnished by none other than Benjamin Franklin to his grandson, Benjamin Franklin Bache.

The small change notes (and a very few metallic objects including two types of church penny from Albany, New York, and a tiny silver threepence from Baltimore, by Standish Barry) rounded out the lower end of the American monetary system at the end of the decade. At the upper, foreign gold and silver coinage would still be used when available. But the other previous commercial mainstay was out: the states were no longer able to issue paper money and the federal power was disinclined to do so. By 1790, there seemed a very real prospect that an increasing amount of American business transactions would have to be carried on by barter once again.

But matters were moving toward a resolution. The preliminary question of the identity of the American currency unit (and the relation of subordinate and multiple denominations to that unit and to each other) had effectively been answered by the end of the 1780s. The new American unit would be an old coin, the Spanish-American Piece of Eight, called by an old name, the dollar, but divided in a new fashion, decimally into dismes and cents. Thomas Jefferson was pointing the way by the mid-1780s, and his suggestions were enacted into law by 1792.

Americans like to believe that they were the first to devise the concept of a stable, orderly arrangement of monetary denominations based on the number ten, but they were not. The ancient Greeks of Syracuse and other areas had *dekadrachms*, huge silver pieces equal to ten *drachms*. And that workhorse of the later Roman Republic and early Roman Empire, the silver *denarius*, was originally equal to ten copper *asses*. Dekadrachms and denarii were both coins in a decimal relationship with other coins, but the dekadrachm was infrequently struck, and then only for commemorative or donative purposes, and the denarius's value was soon raised to sixteen asses, where it remained. Neither ancient precursor left an indelible mark on the world's later money, and it would be another millennium and a half before the decimal monetary concept came to stay.

Then it came to Russia, not America, and it was dragged there by force by that reforming despot, Peter the Great. In 1700, the Tsar decreed that henceforth the *rouble* would be divided into one hundred *kopeks*. And so it was, and so it still is. But this system was not entirely decimal, even if its top and bottom units were related to each other in a decimal fashion. Peter's system took into account other, non-decimal denominations, either retained from tradition or from popularity in various parts of the Empire. So Russians had one-, five-, and ten-kopek coins, but they also had three-, fifteen-, and very briefly four-kopek pieces. The Russian decimal monetary system left no descendants: Americans did not base their coinage arrangements on the Russian precedent, nor did anyone else. On the contrary, the inhabitants of the fledgling United States would see their coinage arrangement (and sometimes the name of the unit which lay at its heart) adopted around the world—first by Revolutionary France, then by Latin Europe and Latin America, and finally by the ancient enemy herself, when British coinage became decimal in 1971.

The United States was to enact its decimal idea into law with the Mint Act of 1792. But there were straws in the wind some years previously. The Massachusetts coinage of 1787–88 hinted at changes to come in one medium, as did the tiny notes of the Bank of North America in another. Having placed the nation on a sound monetary footing (as they saw it) for the future, Hamilton and the Federalists now turned to the country's monetary footing in the immediate present. Late in the first presidential term of General Washington, they secured a Mint Act.

Passed on April 2, 1792, the law addressed three main areas. First, it proclaimed the establishment of a mint at the current national capital, Philadelphia, and it determined the types of employees for the new facility and their salaries. Second, it established a decimal relationship between the members of the new coinage system, and it proclaimed what those members would be, what they would weigh, what quality and quantity of metal they would contain, and what images would be placed on those coins. Finally, it guaranteed that its mint would coin gold and silver for the public free of charge—an absolute necessity, were the new coiner to get the bullion it needed for its coinage.

What would its new coins be? As we might expect, they would center on the dollar, but the chart shows all members of the proposed new system.

A few observations are in order. The word "disme" was shortened rather quickly to dime, which was how the word was pronounced in any case. The copper cents and half cents had their weights reduced before coining began in earnest, for the price of copper had meanwhile risen and the coins would have all gone into the melting pot. And the inclusion of a half cent brings a reminder that this system was a hybrid and indeed divided an old coin in a new fashion.

That old coin, of course, was the Piece of Eight, which had always been divided into eight reales. That old coin would continue to circulate beside its new, American cousin (and indeed it *must* continue to do so: it might be decades before there were enough American dollars in circulation to render Spanish-American ones unnecessary). And any American needing change for a real would need a half-cent coin, because that Spanish-American coin was worth twelve and one-half cents in the new reckoning.

Metal	Name	Value ($)	Weight		Fineness
Gold	EAGLE	10.00	270 grains	(17.496 grams)	.917
Gold	Half	5.00	135 grains	(8.748 grams)	.917
Gold	Quarter	2.50	67.5 grains	(4.374 grams)	.917
Silver	DOLLAR	1.00	416 grains	(26.956 grams)	.892
Silver	Half Dollar	0.50	208 grains	(13.478 grams)	.892
Silver	Quarter	0.25	104 grains	(6.739 grams)	.892
Silver	DISME	0.10	41.6 grains	(2.696 grams)	.892
Silver	Half Disme	0.05	20.8 grains	(1.348 grams)	.892
Copper	CENT	0.01	264 grains	(17.107 grams)	1.000
Copper	Half Cent	0.005	132 grains	(8.553 grams)	1.000

Similarly, the quarter dollar would find a place in the new system, even though common sense tells us that one-fourth is not really part of a decimal system. But the quarter would equal a coin with which all Americans had long been familiar, the two-real or "two bit" piece. And the quarter eagle, one suspects, was introduced because it expressed a decimal concept of sorts, equaling ten quarters. In sum, this decimal system was not complete, but rather it contained comfortingly familiar elements in addition to those which were new, which is probably why it became so successful.

Mexico, eight reales, 1792; and Potosí, real, 1791. Courtesy the NNC.

The Mint Act of 1792 set down designs for the new coinage in a fairly detailed fashion. Although there was a groundswell of sentiment in favor of depicting the President on the obverses of the new coins, General Washington demonstrated a most un-Federalist antipathy to the idea: he said it reminded him too much of monarchical practice. And so the Mint Act stipulated that one side of each coin be devoted to "an impression emblematic of liberty," with a description to that effect. Gold and silver coins were to incorporate an eagle, the national bird, onto their reverse designs, while reverses for cents and half cents were simply required to express the denomination of the coins. The silence of the Mint Act over expression of value on gold and silver coinages left such denominations unstated until the first years of the following century—Congress was obeying British precedent whether or not it realized the fact.

The Mint Act was not as foreordained as we might suppose. In the years between 1789 and 1792 there was a good deal of talk about farming out the coinage to any of several private moneyers in Great Britain, Matthew Boulton's Soho Mint being the leading contender. Boulton's young friend John H. Mitchell of Charleston, South Carolina, did all he could in favor of Soho (having previously been frustrated in securing Boulton's help for a state coinage when the Constitution had gone into effect). Congress mulled over the idea of a foreign coiner, but while Boulton sent no samples, another British firm did. This was William and Alexander Walker, who commissioned John G. Hancock, Sr. to prepare a handsome series of copper pattern cents with Washington's head on the obverse, a large or small eagle on the reverse. Hancock prepared other, rarer pieces without a denomination on the eagle side, perhaps intended as samples of proposed cents (in copper), or half dollars (in silver), or even eagles (represented by a unique piece in gold). The national legislature was impressed, but it was finally swayed by the arguments of Thomas Paine and Thomas Jefferson who believed it simply made no sense to hold American coinage hostage to a European power in such dangerous times. Thomas Jefferson's attempts to lure the gifted Jean-Pierre Droz from Paris to Philadelphia to engrave dies and even direct an American mint met with no success either. For what it was worth, America's new money would be designed and struck in America.

One of the prime movers in favor of a new coinage was Robert Morris, who had been behind the ill-fated trials of 1783. Morris needed metallic samples to show his fellow legislators, and he needed coiners and a mint to create them. He found a mint site in the cellar of a coach house belonging to a saw maker named John Harper, who lived a few blocks from the future federal mint in Philadelphia. Harper hired a self-taught diesinker, goldsmith, and silversmith named Peter Getz to cut the dies. To design his samples, Getz took inspiration from

Hancock's Washington patterns. He made strikings in copper and silver, which were presumably intended as examples of cents and half dollars. Congress was impressed enough to pass the Mint Act, even though it was not particularly taken with Getz' artistry and never employed him once the United States Mint was a reality.

But it continued to use the coach house for minting purposes. Using dies engraved by "Birch" (probably William Russell Birch, an English miniaturist and cameo engraver) the press in John Harper's cellar struck the first American coin legally authorized by the new government, a half disme with a chubby portrait of Liberty rather resembling First Lady Martha Washington on the obverse, and a scrawny eagle on the reverse. Some 1,500 of these coins were minted on July 13, 1792. Even though the Mint Act was law, the coining facility which it had called into being had not yet opened.

It would shortly do so, however. A site at Seventh Street and Sugar Alley was purchased for a trifle over four thousand dollars, and the Republic received the deed to the property on July 18. Work began the following day. The distillery which had stood on the site was demolished, and a foundation and walls strong enough to support the heavy work of coining had been finished five weeks later. Now the mint proper could be erected. As the walls were going up, designers and coiners began their work.

Between September and December 1792 they experimented with three denominations. Adam Eckfeldt contributed an obverse die for a disme companion to Birch's earlier half disme. It was married to a reverse by Birch, and the new Chief Coiner

Pattern disme in copper, 1792. Courtesy the NNC.

Joseph Wright's pattern, 1792. Courtesy the NNC.

Half disme, 1792. Courtesy the NNC.

Henry Voigt then struck a half dozen or so of the new coins in copper and in silver. Eckfeldt would stay on at the United States Mint for decades, working on many other early American coinages.

The career of his more talented colleague Joseph Wright was much briefer, tragically truncated by one of Philadelphia's annual visits of yellow fever. But Wright created a pattern with a charming young head of Liberty and a standing eagle, designs intended either for a quarter dollar or a half eagle. Two specimens have survived in copper as well as an equal number in "white metal," a soft coining alloy composed mostly of tin. Chief Coiner Voigt contributed a pattern of his own, the "silver center" cent. This represented an attempt to create a coin worth a cent in a size more convenient than one made of pure copper. We do not know precisely how Voigt positioned the plug in the center of the planchet, and the difficulty he encountered appears to have tempted him to strike other patterns from the same dies wherein the silver was either mixed with the copper or was absent altogether. Less than twenty pieces of all types are known.

Finally, the man who had designed the half disme struck at one mint designed a cent which was struck at another. The artist Birch recycled his head from the half disme, turned it the other way, and struck a few cents in copper and one in white metal. The latter is particularly interesting because of

a brief reverse legend G*W Pt -for "George Washington President," the final gasp of the movement to honor the nation's chief executive on its coins.

The first true United States coin: the 1793 "chain" cent.

These early pieces are among the most revered members of American numismatics, but with the exception of the Birch half disme, none would have been seen by the average citizen of the day. That citizen was beginning to see the first "real" United States coins within a few months, though. In March 1793, the first issues began trickling from the new United States Mint (copper cents designed by Henry Voigt). For his obverse, Voigt employed a wild-haired, right-facing head of Liberty. His treatment of the goddess' hair and the shallow, almost tentative quality of the molding suggests that Voigt would have been more at home engraving paper currency than copper money, and his

Henry Voight's pattern cent with a silver center, 1792. Courtesy the NNC.

obverse for the cent was widely criticized. But the real adverse comment was reserved for his reverse.

There, Voigt reintroduced a design idea which had been in existence since 1776—the linked rings, symbolic of national unity. He doubtless got the idea from the Fugio cent, but he flattened the circular rings to make room for the surrounding legend. What had begun as conjoined rings of freedom now appeared uncomfortably close to a chain of slavery. The fact that Voigt had miscalculated and was forced to abbreviate the name of the country to AMERI. on his first die did not add to the appeal of his effort: in the following month, it was replaced by designs suggested by Mint Director David Rittenhouse and engraved by Adam Eckfeldt. Cents with those second designs were struck through the summer of 1793, replaced that September by yet a third try, the final labor of the gifted Joseph Wright. Wright's Liberty borrowed heavily from Augustin Dupré's "Libertas Americana" medal of 1783, down to the Phrygian cap (an ancient symbol of the newly-manumitted) behind her head. When he died in mid-September, his successors at the mint took up and continued the idea of the Liberty cap, an element which would adorn most American coins in one guise or another for the next century.

Meanwhile, Adam Eckfeldt had engraved dies for the companion to the cent, his first copper half cents being struck between July and September 1793. His Liberty also featured a Phrygian cap, and she was based on sketches by Mint Director Rittenhouse. The half cent was never as popular as the cent, but it was struck intermittently down to 1857, its designs generally replicating whatever had been introduced on the cent a few years previously.

All told, the new mint struck 111,512 cents and 35,334 half cents that first year—not bad for a first effort, but scarcely guaranteed to alleviate American monetary difficulties on the lower end of the coinage scale. The new national coiners expanded their copper output the following year, and the year after that, but their fellow-citizens still had recourse to more tra-ditional sources for most of their small change. They kept those small-denomination, local notes in commerce, and they printed even more (now denominated in terms of cents in the case of issues of the Society for Establishing Useful Manufactures of Paterson, New Jersey; other issuers stayed with pence for the time being). They also imported cent-sized tokens from Great Britain.

Britons were currently experiencing their own shortage of official small change, a scarcity which made that suffered by Americans pale in comparison. The last time they had had legal copper money put into circulation had been some two decades previously, early in the reign of George III. By the opening of the nineties, the country was in the beginning stages of the Industrial Revolution, which meant among other things that vast amounts of low-value coinage would be needed to pay the new, salaried workers. But the Royal Mint was reluctant to provide public copper coin, and so private copper would fill in (penny, halfpenny, and farthing tokens).

Their issue began in North Wales in 1787. By the middle of the next decade, hundreds of merchants and firms across England, Scotland, Wales, and Ireland were busily providing the coppers which the Royal Mint would not. And by that time, members of the upper and middle classes were beginning to treasure them for their collector interest as well as for their economic utility.

The collector coppers celebrated popular places, called attention to noteworthy historical events, and paid homage to the famous people of the day. It was probably inevitable that Americana would make its appearance. Ben Franklin's press showed up on a halfpenny token of 1794, while the new state of Kentucky received oblique mention on another token, the "starry pyramid" halfpenny, which was undated but struck between 1792 and 1794. There is no indication that the "Franklin Press" coppers were ever targeted for anyone other than British collectors, but the starry pyramid pieces were indeed shipped to America, where they circulated up and down the

East Coast in the 1790s. Several pieces celebratory of General Washington were designed by Hancock, Thomas Wyon, and others, struck at a number of private mints in Birmingham and possibly London. British collectors snapped up the more artistic of the Washington creations. The less successful, such as a 1793-dated halfpenny with Washington on the obverse and a ship under sail on the reverse, appear to have been sent over to the United States, to circulate there beside the new national cents.

In addition to all of this, the 1790s saw the production of two types of copper tokens specifically intended for circulation among Americans, not simply sent there when rejected at home. The first of these was the Talbot, Allum & Lee cents of 1794–95. Designed by Thomas Wyon and struck by Peter Kempson in Birmingham, these coppers were ordered by a merchant house at 241 Water Street in Lower Manhattan, New York City. Their obverse bore an attractive, standing female figure, whose cap and bale

Well-worn Washington halfpenny tokens, produced in Great Britain but used in America. Courtesy the NNC.

Talbot, Allum & Lee cent, 1795. Courtesy the NNC.

carried out the sentiment expressed by the legend, "LIBERTY & COMMERCE." Their reverse bore a sailing ship, another emblem of commercial enterprise. Their edge bore a promise to pay "real" money in exchange for them, just as did most of the legitimate British trade tokens of the period. The Talbot, Allum & Lee tokens found instant favor as cents, even though they were slightly lighter than the official issue. Emboldened by the reception of its 1794 coppers, the firm or-dered a second shipment in 1795. Along with the public, the fledgling United States Mint found these coppers appealing as well: need-ing rolled copper for half cent planchets in the spring of 1795, Mint Director Ritten-house bought some 1,076 pounds of the to-kens (around fifty-two thousand of them) from William Talbot and recycled them into the national coining process. Many 1795 half cents (and a few 1795 cents as well) were struck on these former British tokens.

Myddelton token, 1796. Courtesy Bowers and Merena.

Trial piece, in copper, of the first United States dollar, 1794. Courtesy the NNC.

Ten dollars, 1795, with a peaceable eagle.
Courtesy Stacks Rare Coins, New York,
Krause Publications photo file.

Ten dollars, 1799, with a heraldic eagle.
Courtesy Stacks Rare Coins, New York,
Krause Publications photo file.

The second made-for-America piece was created by Matthew Boulton for Philip Parry Price Myddelton in 1796. Myddelton had come into possession of a huge tract of land in Kentucky. During 1795 and 1796, he was busily persuading poor British farmers and laborers to come with him to seek the New Jerusalem in America. His colony would need small change, which was where Matthew Boulton entered the story.

Myddelton persuaded the coiner to employ the talented Conrad Heinrich Küchler to design copper tokens for the project. For his obverse, Küchler depicted Hope presenting two children to Liberty. Behind the latter is a cornucopia, probably a reference to the fecundity of the new colony. Küchler's reverse was more pointed: here Britannia sits with a downcast gaze, her inverted sword suggestive of her defeat at Yorktown. It is curious that Matthew Boulton (who was ordinarily a very cautious man, especially now that he was attempting to get a coining contract from the British Government) would have taken on this project. But it never got beyond the pattern stage in any case, because in August 1796, Myddelton was thrown in prison for his ambitious plan: encouraging the departure of British artisans

was illegal. And Boulton never got paid for Küchler's artistry.

By the time of the Myddelton fiasco, the federal mint had managed to expand its production into metals in addition to copper. In October 1794 the first half dollars were coined, and on the fifteenth of that month, the first representatives of the new American dollar also left the coining press. Some 1,758 of them were struck on that single day, and no more until the following year. By that time, the mint was also striking half dimes.

But those dollars are what interests us, because they have much to say about the early mint and its first products. They were designed by Robert Scot, who would be responsible for most of America's coinage designs over the next decade. Scot was not particularly gifted, and his eyesight eventually began failing him, with lamentable effects on his products, but he was faithful, and consistent. His dollar Liberty head and eagle were criticized for their delicacy of execution, but that was hardly Scot's fault: the new mint had no press strong enough to give its dollars a sharp impression, nor would it have until the following year—after which Scot's designs were seen to have improved.

Robert Scot's second try: dollar, 1795. Courtesy the NNC.

The new dollars would serve as the flagship for American silver coins: any design changes adopted there would tend to be later extended to lower denominations. Thus, Scot replaced his simple Liberty head with a draped bust of the goddess on dollars in 1795. This was extended to half dimes and half dollars the following year, and to two new coins, the dime and the quarter, at the same time. When Scot abandoned his simple eagle for a heraldic one on the dollar, subsidiary silver designs replicated this substitution as well—as would gold coinage.

The United States Mint struck its first gold in 1795 (eagles and their halves, designed once more by Robert Scot). Here, Scot's right-facing Liberty wore a turban instead of a *pileus* or liberty cap, a bonnet reminiscent of contemporary high fashion, and low drapery, soon to be extended to coins of all metals. But Scot's eagle for his gold was unique. It was a small, peaceable bird with an olive wreath in its beak, a palm branch at its feet. This design was shortly abandoned in favor of the heraldic, bellicose eagle as seen on the silver.

The switch of eagles happened to coincide with a stiffening of foreign policy against French and British meddling with American commerce. This harder line would soon result in an undeclared war with the French (and it would materially contribute to the ending of Federalist control of the national government at the end of the old century). And in time, continued British interference with American commerce (and American designs on British Canada) would lead to a second conflict with England, the War of 1812. This war would have a malign but interesting effect upon our money.

By the time the last of the legally-mandated denominations was being coined (the quarter eagle, which appeared in mid-1796), it was becoming apparent that at least a portion of the mint's production could not be achieved in the ordinary way. Trouble centered on the half cent and particularly on the cent. The difficulty stemmed from two considerations: the coins' low value and the time and trouble it took to make them.

Consider for a moment. If you were a Mint Director in the late 1790s, and you had a set amount of money to produce during a given term, would you not prefer to meet it by striking eagles rather than cents? Those cents took as much labor to make as did the ten-dollar pieces—more, in fact, because copper was harder to roll and strike than gold. And yet when you got done, you had a cent instead of an eagle, and you still had virtually all of your coining left to do.

We tend to assume that the most difficult labor at a mint lies in the striking of a coin, which is not necessarily so. In the eighteenth century, the most difficult labor involved the rolling of metal into sheets, then cutting planchets from those sheets. The rolling was especially difficult, because it required the application of great and precise force. At the United States Mint, early personnel must have looked at the huge amount of copper required for a few dollars' worth of cents, and shuddered. If only they could get their copper already rolled and cut out!

This was not the only problem, because as far as anyone knew, the United States was still short of native coining metals. The simple winning of independence had done nothing to alleviate this problem. Americans had little domestic gold, silver—or copper, which meant that their coiners had to scrounge for it. A 1798 cent exists which was overstruck on a halfpenny token from Anglesey, North Wales. One wonders whether this was accidental.

Of course, there *was* an area blessed with much copper and the technological wherewithal to turn it into blanks. This was the old enemy, Great Britain. By early 1796, the new Mint Director Elias Boudinot was preparing to hold his nose and ask Albion for help.

She responded: between 1796 and 1837, Cornish and Welsh copper were made into planchets of two sizes, then sent across the Atlantic to be elaborated into half cents and cents at Philadelphia. While two other firms participated, the favored agency was Boulton, Watt & Company—one more instance of the enterprising Matthew Boulton capitalizing on his contacts with Americans in other areas, ties which stretched back to the 1760s. Boulton's planchets were of the best copper. They were of the correct weight and they were carefully finished, so that they could be coined just as they came ashore in the keg. But they were not always available when needed.

On two occasions, their tardy delivery helped change the course of American numismatic history. The first was in the late 1790s, when Boulton delayed so long in sending copper that the mint virtually ceased production in that metal, striking only a few thousand cents in 1799 and no half cents whatsoever between 1797 and 1800. The second occasion took place about fifteen years later, but was scarcely Boulton, Watt's fault: America declared war on Great Britain in the spring of 1812, and the two countries remained cut off from each other for nearly three years. The worsening relationship had already resulted in a stoppage of planchet shipments by January 1811, and they were not resumed until September 1815. During those years, the mint struck no half cents and a dwindling number of cents, until it halted production altogether with the last of the 1814-dated coins. There is only one year in American history unrepresented in the story of the cent, and that is the year 1815. But cent coinage resumed with the end of the war, and it steadily expanded through the 1820s.

By then, Americans were essentially doing business with only three of the ten denominations stipulated in the Mint Act: cents, half dollars, and half eagles. The cent was becoming essential on the lower end of the monetary scale, especially as the supply of genuine and counterfeit British and Irish halfpennies dwindled through attrition. The half dollar represented a handy amount of money in the United States (and probably circulated in Mexico as well; struck Mexican copies of this coin exist, in base-metal alloys). And the half eagle was popular because its gold value was conveniently close to other gold coins which Americans had previously used and were still using: the British guinea, the French *louis d'or*, and the Spanish-American double *escudo*.

But what about the other seven stars in the American monetary constellation? Several were unpopular and rarely struck because there existed better-known foreign coins which were preferred in trade. Thus, the half dime and dime yielded place to the half real and real, while the quarter dollar

Three pillars of our early monetary system: a cent, a half dollar, and a half eagle, all from 1807. Courtesy the NNC.

was rarely struck because it was the exact equivalent of the Latin American double real—and the early United States Mint would cut production corners when and where it could.

Other members could not be kept in circulation, most notably the silver dollar. This coin had been overvalued in relation to the Piece of Eight, because it was slightly lighter, of slightly less pure silver than the Spanish-American coin after which it had been modeled. This was of no concern to the average American, but sharper members of the community discovered an interesting and profitable fact: the coins would pass at par in the West Indies, where they could be freely exchanged for Pieces of Eight. The latter could be carried to Philadelphia, coined into dollars for free, and then carried south to be exchanged for more pesos.

The gold eagle suffered from similar problems. In 1803, France adopted a new silver-to-gold ratio of 15-1/2:1, and it now became profitable to ship American gold coins to France for melting. Seeking to end both evils, an irate Elias Boudinot suspended coinage of both eagles and dollars in the following year, a suspension which would hold for nearly four decades. The Mint Director must have been relieved in a way, for the policy meant that he had two fewer denominations to produce.

And this was a material consideration: the early United States Mint was a most inefficient coiner. Its equipment was ancient, made up of the cast-offs and hand-me-downs of other countries and other coiners and creaking machinery originally intended for other purposes, now jury-rigged for service in a noble national cause. Its coiners were largely journeymen, as were its designers. All were receiving the most basic sorts of on-the-job training, to the detriment of the product they created. Mint Directors were seeking help from the beginning, and Matthew Boulton and his son were approached several times for technical aid ranging from better die steel to a plea for a new steam-powered mint—an idea which had to be scrapped from financial and political considerations.

The political climate was most hostile to this new mint. Many Congressmen found (as have their successors) that political capital could be made with the folks back home by lambasting a bungling federal institution. The mint regularly came up for review and

Peruvian successors to the Spanish-American Piece of Eight, widely accepted in American commerce. Courtesy the NNC.

could have been voted out of existence whenever such examination was made—and indeed came close to being abolished in 1800 and again in 1802. In the latter year, a harried Robert Scot threatened to resign, and a harried Elias Boudinot drew up an inventory of mint machinery and property preparatory to closing out the operation. An eleventh-hour decision kept the facility open, but the morale of its employees was hardly raised by the recurrent threat of unemployment. Not until May 19, 1828, would the mint be authorized to remain "in force and operation, unless otherwise provided by law." Even by that period, though, its production had come nowhere close to meeting the demands of the people it attempted to serve.

The same two considerations we saw in the beginning of America's history were still true now. The country was metal-poor, just as it always had been, and this was a natural hindrance to the success of its mint. And while this ramshackle institution might in time have scraped together domestic coining metal and gotten proficient enough at its craft to meet the requirements of a stable population, it had no chance whatsoever of matching those of a people, which was literally doubling itself every two decades—especially as this

population's money-based economy was growing even faster than it was.

If Americans could not turn to their local coiner for the specie they required, they would do as they had done since the beginning. They would turn to other people's coiners for help, and they were legally empowered to do so. The framers of the Constitution were nothing if not realistic, and the business element among them realized that a legal provision must be made for the circulation of foreign coins if commerce were not to grind to a halt. But they wanted to ensure that their new federal creation played a key role in such circulation, which was why Section 8 of Article I of the Constitution expressly gave Congress the power to "regulate the Value...of foreign Coin." Just as the mint was opening its doors for business, Congress elaborated on the foreign coinage theme.

On February 9, 1793, Congress passed "An act regulating foreign coins, and for other purposes," which went into effect on the following first of July. The new law demonetized all foreign coinage *except* the gold coins of Great Britain, Portugal, France, Spain, and Spanish America, and the silver coins of France and Spain. It also established values at which those coins were to circulate:

Competition to the Mexican dollar: France, five francs, 1830, and Brazil, 960 reis, 1815, struck over a Spanish-American peso. The Brazilian coin still shows traces of its origins. Courtesy the NNC.

the Spanish dollar, for example, at 100 cents, and its French equivalent at 110.

The new law was intended as a stopgap. It stipulated that three years from the beginning of American silver and gold coinage, everything except the Spanish and Spanish-American Piece of Eight would be demonetized. The new President John Adams duly proclaimed as much in July 1797, but his proclamation soon became a dead letter: regardless of his or Congress' aspirations or enactments, the United States Mint simply could not make enough domestic coins to replace the foreign ones.

And so Congress climbed down from its lofty pinnacle of self-sufficiency. It renewed the Act of 1793 on February 1, 1798, and again on April 30, 1802 and April 10, 1806. The Act was then allowed to expire, but foreign coins were allowed to circulate regardless. Shortly after the War of 1812, a group of Maryland bank presidents (who had become the unhappy possessors of a host of for-eign coins of which they could not legally dispose) secured an Act which renewed the circulation of foreign gold and silver coins (on April 29, 1816). The provision was renewed periodically, and foreign gold and silver coinage remained legal tender in the United States until 1857.

Which foreign coins circulated there? The Spanish and Spanish-American Piece of Eight led the way in silver, although coins like the Brazilian 960 *reis* (which was actually a recycled Latin American peso, restruck at Bahia or Rio de Janeiro) gave it much competition in the teens and twenties, as did the French five *francs* in the thirties. In the case of coinage from the Spanish world, pieces from Mexico City and Lima were predominant, both of those from the closing days of the viceroyalties and from the beginning days of the independent republics. In time, they were joined by issues from Bolivia, the Central American Republic, and Colombia, but the Mexican Piece of Eight

British sovereign, 1838. This particular coin was part of James Smithson's gift to the United States. Courtesy the NNC.

was always king, its obverse eagle and reverse liberty cap becoming known to generations of merchants and farmers from one end of the United States to the other.

Thus far, we have been speaking of equivalents to the now-suspended American silver dollar. Common sense suggests that the popularity of these foreign substitutes was founded in part on the unavailability of their American competitor. But what of subsidiary silver? There, the American half dollar was king. One reason why so many half dollars were struck relative to other United States denominations (and indeed, they were the *only* silver coins struck by the United States Mint in 1810, 1812, 1813, 1817, and 1826) was that they filled a need which foreign coins did not. There was no such thing as a two-and-one-half franc piece, and while Spanish America indeed coined a four-real coin, it rarely did so in sufficient quantities for export to the United States. Elsewhere, the two-real coin obviated the need for quarter dollars, as we have seen, and the real and half real tended to do the same for the dime and its half. Indeed, no half dimes were struck between 1805 and 1829, suggesting that Americans were coping quite well without them.

In gold, British, French, Spanish-American, and Brazilian pieces held sway. The guinea was important, but the last representatives of this denomination were struck in 1813. Four years later, a new gold coin, the *sovereign*, began issuing from a rebuilt Tower Mint in large numbers, and it would henceforward be a dominant player in international and intra-American commerce. When the legacy of James Smithson was paid to the United States (so that an institution could be built in Smithson's name in the federal capital), it was remitted in the form of sovereigns, some 104,960 of them. All but two were melted down, recycled into new American coinage. Those two still repose in the National Numismatic Collection of the Smithsonian Institution. In terms of sheer popularity, the sovereign would have frequently yielded place to the Spanish and Spanish-American *onza* or doubloon, which traded well across the country, and particularly in border areas of the Old Southwest, places which rarely saw United States coinage of any kind, including gold.

Aided by recurrent infusions of fresh foreign coinage, the American monetary system limped along. But its dependence on other people's monies was obviously galling to

Onzas, or "doubloons," from Central America, 1820s. Courtesy the NNC.

Hamilton, his fellow Federalists, and any later American with a nationalistic turn of mind. That was not the worst of it, though. Had Americans had enough coinage of any kind for commercial use, they would have been satisfied. But they did not. Even with the Piece of Eight, the sovereign, the gold of Brazil and the silver of France, they were not receiving all the money they needed to keep up with their present and prospective rates of economic development. What had been true before still held true now: America was a demographic and commercial success, and the normal rules of monetary usage did not hold. Faced with an economy which constantly outstripped the orthodox money supply, Americans did what they had done before: they replied with an unorthodox one. Just as the Constitution was taking force, just as it was seeking to channel America's money into a particular direction, the prospective users of that money were cutting a path of their own, with the paper note, from the private bank. And paper money, not coinage, would be king for the next three-quarters of a century.

CHAPTER 4

'RAG' TIMES: THE ERA OF THE PRIVATE BANK NOTE (1789–1865)

CHAPTER 4

'RAG' TIMES: THE ERA OF THE PRIVATE BANK NOTE (1789–1865)

The low-denomination notes printed by Ben Franklin's grandson offered a hint of things to come: they were issued by a bank, to provide money during times of a shortage of coins. If one were to multiply this response by infinity and spread it across three thousand miles and three-quarters of a century, one would have a fairly accurate blueprint of what actually took place. Private paper money would dominate, spur, and to a degree channel the economic development of the United States until a crisis comparable with that of the War for Independence would once more bring the public printer into the picture.

If Americans know anything about the years of "rag" money, of the private bank note, they tend to view them with an amused and nostalgic skepticism. There was an odor of fraud, flimflam, and humbuggery surrounding these notes when they were printed and circulated, and we can still catch a whiff of the scent today. It is believed that the notes were circulated by confidence men, forged by common criminals. Many of them were. In a country with a growth rate as dramatic as that of nineteenth-century America, a good deal of mischief will occur while everyone is concerned with making money, and most are actually succeeding in doing so. But fraud should not be seen everywhere; the truth is more complex, as truth always is. While many of the note-issuing banks failed, leaving those who held their paper penniless, many others were sober, carefully-run institutions, whose direct corporate descendants are still players on today's banking scene. And there is more: like it or not, the miracle of nineteenth-century American growth, ranging from grand finance on the East Coast to family farms on the West, simply could have not occurred without those private notes. Paper alone would give the United States the peculiar capital elasticity it required—and if the elastic paper system contracted as well as expanded, that was inherent in elasticity itself. Had there been no paper, we would now be speaking of the numismatic history of a much smaller, and a much lesser, country.

The era of the private bank note, also called the "broken bank note" by the disrespectful and the "obsolete note" by the serious, lasted for about three-quarters of a century, from approximately 1790 to 1865. We may hedge it a bit either way, but we may safely say that the era of the private bank note coincided rather nicely with the "first American republic." While thumbnail generalizations must always be suspect, we can cautiously say the following about the period. Agriculture was still predominant during this period (and certainly formed the core of the average citizen's life), but at the same time yielded primacy here and there to the beginnings of the American version of the Industrial Revolution. The role of government was small in good times and virtually nonexistent in bad. It was primarily concerned with keeping the peace; moving the more objectionable members of society (Native Americans) out of the way and beyond the concern of the European-base majority; encouraging the spread of agriculture and industry at little cost to itself; securing the respect of the outside world for the Republic, its people, and their institutions; and with ensuring that discussion of one particular institution did not get out of hand, that it did not in fact bring the Edifice of Liberty down on the heads of those who had built it. That issue was human slavery, of course, and it would finally demand a set of answers which this "first American republic" could only meet by sacrificing its peculiar identity— and in so doing bring the era of the private bank note to a close as well.

The first representatives of America's private currency predated this first American republic by a few years (indeed, the very earliest of them came from a bank organized during the last days of the Revolutionary War). Some ten weeks after Yorktown, the Bank of North America opened its doors in Philadelphia. The brainchild of war financier Robert Morris (who had recently been appointed Superintendent of Finance of the United States), the new bank began its life with a capitalization of $400,000 in a thousand shares of $400 each. The United States purchased nearly two-thirds of these shares and then borrowed the money back to finance its own operations. Private parties subscribed the remainder. The Bank of North America began doing business in Philadelphia on January 7, 1782. It extended its operations to Massachusetts, New York, Connecticut, and Rhode Island during that year, and to other states as the decade progressed. It was soon joined by two other note-emitting banks (the Bank of New York in June 1784 and the Massachusetts Bank a month later), but the real spur to private bank note issue only came after the establishment of Hamilton's Bank of the United States in 1791.

That institution had the right to circulate notes from the central office, a power which was used with extreme care by the young financier and his adherents. It also had the authority to set up branches and emit notes there as well, a power which it first exercised by opening offices in several commercial centers along the East Coast (in Boston, New York, Baltimore, and Charleston in 1792, Savannah in 1793, and Norfolk, Virginia, in 1795), but which it later employed in response to new political realities (a branch at the new national capital in 1800) and opportunities (a branch in New Orleans, set up in 1804, on the heels of the departing French). These branch notes, and indeed all issues of Hamilton's Bank of the United States, are excessively rare today, for almost all were redeemed upon that institution's liquidation in 1811.

The rise and spread of the branch bank idea seems to have acted as a spur to the formation of purely private, note-emitting banks. These first came to states which had no local branch of the Bank of the United States—for example to Connecticut, where the Union Bank, the Hartford Bank, and the New Haven Bank all opened their doors in 1792, followed by the Middletown Bank

Bank of the United States, thirty dollars, 1791. It is a contemporary, possibly British, counterfeit. Courtesy the NNC.

in 1795 and the Norwich Bank in 1796. A similar pattern took place in Delaware (the Bank of Delaware, 1795), New Hampshire (New Hampshire Bank, 1792), and Rhode Island (Providence Bank, 1791, and Bank of Rhode Island at Newport, 1795). Additional banks were organized in New York, Pennsylvania, and the other states also served by the Bank of the United States and its branches. By the end of the eighteenth century, about twenty banks were injecting new, private paper notes, in denominations ranging from one dollar to one thousand, into the anemic fiscal bloodstream of the new nation. In passing, the very fact that these banks and their immediate successors denominated their currency in dollars rather than sterling (and a few had indeed begun

Unissued sheet of notes from the Washington Bank (Waverly, Rhode Island), 1800. All of the engraving was done by hand, resulting in minor differences on the notes. Courtesy the NNC.

in one currency system before switching to dollars by the mid-1790s) helped to ensure that the dollar would be paramount in notational systems, even if the average inhabitant was unlikely to see one of the new dollar coins for many years.

By 1800, the appeal of the private bank note had become permanently established. Also by that time, its possibilities for further development of the national economy were becoming evident—and well-nigh mandatory. Americans were standing at the outskirts of their Industrial Revolution; soon they would need a rapid and sustained growth of the money supply for the payment of wages in factories and workshops. Moreover, they were about to secure a new national domain nearly as large as the one they already possessed (the Louisiana country of the Mississippi Basin, which their representatives would purchase from Napoleon at the end of 1803).

By the beginning years of the new century, two more characteristics of the bank note were becoming manifest. It would need to be produced in larger quantities than ever before to pay for all of the possibilities now suddenly opening. And it would have to be made much safer than was currently the case, or it could not play its part in the fulfilling of the American prospect.

The first generation of private notes was engraved and printed from copper plates. As was previously mentioned, the use of this technique yielded a delicate line and a product very difficult to forge. But it did not result in a large number of impressions without the necessity of fairly frequent re-engraving, a process which would rob its products of their perfect consistency. As long as banks were small and their paper issued sparingly, the problems inherent with printing from copper would likewise remain minor. But by 1800, two things were happening: more banks were entering the game, and the size of the printings circulated by a number of them was growing as well. That called note consistency into question, and the fact that the notes' designs were simple affairs (for copper, while soft, is still difficult to engrave by hand) made matters still worse. Those modest, tentative attempts at pictorial representation—an American eagle here, a seated Liberty there, a bit of fancywork, a scroll, a simple bust of General Washington on a Rhode Island note from a bank which bore his name—were as easy to prepare by a dishonest craftsman as an honest one.

And so a bottleneck was coming into existence by the turn of the new century. If left unopened, it would soon mean that Americans would not get the notes they needed in sufficient numbers and could not trust the ones they already had. It is a matter of record that many of the early notes (especially those of the Bank of the United States) are known today only from counterfeits. It may be argued that the survival of these notes stems from the fact that they were not redeemable, unlike genuine notes, but the spread of the fakes from one end of the Republic to the other suggests that the problem was real, general, and might one day become fatal.

Fortunately, a savior was in the wings. Elsewhere, it has been noted that the British Industrial Revolution produced a monetary crisis (a shortage of safe coins of low value for wage payments to the new proletariat), which was solved by turning to some of Matthew Boulton's new technology (he used the power of steam to mass-produce coins and coin dies, achieving consistency and unforgeability at once). In Britain the essential form of money was the coin, but what about America where the essential form of money was fast becoming the note?

One of the pivotal figures in the industrialization of money lived in Newburyport, Massachusetts. His name was Jacob Perkins. He had once been a silversmith and was later a diesinker (he had made many of the moneying tools for the Massachusetts copper coinage of the 1780s). More recently, Perkins had turned his hand to the mechanization of nail-making. By the dawn of the new century he was thirty-five and well-established, but always with an eye out for more renumerative opportunities. He was about to find one.

In the early 1790s he had begun experimenting with engraving on steel. The advantages of this metal for security printing were obvious, for steel would outlast copper by a factor of at least six to one. But it was difficult to engrave and nearly impossible to roll into flat sheets for engraving with the rudimentary motive force traditionally available, so steel had remained an attractive idea and no more.

Massachusetts cent, 1788. Die by Jacob Perkins. Courtesy the NNC.

Perkins set out to conquer the metal. He began selecting steel of a particular type, one soft enough to be rolled out and engraved, but which could be hardened after it had received its design. The fact that the Industrial Revolution was now producing such steel in modest quantities made Perkins' work easier and indeed possible. Once he had found his steel, he developed methods of hardening and softening it again, until he could produce any degree of ductility desired. This was essential for what he next had in mind.

Perkins not only wished to use steel for engraving, but he wanted to mass-produce what he had engraved on other pieces of steel. In short, he wanted to do for currency what Matthew Boulton had already done for coinage: make the tools which produced money infinitely replicable by the official producer, infinitely difficult of replication by the unofficial. He would achieve his goal in two stages.

The first was by an invention created around 1792, patented in 1799. Perkins called it a "check plate protector," which we know better as a stereotype steel plate. Here, its inventor would create a number (as many as sixty-four) of tiny steel dies with letters, numbers, or fancywork on them. These dies might include the name of an issuing bank on one die, its location on another, the denomination in words on a third, and the same information in figures on a fourth. Literally anything could be engraved on the dozens of small dies, and, when all had been completed, they were clamped together into a single printing plate or matrix. Perkins' goal here was twofold: to render counterfeiting infer-

nally difficult, and to render easier the creation of related notes of different denominations. He had perfected all of this by the end of the 1790s, although no notes from this early period appear to have survived. We might never have heard of him, had it not been for that second invention, the hardening and softening of steel at will.

Perkins created the process, and the idea soon occurred to him of combining it with his stereotype plate. He was doing so by 1804, leading a quiet revolution in the way in which Americans would get the paper money they required. Perkins' methodology is forgotten today, but the United States would have developed differently had he or someone else not invented it.

What he devised (and what he soon patented) was nothing less than the mass-production of unforgeable paper currency. He took his new, soft steel, engraved an image on bits of it, combined those bits into a plate, then hardened the lot. Next, he took another

An early Perkins note: Gloucester Bank (Gloucester, Massachusetts), ten dollars, 1814. Courtesy the NNC

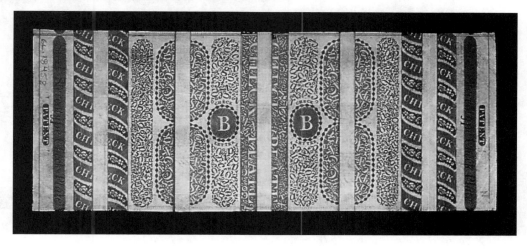

piece of soft steel, fashioned it into a roller, and passed it repeatedly over the designs on the plate (he had devised an improved transfer press to accomplish this portion of the labor) until the intricate designs had been completely carried over to the roller. Then that roller was hardened and could be used to replicate its designs onto soft steel plates, which were then hardened. Openings were left in these plates to accommodate small rectangular steel dies with the name of banks, their locations, and the denominations of the notes to be issued. When these smaller dies were dropped into their proper positions in the blank spaces of the larger plates, the preparatory process was finished and production could begin.

By 1804, Perkins was printing notes from such steel plates. By the following year, he was creating currency for sixteen area banks, and by 1806 the inventor was doing so well that he had ceased most of his other gainful activities. He built a three-story printing plant on Fruit Street in Newburyport in 1808. A Massachusetts law of the subsequent year would bring more business his way: henceforth, all paper money printed in the state (whose jurisdiction included Maine until 1820) would have to be created by Perkins' stereotype steel plates.

Jacob Perkins eventually went to Philadelphia where he helped revolutionize security printing in the former capital. He finally moved on to London at the beginning of the 1820s, where his attempts to replicate his American successes met with stiff patriotic resistance from Matthew Boulton's son, from William Congreve, and from others. He lived the life of a wealthy tinkerer, keeping his neighbors on the Thames awake nights with his experiments with a steam-powered cannon. He lived until 1851, but his essential work had ended, and his niche in American history had been securely carved many years before.

Perkins' notes lacked esthetic appeal, and to be blunt, they were downright homely, but they were difficult to counterfeit. They were so challenging, in fact, that they were never seriously attacked. They had an additional, if unforeseen, advantage over other notes of the day: they all looked alike, regardless of denomination, issuer, or place. And so an early note of the Detroit Bank, the first such institution west of the Mississippi, looks very much like one from New England (even though the note from Detroit is of greater historic interest because it was signed by the city's founder, Judge A. B. Woodward).

Perkins continued his currency improvements for some years. As the state of Massachusetts was adopting his stereotype system for the front of its notes, he was ex-

State Bank (Trenton, New Jersey), ten dollars, 1822. The basic processes were by Perkins, and the refinements by Spencer. Courtesy the NNC.

tending his attentions to the back, a side traditionally ignored by security engravers up to that point. Perkins had created a way of mass-producing an intricate, virtually random arrangement of letters and words for that side of the currency by the time the 1809 law went into effect, but it never achieved the popularity of what he had created for the faces of his notes.

The firm he founded continued to print its distinctive notes long after he had left New England, but other inventors had already begun taking American currency in new, more artistic directions. Murray, Draper, Fairman & Company of Philadelphia organized in 1810, hired the finest engravers available, and in 1815 lured the man who could mass-produce their artistry to Philadelphia to assist them. Jacob Perkins only remained with Murray, Draper, Fairman for four years, but he left his mark there for all time, marrying his techniques of mass-production to the excellence of imagery already attained by the firm. His new employers would use his system to create the major elements on working plates from his steel rollers, abandoning his idea of individual slugs for name, place, and denomination, and subsequent printers would tend to follow in their path.

Another inventor had joined Messrs. Murray, Draper, and Fairman immediately prior to Perkins' arrival. That was a Connecticut Yankee named Asa Spencer. Spencer had invented a geometric lathe, a contrivance which would add an important new weapon to the arsenal of security printing. It made possible the creation of precise, curving lines of essentially infinite variety, useful for rosettes, for borders, for the "medallions" upon which could be added the denominations of the notes or the names of the issuing banks. With Spencer, the basic outlines of the American note, and the path it would take up to the present day, had been plotted.

This is not to say that the printers rested on their laurels. They did not dare to, because there were still many who wished to mimic their products. The nineteenth-century private American bank note was one of the most counterfeited of all fiscal documents, and its forgery would be a permanent problem for issuers, printers, and the public alike. How could this be?

In a sense, the private note was a victim of its own success. When the first few private banks had become going concerns, they naturally attracted the attention of ambitious businessmen and local civic leaders alike. Consequently the number of note-issuing banks had grown to dozens by 1810, hundreds by 1830, and thousands by 1850. At the same time, the success of Murray, Draper, Fairman & Company and its competitors meant that bankers were no longer restricted to the trite if safe designs of Perkins' plates: they could have anything they wanted, and they promptly acted on the new freedom of design. Unfortunately, that meant that there would no longer be standardization in design—which was, after all, what Perkins had wanted, and which was still at the heart of an effective counterfeiting deterrent. And so the Republic entered the great days of the private bank note with a multiplicity of excellent designs, all of them at risk from the forger. When we combine this abundance of imagery with two other considerations (a widespread illiteracy and unfamiliarity with printing of any type, and the very real possibility of genuine notes issued for fraudulent purposes) we begin to see the rich potential for trouble inherent in the new fiscal tool.

The printers did what they could to reduce the problem of forgery, if not of fraud. Their efforts went in several directions. One of the earliest defenses which occurred to them was to print their notes on special paper, whose dispersal was jealously guarded. This expedient had been employed for Continental Currency (and even for some of the later colonial issues), and it would have been a logical thought to those who had handled those notes when very young. Murray, Draper, Fairman & Company used paper with a pinkish cast and imbedded red fibers, and

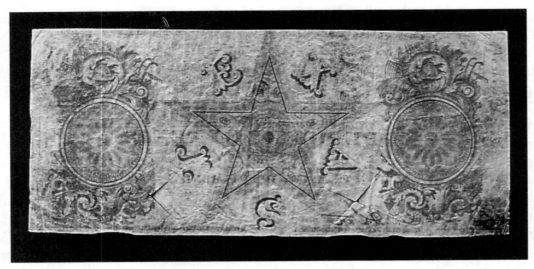

Republic of Texas, back of a hundred-dollar bill, 1839. Courtesy the NNC.

Peter Maverick and a few of the other early printers made efforts in similar directions, but that other tried and true paper expedient, the watermark, was rarely employed by any American printers. It soon became apparent that notes got dirty so rapidly that any protection offered by special paper was temporary anyway.

As a result most of the printers concentrated on what was on the notes, not what they were printed on. Here, their efforts went in three basic directions. First, they began printing notes with back designs as well as front ones. Second, they added secondary colors to the faces of their notes. Finally, they made the artwork on both sides ever more complex.

The first expedient never became universal: down to the end of their career, most private bank notes were only printed on the face. Back printing, though, achieved popularity in certain areas fairly early—particularly the South and some frontier areas such as Texas (which had printed its own notes by the typeset method immediately after gaining independence from Mexico in 1836, but soon resorted to United States printers and engravers instead). The South was even more short of specie than were other sections, and it was correspondingly more dependent on paper money, so its notes had to be as difficult to counterfeit as possible. Ear-

ly back designs featured simple "engine-turned" arrangements, whose loops and whorls may have been trite but whose presence made forgery much more difficult. The backs of Republic of Texas issues show a somewhat later stage of artistic development, wherein a fancy five-pointed star (with letters spelling out TEXAS in the interstices, just to make certain everyone got the point) was flanked by two identical assemblages of agricultural and maritime symbols, flanking a medallion produced by the geometric lathe. The Republic of Texas employed this design on all of its issues of the early 1840s, without indication of value. Back printing was ordinarily applied in a color different from that used on the front. Gray, orange, and light blue were favored, as was the color Americans use on their money today—green.

For the fronts of the notes, black enjoyed a monopoly until the 1840s, but then a strange thing happened. The first photographic methods were invented, and as one might expect, they were immediately turned to two illicit uses: pornography and counterfeiting. We are not concerned with the former, but the latter interests us because it led directly to the second of the anticounterfeiting practices, the addition of one or more colors to the faces of the notes.

The first, tentative efforts in this direction were occurring by 1845, and they were modest. Color was applied to the area where the note's denomination was spelled out. This would make matters more difficult for the darkroom forgers, but its primary purpose was to discourage the upward raising of a note's value by those good with the pen or the pastepot. That second color would show any disturbance attempted in that area. Bars of different colors were tried, and red and orange long enjoyed popularity. But they gradually yielded their places to green, when it was discovered that that tint also offered greater challenges to the crooked photographer than any other.

City Bank (New York, New York), three dollars, 1852. This is a photographic counterfeit. Courtesy the NNC.

State Bank (New Brunswick, New Jersey), a hundred-dollar bill without "protector," c. 1850, and with "protector," c. 1855. Back printing was added at the same time. Courtesy the NNC.

The domain of the second hue was gradually extended across the faces of the notes—to fancy ornaments along the left and right margins, to small, subsidiary engravings of figures, numerals, and objects, even to a precise juxtaposition with ordinary black printing in the name of a bank or the medallions containing the denomination. Upon occasion, a third color was added to the notes, but its use was ordinarily highly restricted. The second and third colors were reserved for faces alone: I have never seen an American obsolete note with a bicolor back.

While these chromatic experiments were taking place, the private bank note was undergoing a final evolution: the designs employed on its face were becoming larger, more detailed, more complex, moving toward a legitimate position among the minor decorative arts in America. The printers were hiring the best artists they could afford and improving Perkins' and Spencer's technologies to keep apace with what those artists created. They were doing so primarily to make their notes ever more difficult to counterfeit, but an element of competitive pride must surely have entered into their considerations: for one of the few times in American history, the money-makers were creating beautiful objects simply because they wanted to do so, because they wanted to see how far they could take their new medium. The users of their products would receive an entire liberal education from them—and so can we.

End-point of evolution, Hartford Bank (Hartford, Connecticut), three dollars, 1862. Courtesy the NNC.

But for now we are interested in the technological nature of those images, and here we can make several generalizations. The most important is that there was a direct relationship between the date on a note and the size and complexity of its images or "vignettes." If the notes were being created by the technology which predated Jacob Perkins and his fellows, those images were likely to be quite small, and there would be differences between those employed on the same denomination of a note even if an identity were sought, for each of the vignettes would have to be painfully carved by hand, dot by dot. When Perkins' transfer process came into common use (say by the 1820s), the identity of vignettes was assured, for they would now be created from transfer rolls. Their positions would tend to vary slightly relative to other elements, for the printers created their note plates by combining elements from several transfer rolls, separately applied. But this variation still represented an immense improvement over the variety previously inherent between one rendition of a design and the next. But the central vignettes and other lesser elements still tended to be modest in the early days, because it obviously required less pressure to impress a design from a small transfer roll than a large one; more importantly, designs tended to be fairly limited in subject choice.

This was because the creation of a master took a great deal of effort, and printers had a natural disinclination to expend efforts on more images when decent ones already existed. And so a distinctly limited number of national figures appeared on the early notes. For example, the Marquis de Lafayette's somewhat glum countenance graces paper from one end of the Republic to the other—now as the centerpiece, now as a border element, now in a square frame, now in an oval. DeWitt Clinton was similarly popular—not because anyone remembered precisely what he had done (he was governor of New York when the Erie Canal opened for traffic in 1825, had unsuccessfully run for President back in 1812), but because he was available,

in the form of a portrait suitable for the notes. The same scenes tended to show up on notes as well—a canal boat here, an early train there—as did selected views and figures from mythology. A twentieth-century historian whose knowledge of early American life was based on those early issues and vignettes would form an erroneous impression indeed of what the country was actually like in the twenties and early thirties of the last century.

The mid-1830s saw the beginnings of an artistic golden age for the private note. More printers came into the business, and they sought and hired more and better artists. Because the counterfeiters were now becoming adept at copying small and simple images, the artists and the firms for which they worked expanded the size and subject matter of the pictorial elements on their products. In time, scenes of great beauty and complexity were achieved, artwork which occasionally employed the entire canvas represented by the face of the note to tell a story, reproduce a scene, point out a moral. The earlier "cut-and-paste" appearance of the bank note yielded place to an artistic unity, one suggesting that larger and larger portions of the design, although not all of it, were being applied by larger rollers and more powerful presses. All of these improvements in design and color were created to guard the notes against counterfeiting, but they were also intended as emblems of pride, as advertisements for the skills of artists and the ingenuity of printers, leading to additional printing work. They meant that, for a brief period in the middle years of the nineteenth century, the American bank note was the finest in the world. They also meant that the number of firms doing security printing was about to become severely restricted.

It could not have been otherwise. All of those perfectly-centered vignettes, those fancy, machine-engraved rosettes, those painstaking printings in two or more colors on the finest rag paper, all of those elements, and the artists and mechanics necessary to produce them, represented an enormous capital investment. By the 1850s, a process of consolidation was at work, and it soon came to fruition. On April 29, 1858, the seven premier printers of paper money in the United States (Rawdon, Wright, Hatch & Edson; Toppan, Carpenter & Company; Danforth, Perkins & Company; Bald, Cousland & Company; Jocelyn, Draper, Welsh & Company; Wellstood, Hay & Whiting; and John E. Gavit) combined to become the American Bank Note Company, with headquarters in New York City. Eighteen months later, a few printers who had refused to join the merger created a firm of their own, the National Bank Note Company. Between them, these two organizations would print virtually all of the remaining private bank notes. They would also be instrumental in providing fiscal paper for the national government, soon to be involved in the Civil War and accordingly forced to rethink its position on its own currency.

For the student of American business history, the American Bank Note Company might be worth researching, for it combined most of the elements of a horizontal trust (an organization which achieves a monopoly or near monopoly over a commodity by securing a control over the various firms connected with its product) some twenty years before the practice occurred elsewhere in American business. The men who brought off the merger would have seen it in a more modest light: a way of making more money (literally and otherwise), a way of combining techniques and talents in the most efficient way. And so it was.

By the time of the creation of the American Bank Note Company, Americans had been using private paper for two-thirds of a century. It had fueled their industries, financed their ships, and fostered their farms. It had gone with them everywhere, and the spread of the private bank note reflected the westward expansion of the Republic itself.

The first private notes had circulated along the Eastern Seaboard, because that was where most people lived. But the United States had been granted wider territories un-der the Treaty of Paris (1783), and many spots within these territories were being settled as the eighteenth century was drawing to its close. New states began to emerge—Kentucky (1792), Tennessee (1796), and then, with the new century, Ohio (1803)—towns grew up, legislatures were elected, laws were written, professionals were attracted, and banks were established. The sway of the private note also expanded, to Kentucky (1802), Tennessee (1807), and Ohio (1807). While the Louisiana Purchase of 1803 led to an expansion to the south, new states were entering the Union from the opposite direction as well, as the Old Northwest began making its influence felt. Louisiana became a state in 1812, followed by Mississippi (1817), Alabama (1819), Missouri (1821), and Arkansas (1836). The private note spread less rapidly to these last four places than it did to Louisiana, which received its first note-issuing bank some eight years prior to statehood, in 1804. Missouri saw its first issues in 1816, Mississippi in 1817, and Alabama in 1819. Arkansas waited until 1837, because its degree of economic need was more modest there than elsewhere.

The spread of the private bank note in the Old Northwest was even more dramatic: as we have noted, Detroit got its first local notes in 1806, some thirty-one years before Michigan became a state! Similarly, Indiana was seeing its own bank notes at least two years prior to statehood, while neighboring Illinois saw its first notes some five years before becoming a state. This pattern repeated itself across the Midwest, as settlement spread to Wisconsin and then across the Mississippi, to Iowa, Kansas, and Nebraska. The latter was seeing heavy settlement by the mid-1850s, and it was shortly seeing a remarkable number of note-issuing banks and related institutions as well, serving established residents and newcomers alike. All of this was more than a decade before the territory became a state.

By the end of the 1840s, the United States was achieving its present boundaries. Texas had been admitted to the Union late in 1845, and the Territory of Florida earlier that

Miner's Bank (San Francisco, California), one dollar, 1849. Courtesy the NNC.

same year. Both areas had had private banks which issued notes. Some of the Texan issues were bilingual, and Florida was seeing notes from half a dozen banks by the early 1830s, issues from such metropoli as Apalachicola, Magnolia, and Marianna.

Texas had come into the Union with a quantity of unwanted baggage, including a large public debt from its days as an independent country (1836–1845) and an ongoing boundary dispute with its erstwhile owner, Mexico. The United States absorbed the former and took responsibility for the latter: by the spring of 1846, ambitious James K. Polk had sent troops into the disputed area. The Mexican authorities obliged by firing on them, and Mr. Polk had the pretext for what no less an authority than Ulysses S. Grant (who served in Mexico) later referred to as the most unjust war ever waged by a strong country upon a weak. Morality disregarded, the United States had won the contest within eighteen months — and one of its commanders would soon grace dozens of bank notes, placed there by order of the bankers of a grateful Republic. One such issuer was the Miner's Bank, which placed Zachary Taylor's portrait on a dollar bill early in 1849. There was nothing particularly noteworthy about that except for

one thing: the Miner's Bank was located in San Francisco, California. And it was connected with something of some importance which was gathering momentum that year: the Gold Rush.

The vast deposits of precious metal which were found and extracted from the new lands taken from Mexico would in time allow Americans to shift their numismatic emphasis from paper to coinage. But for the moment, the surge of new metal merely served to encourage more speculation, more private banks, and more fiscal misery whenever those banks collapsed. Here is what we may call the underside of the private note phenomenon. While many of the banks continued to issue safe currency decade after decade, many others were financially unsound from the very beginning and went under at the first sign of economic uncertainty. Others still were outright frauds, which never offered banking services at all and existed only on paper to circulate worthless currency among the unsuspecting.

Consider a state of the Upper Midwest, for instance. Michigan had some excellent and safe note-circulating banks. But it had many unsafe and fraudulent ones as well. All are detailed in the following:

ROSTER OF MICHIGAN NOTE-ISSUING BANKS

Name	Fate
Bank of Adrian, 1838–39	Became the Adrian Insurance Co.
Erie & Kalamazoo R.R. Bank, 1835	Organized 1835, failed c.1841; c.1841, 1853-54, revived 1853, failed 1854.
Bank of Allegan, 1837–39	Closed/failed.
Kalamazoo River Bank, 1838	Never opened.
Bank of Ann Arbor, 1837	Never opened.
Citizens Bank of Michigan, 1838	Probably never opened.
Exchange Bank, 1838	Never opened.
Government Stock Bank, 1849–54	Failed.
Millers Bank of Washtenaw, 1837–39	Closed/failed.
Bank of Washtenaw, 1835–1854	Failed in 1839; revived and failed again, 1854.
Bank of Auburn, 1838–41	Closed/failed.
Farmers Bank of Sandstone, 1837–38	Closed/failed.
Bank of Battle Creek, 1838–40	Closed/failed.
Bank of Lake St. Clair, 1838	Never opened.
Berrien County Bank	Closed/failed.
Branch County Bank, 1837–38	Closed/failed.
Bank of Brest, 1837–38	Closed/failed.
Merchants Bank of Jackson County, 1838–41	Closed/failed.
St. Joseph County Bank, 1837–38	Closed/failed.
Bank of Clinton, 1837–38	Closed/failed.
Bank of Cold-Water, 1837–38	Closed/failed.
Bank of Constantine, 1836–41	Closed/failed.
Detroit Bank, 1806–08	Closed.
Detroit City Bank, 1837–39	Closed/failed.
Farmers & Mechanics' Bank Bank of Michigan 1829–39, 1841–69	Closed in 1839; revived 1841 finally closed in 1869.
Bank of Michigan, 1818–42	Closed.
"Michigan Bank of Detroit," c.1818	Non-existent bank; issued notes intended to pass as those of Bank of Michigan.
Michigan Insurance Bank, 1860–65	SURVIVED the period; became the National Insurance Bank.
Michigan State Bank, 1835–39	Closed in 1839; revived in 1845–55 in 1845 and closed or failed in 1855.
Peninsular Bank, 1849–70	Closed.
State Bank of Michigan, 1859–64	SURVIVED the period; merged to become the First National Bank Detroit.
Erie Banking Company, c.1840	Unknown.
Farmers Bank of Genesee County, 1838	Closed/failed.
Genesee County Bank, 1837–37	Closed/failed.
Bank of Gibraltar, 1838	Closed/failed.
Goodrich Bank, 1838	Closed/failed.
Grand River Bank, 1837–39	Closed/failed.
Peoples Bank of Grand River, 1837–38	Closed/failed.
Commercial Bank, 1838	Never opened.
Farmers Bank of Homer, 1837–39	Closed/failed.
Detroit & St. Joseph R.R. Bank, 1838–40	Failed.
Jackson County Bank, 1837-38	Closed/failed.
Bank of Kensington, 1837-38	Closed/failed.
Van Buren County Bank, 1838	Never opened.

Name	Fate
Bank of the Capitol, c.1859	Unknown.
Bank of Lapeer, 1837-38	Closed/failed.
Lapeer County Bank, 1838	Never opened.
Saginaw County Bank, 1838	Never opened.
Bank of Manchester, 1837–39	Closed.
Calhoun County Bank, 1836–40	Closed/failed.
Bank of Marshall, 1837–41	Closed/failed.
Bank of Michigan, 1862–65	SURVIVED the period, to become the National Bank of Michigan
Bank of Michigan Centre, 1837–38	Closed/failed.
Merchants & Mechanics Bank of the City of Monroe, 1837–39	Closed/failed.
Bank of Monroe, 1827–30, 1835–38	Closed/failed c.1830; revived 1835, failed 1838.
Bank of River Raisin, 1832-39, 1841–46	Closed in 1839; revived 1841, failed 1846.
Bank of Macomb County, 1836–41	Closed in 1841; revived 1851, 1851-58, failed 1858.
Bank of Niles, 1837–39	Closed/failed.
Bank of Owasso, 1838	Never opened.
Bank of Shiawassee, 1837–38	Closed/failed.
Lenawee County Bank, 1837–38	Closed/failed.
Wayne County Bank at Plymouth, 1837–38	Closed/failed.
Clinton Canal Bank at Pontiac, 1837–38	Closed/failed.
Farmers & Mechanics Bank at Pontiac, 1837–38	Closed/failed.
Bank of Oakland at Pontiac, 1837–38	Closed/failed.
Oakland County Bank, 1836–46	Closed/failed.
Bank of Pontiac, 1835–1840s, 1860s	Closed in the early 1840s; revived in the early 1860s and SURVIVED the period, merged into the First National Bank of Pontiac.
Farmers' Bank of Romeo, late 1830s	Failed.
Farmers Bank of Oakland, 1837–38	Closed/failed.
Saginaw City Bank, 1837–38	Closed/failed.
Bank of St. Clair, 1836–45	Moved to Detroit 1842; closed 1845.
Commercial Bank of Michigan, 1837–39	Closed/failed.
Farmers & Merchants Bank of St. Joseph, 1838	Closed/failed.
Bank of Saline, 1837–38	Closed/failed.
Chippeway County Bank, 1838	Closed/failed.
Bank of Chippeway, 1838	Closed/failed.
Farmers Bank of Prairie Ronde, 1838	Never opened.
Schwarzburgh Bank, 1838	Never opened.
Farmers Bank of Sharon, 1837–38	Closed/failed.
Exchange Bank at Shiawassee, 1838	Closed/failed.
Bank of Singapore, 1837–39	Closed/failed.
Bank of Superior, 1838–39	Closed/failed.
Commonwealth Bank, late 1830s	Probably never opened.
Bank of Tecumseh, 1836–39, 1855–60	Closed 1839; revived 1855, failed 1860.
Tecumseh Bank, 1838	Never opened.
Urbana Banking Company, 1830s	Unknown.
Bank of Utica, 1837–39	Closed/failed.
Clinton County Bank, late 1830s	Probably never opened.
Bank of White Pigeon, 1838	Never opened.
Huron County Bank, 1838–39	Closed/failed.
Bank of Ypsilanti, 1836–39	Closed/failed.

SOURCE: James A. Haxby. *Standard Catalog of United States Obsolete Bank Notes, 1782-1866*, II, pp.1035–1091.

The simple citation of the above table tells us a great deal about the nature of early banking and the notes which the system created. Michigan was something of a special case, for there was a real banking scramble there in the middle and late 1830s, but not that special: there was very little regulation of banking in nineteenth-century America, and boom times were likely to attract more than their share of bankers, and bank notes. There is no mystery as to why so many of the high banking hopes abruptly guttered out in 1838 and 1839: those were probably the worst years of the worst depression the country had ever suffered. The hard times had a major effect upon other aspects of the United States, and upon its money. Lean years fostered emergency monetary issues, copper cent-sized tokens and low-denomination notes called scrip, issues which flooded the eastern half of the country between 1837 and 1842. They fostered westward expansion, which was accelerating by the early 1840s, once the worst of the depression had passed. They fostered greater idealism and social concern—including concern over slavery. The abolition movement began a growth in the late 1830s which would finally carry it into the White House a quarter-century later. And hard times fostered a revival of old religions and encouraged new ones. Out in Ohio, the Kirtland Safety Society was issuing paper money in the late 1830s, but the primary concern of its personnel was theological rather than financial. Its cashier was a visionary named Joseph Smith, founder of the Church of Jesus Christ of Latter Day Saints. Smith would be martyred in time, but his followers would soon emigrate to the West along with thousands of others, whose desire for economic betterment might or might not be combined with a search for religious freedom. Smith's people are better known as Mormons, and they will soon make another appearance in our story.

The Kirtland Safety Society suggests an important aspect of private currency in nineteenth-century America, but by no means was all of it the product of ordinary banks. The Kirtland people were far more engaged in setting up a mutual aid and religious institution than they were in banking. In many other cases, the persons responsible for issuing notes had nothing whatsoever to do with banking in the sense with which we associate the word.

It must always be remembered that all those banks existed to create money. But it was perfectly possible for other types of financial institution to create currency as

Kirtland Safety Society Bank (Kirtland, Ohio), five dollars, 1837. This was signed by Joseph Smith. Courtesy the NNC.

well, promising payment in specie in exchange for paper notes. And many other types of business did in fact issue money, especially railroads, plank roads, turnpikes, and canals, concerns which literally used the paper they issued to create the capital to see their projects to conclusion. Railroad notes are particularly interesting, for

Small-change or scrip issues from the War of 1812 (above) and the Panic of 1837 (below). Courtesy the NNC.

they generally depict early locomotives, going back to the dawn of the invention itself. Railroads circulated their notes throughout the period, but their great days were the 1830s and the 1860s, the former a time when the novelty of this form of transportation attracted the attention of investors and public alike. Many of the railroad notes of the 1860s came from the Southern Confederacy, pressed into service during a period of economic emergency there.

Insurance companies were also frequent issuers of notes, as were mechanics' and other mutual aid societies (including the Kirtland group). Other players included factories, political organizations of various sorts (wards, city and borough councils, etc.), a lumber company (in Maine), a hotel (in Illinois), an import-export company (in the District of Columbia), an orphans' institute (in Ohio), and individual citizens (in many states). This roster only includes "normal" notes (those worth a dollar or more). If we included scrip in our calculation, the list could be greatly extended.

We should devote some space to the scrip phenomenon. In periods of political and/or economic dislocation in the nineteenth century, scrip and tokens both played a role. We

Patriotic Hard Times token, 1837.

previously saw scrip around 1790, when private, low-denomination paper was used for small change, to tide the Republic over until its new minor coinage could appear and take hold. Low-value notes appeared again during the War of 1812, when an actual British invasion created fears for the future and a hoarding of small change (a hoarding compounded by the fact that the United States Mint was concentrating most of its efforts on larger coins at the time). Scrip would also be a feature at mid-century, when a panic in 1857 again caused economic uncertainty, and this numismatic medium would play another major role, North and South, during the Civil War of the 1860s. But one of scrip's high points had been reached during the 1830s, when the Panic of 1837 hardened into the worst depression the country had yet known, perhaps the worst it has ever known.

Across America, specie went into hiding. We might expect such a reaction relative to large silver coins and gold coins of any size, but people of the late thirties indiscriminately hoarded copper, small silver, large silver, and gold. And so emergency money was created. On the lowest end, cent-sized copper tokens, some containing advertisements for store owners, others making sarcastic reference to the unsafe federal fiscal policies which had led to the national ruin, fulfilled the role of real cents, while still providing a profit to their makers and circulators. (A cent token could contain far less than a cent's worth of copper because the official version already did so. Britons of the 1790s had discovered the same phenomenon; Americans in the 1860s would rediscover it, as we shall see.) And for higher denominations, paper scrip came into play.

Washington, D.C. is a good example. There, around thirty merchants and organizations issued small-denomination notes between 1837 and 1841. Professions represented included those of butcher, grocer, singing-master, restaurant-owner, hotelier, dry goods merchant, printer, and druggist. Denominations included notes for five and ten cents, but six-and-one-quarter and twelve-and-one-half cent notes were far more popular, for they would replace Spanish-American reales and their halves, which still circulated widely in Washington and adjacent areas during normal times. Many of these notes were prepared from engraved plates, and they closely resembled normal

Store card Hard Times token.

currency except for size. Others were printed from type, simple affairs which favored a bit of artwork in the form of an American eagle or a portrait of George Washington. Whenever times got better, scrip went into hiding, its issue restricted to isolated areas which had difficulty getting normal money in good times or bad. But it would regularly reappear in times of trouble, throughout the days of the private American bank note.

Notes in the obsolete series were ordinarily printed in English—but not always. Mention has been made of Texan notes (on the Commercial & Agricultural Bank, located in the hamlet of Columbia) which were printed in Spanish as well as English, which was a sensible practice in an area which had recently been part of a Spanish-speaking country. This bank never seems to have opened, and I know of no other American bank which included the Spanish language on its products. But there were several banks in Pennsylvania which employed the German language on their notes, for German settlement was fairly heavy there. The Western Bank of Philadelphia issued English-only and German-only notes, the latter denominated in *thaler* rather than dollars. The Northampton Bank followed the same practice, and it placed such luminaries of German

Northampton Bank (Northampton, Pennsylvania), ten thaler or dollars, 1835. Courtesy the NNC.

A "dix" note from the Citizens' Bank of Louisiana, ten dollars, c. 1860. Courtesy the NNC.

A sophisticated counterfeit note: Bank of America (New York, New York), five dollars, 1861. Courtesy the NNC.

culture as Goethe and Haydn (who was actually Austrian, but never mind) in prominent places on its five- and ten-dollar bills of the mid-1830s.

In Louisiana, the second language was French, a reflection of the state's Gallic heritage. Several Louisiana banks and other institutions issued bilingual notes, expressing denominations in dollars and piastres, their French equivalent. One of these notes gained a peculiar immortality. In the mid-1850s, the Citizens' Bank of Louisiana was issuing a splendid ten-dollar note, whose value was expressed as DIX on face and back. The French word means "ten," of course, and the engravers used the English word on both sides of the note in addition to the French. But the French word appears to have captured the fancy of the public, and soon the bill was being referred to as a "dix note" or "dixie note," and Louisiana, and soon the South itself, became known as the "land of the dixie notes."

In 1859, an Ohioan named Daniel Decatur Emmett (who happened to be connected with a popular minstrel show in New York City) wrote a song about the South and its money. He called it "Dixie's Land," and soon Northern and Southern boys alike would be marching to Mr. Emmett's new topical song.

The bilingual notes of Texas, Pennsylvania, and Louisiana had an additional distinction besides language: at the time, it must have seemed that they were the only notes which someone, somewhere, was not attempting to alter or counterfeit. The new printing techniques of Jacob Perkins, his contemporaries, and those who followed had all been intended to make alteration and forgery more difficult, and they succeeded to a degree: without them, all currency would have been attacked, but with them, only part of it was.

How much? The answer would depend in part upon location, for isolated areas with few banks (such as Utah in the late 1850s) were served by so few issuers that a new or different product would have immediately been suspect. It was much easier to pass bad currency in larger, more chaotic places, and that was where most of it surfaced. To this day, the New York Police Department has a collection of counterfeit notes which its people acquired directly from commerce in the 1850s and 1860s. The collection is large, for the problem was great.

How great? I have been working with obsolete notes for twenty years, have seen perhaps a hundred thousand of them. I would estimate that at least twenty-five percent of the notes I have seen were spurious (representing nonexistent banks), counterfeits (fakes of real notes, but sometimes of spurious ones as well), or altered or raised (altered from a failed bank to a solvent one, raised from a lower denomination to a higher). Some of the fakes were printed on good paper, created by skilled engravers who might have brought laurels to a legitimate establishment. Others were so poorly done that one wonders why anyone would have accepted them, but accept them they did.

By the 1850s, many of the fakes were being printed in two colors, just as the real ones were. And by that time, enterprising printers of another sort were making money off the currency as well: Laban Heath and others were printing "counterfeit detectors," state-by-state listings of every current genuine note, with thumbnail descriptions of denominations and types. Mr. Heath's detectors would find ready buyers throughout the remaining years of the private bank note.

All of the counterfeits and related problems created a curious, chaotic effect on nineteenth-century American money. There was no single, universal value for any given note, from any given bank. Instead, the worth of any note varied against that of every other note, and all fluctuated against specie. So a five-dollar note from Plainfield, New Jersey, might be worth $4.70 against gold in that town, but $4.20 in Philadelphia, $3.90 in Boston, $3.00 in Cincinnati. The same note would vary in value against every

other note coming out of Plainfield as well, based on the reputed soundness of the issuing institution, the number of counterfeits it had inspired, etc. In short, what had taken place with paper in the eighteenth century was being repeated in the nineteenth, and with a vengeance. But Americans of 1850 would have joined their counterparts of a century earlier in observing that shifting money was far preferable to no money at all. And there was a minor consideration, of greater importance to us than to either of them: the notes of the nineteenth century were among the most beautiful and evocative financial documents ever created. They are our best, most easily obtainable visual representation of the American nineteenth century—not in terms of what it actually was, but in terms of what those who lived through it thought it was.

Let me explain. If you seek an accurate depiction of an 1855 railway locomotive, seek elsewhere. But if you seek to learn what a railway locomotive actually meant to an average American of 1855, you could do far worse than begin with the obsolete note.

Those things which Americans valued, thought important, lived with or by are all here, displayed with a more-than-photographic intensity and immediacy. Workingmen are here, in field and factory, in logging camp and mine, on seas and rivers, in sailing ships and on flatboats and rafts: every conceivable male profession is represented, during every stage of the working day. Pride

Government Bank (Washington D.C.), five dollars, 1862. Courtesy the NNC.

Ocmulgee Bank (Macon, Georgia), twenty dollars, 1840 (detail). Courtesy the NNC.

shows in the faces of these men—pride of profession, pride of nationality.

A national element is generally present, whatever the actual subject matter of the notes' vignettes. These were days of a very tender, somewhat insecure American identity—feelings and fears of a people which desperately wanted to be taken seriously by the older members of the family of nations, which was likely to be somewhat bellicose and shrill when others did not see it as it wished to see itself. The Screaming Eagle is everywhere. One popular image late in the period has him rising the seas with a portion of the Transatlantic Cable and lightning bolts in his talons, and in another, he is perched atop a globe, surrounded by the flags of the states. Heroes from the distant and recent past abound as well: George Washington is everywhere, as are Thomas Jefferson, Benjamin Franklin, and as for Southerners, John C. Calhoun. Current politicians may also appear: as soon as Franklin Pierce was elected President in 1852, at least one bank in Connecticut was searching for a daguerreotype of the new chief executive so

Central Bank (Nashville, Tennessee; Dandridge Branch), five dollars, 1853. Courtesy the NNC.

Bank of Lewistown (Lewistown, Pennsylvania), ten dollars, 1844. Courtesy the NNC.

that he could be put on one of its new notes. Zachary Taylor was similarly honored, as was James Polk, Abraham Lincoln, and the disastrous James Buchanan—usually on issues from his native Pennsylvania.

Scenes of national remembrance are plentiful. Sometimes they made a logical connection with the venue of a bank, as with a note depicting the ruins of Jamestown from a bank in nearby Norfolk, Virginia, or another showing the signing of the Declaration of Independence, from a bank in Philadelphia. But scenes from the past might turn up anywhere, for the past belonged to everyone. And the scene might be from the recent past, and involve ordinary citizens rather than national icons. For example there is a five-dollar bill from the Central Bank of Tennessee which shows the homecoming of a veteran of the recent Mexican War. A figure of General Washington appears at the opposite corner, stretching his hand toward the homecoming scene, blessing it, enfolding it in the ongoing American experience.

Thus men and their occupations and their deeds—or rather, white males—were depict-ed. The private bank note depicted non-white males too, and women of all colors. Let us go deeper and see how these other Americans are seen through the medium of the obsolete note.

We begin with women. Among female subjects, those of European extraction dominate, just as with males. The earliest depictions of women on notes were as goddesses, Juno, Diana, Liberty, and the like. Some of them strike us as silly or even risqué—the nineteenth-century equivalent of soft-core pornography. By the later 1830s, the mythological rendition is yielding place to one of virtuous attributes: women in recognizably nineteenth-century dress, representing Commerce, Agriculture, Navigation, and Science. Still later, engravers begin depicting women as women, involved with normal pursuits ranging from child-rearing to factory work to work on the farm, and to taking a walk with a special young man once the work has been done (Bank of Lewiston, ten dollars, 1844). This greater realism is welcome, but we should not take it too far, because on many of the notes, women are still

Ocoee Bank (Cleveland, Tennessee), two dollars, 1859. Courtesy the NNC.

Eagle Bank (Bristol, Rhode Island), one dollar, 1848. Courtesy the NNC.

portrayed as temptresses, delicate flowers needing the protection of their menfolk, or as incipient consumptives, for whom such protection is probably too late. These other views should not surprise us: we are speaking of how an age saw itself and its inhabitants, how it replicated those views through the media of ink and paper.

Thus far, I have been speaking of white American females, but Native American and African American females, and males, also graced the notes. How were they depicted?

Here, the gap between perceived and photographic reality widened. We must always bear in mind that those who were ordering, creating, and using the notes were predominantly white males; the depiction of others would therefore be filtered through the dominant group's perception of the truth. We have already seen a certain romanticizing of American wives and daughters as their husbands and fathers wished to perceive them, but the phenomenon goes much further with these other groups.

Native Americans were distorted most. While bank notes of the 1850s were beginning to portray members of this group as they really were (or even with affection and sympathy, as on a two-dollar Tennessee note of 1859, which purports to show members of a family out for a Sunday canoe ride), earlier notes and many current ones presented Native Americans in a light unfavorable to them, flattering to the white majority. A note from the Eagle Bank of Bristol, Rhode Island, displays this image in its most complete form: here, a Native American wife is attempting to convince her husband of the blessings of (European) civilization, pointing down to a busy harbor scene, one which in she and her family can never participate due to their insistence on remaining Native Americans. Related images include a white American female instructing her Native American counterpart in the blessings of agriculture (which is a bit self-serving, considering that Native Americans had introduced corn, potatoes, tobacco, and a host of other farming plants to the attention of Europeans), and my favorite, a warrior seated on a tree stump, gazing down at a log cabin with a frustrated look on his face: I imagine he is annoyed because he can't understand the concept of civilization, and knows it.

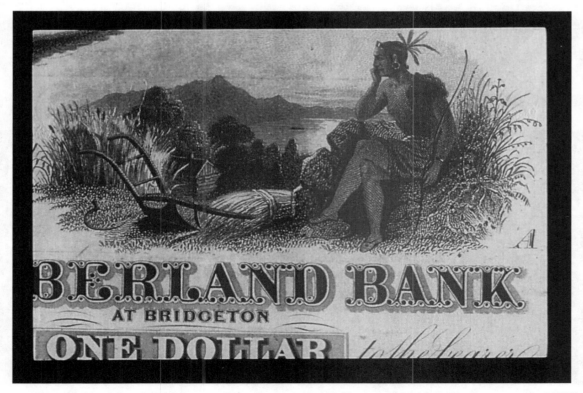

Cumberland Bank (Bridgeton, New Jersey), one dollar, c. 1850 (detail). Courtesy the NNC.

Manufacturers Bank (Macon, Georgia), twenty dollars, 1862 (detail). Courtesy the NNC.

Bank of Hamburg (Hamburg, South Carolina), five dollars, 1860 (detail). Courtesy the NNC.

Timber Cutter's Bank (Savannah, Georgia), two dollars, 1858. Courtesy the NNC.

African Americans were portrayed with a similar lack of realism, which flattered the dominant as it idealized the supine. Whites and blacks may appear together in work scenes (as they most certainly did in real life), but there is never any question about who is in charge. African Americans are also depicted alone or with others of their race in scenes of plantation work, as haulers of goods, workers on the docks. One rarely sees them in factories, however, because the image of the slave in the mill touched the nerves of the white majority in both the North and the South.

And we are talking about slaves, of course, for that was the identity of nearly every African American in the mid-nineteenth-century United States. Their depiction on the notes nearly always involved work, because that was what they were in America to do. The scenes might be a realistic, bald statement of the activities of a particular group at a particular time. They could also be romanticized, the slave now appear-ing as the lovable incompetent of contemporary white folklore. We may see him drowsing on a wagon, letting the time go by, as on a twenty-dollar bill of the Manufacturers Bank of Macon, Georgia, or in the guise of a docile young boy, helping his master sharpen a scythe (Bank of Hamburg, five dollars, 1860). But the most self-serving image of African Americans ever to appear on an obsolete note must surely be found on a two-dollar bill of the Timber Cutter's Bank of Savannah, Georgia. Here, a smiling mother holds a chuckling infant on her shoulder, and he in turn holds a bough from a cotton plant, which enslaves them both.

A final aspect of the imagery of the obsolete note deserves mention, because it was at the very heart of how the age perceived itself. This was Progress—as the age determined it. We might not see the factories spewing smoke on a Massachusetts or Ohio note as symbolic of a better way of life, but for those who used that note, they were harbingers indeed. Compared with the back-

Susquehanna Bridge & Bank Company (Port Deposit, Maryland), ten dollars, 1831 (detail). Courtesy the NNC

breaking drudgery of the field and farm, the smoke from a factory chimney was progress, the very promise of a better life. Images of improvement abound on these notes, including steamboats, power looms, and canals full of traffic. But one image overshadows them all: the railroad.

For many nineteenth-century Americans, the railway train was progress promised and personified. It spanned rivers and burrowed through mountains, carried products to market and people to new lives, and knit a disintegrating republic back together. Trains fascinated Americans from the beginning: the earliest note I have seen with a railway vignette dates from 1831, the product of the Susquehanna Bridge & Bank Company of Port Deposit, Maryland. The vignette is tiny, less than an inch broad, but there it is, one of the first trains, happily chugging its way into the American consciousness.

Trains were depicted at stations, hauling freight, carrying passengers, crossing marvelous suspension bridges, and entering or leaving tunnels. But one of the most telling images of all appears on a note of the Talla-hassee Rail Road Company, printed around 1860. A group of people has gathered to watch for the appearance of a passenger train. And here it comes! A child waves, as do two young men. A backwoodsman strikes a jaunty pose and salutes the engineer. The latter slows his engine, nodding toward the spectators. Scenes like this must have occurred across the Republic, as a generation of Americans welcomed the new era. In this case at least, the bank note tells the truth.

By the time this note was printed, the great days of the private note (and indeed, the great days of American currency itself) were nearly over. A combination of factors would soon ensure that what had taken nearly three-quarters of a century to construct would only take half a decade to demolish. One of these factors was the Civil War, but earlier, the inevitability of the private note had been challenged by a second, even more surprising event: for the first time in their history, Americans were getting enough precious metal, and enough expertise in coining it, to reduce their age-old dependence on paper.

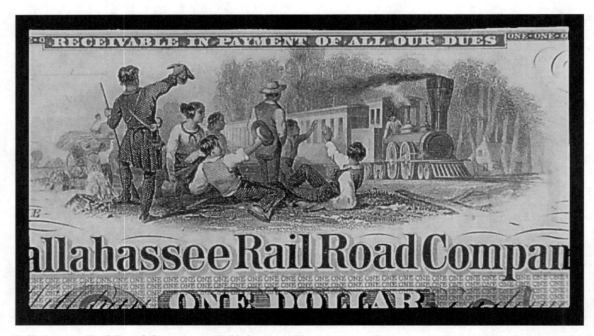

Tallahassee Rail Road Company (Tallahassee, Florida), one dollar, c. 1860 (detail). Courtesy the NNC.

CHAPTER 5

GOLD!

CHAPTER 5

GOLD!

Toward the end of the year 1848, an observant Philadelphia merchant might have encountered one of the new quarter eagles just struck by the federal mint, with the head of Liberty and the current year on one side, a bellicose American eagle and the denomination on the other. There was nothing particularly noteworthy about this piece because the Philadelphia Mint had been striking coins just like it ever since 1840, and would make nearly nine thousand of them in this very year. But there was one odd feature about the new coin: above the eagle on the reverse, this piece and a few of its fellows had the letters CAL. punched in. And thus was quietly announced one of the most momentous events in the story of numismatics.

The gold in this coin had come from California, which the United States had recently acquired by conquest and by purchase. The formal acquisition had taken place in Mexico City at the beginning of February 1848, with the Treaty of Guadalupe Hidalgo. Under its terms, Mexico got fifteen million dollars and the cancellation of all claims against it by American citizens. The United States got assurance of its title to all of Texas (which was the ostensible cause of the late war), plus New Mexico, Arizona, Nevada, Utah, part of Colorado, and California.

From the United States' perspective, it was just as well that there were no instantaneous communications in those days: a week before the treaty was signed, a recent Mormon arrival named James Marshall had observed a glint of bright yellow metal in the tailrace at Sutter's Mill on the American River, near Sacramento. Nothing happened for several weeks because John Augustus Sutter (who owned the mill where the gold was found) rightly figured that broadcast of the discovery would upset the placid life he and his people had found there and so did all he could to keep the discovery hidden. But another Mormon named Sam Brannan happened by, found out what had happened, and promptly rode back to San Francisco yelling "Gold! Gold! Gold on the American River!" at the top of his lungs. And as the saying goes, there went the neighborhood...

Within the next eighteen months, some seventy-five thousand gold seekers arrived from

1848 quarter eagle with CAL. Countermark, made from California gold. Courtesy the NNC.

1848 Congressional medal given to Winfield Scott, made from California gold. Courtesy the NNC.

the East Coast, more from Europe, and even a few from Australia—the dreaded "Sydney Ducks," who were hardened criminals even by the generous standards of San Francisco. Meanwhile, Col. Richard B. Mason, Military Governor of the Territory of California, detailed Lieutenant Lycien Moeser to carry some 230 ounces of native gold back to Philadelphia. Some of it was struck into medals given to Winfield Scott and Zachary Taylor (the two generals who had won the recent war for the United States). But the majority of it was struck into some 1,389 quarter eagles, one of which might have found its way to the hand of our Philadelphia merchant in the autumn of 1848.

The effects of the California Gold Rush are almost too large to calculate. The discovery upset the old ratio between gold and silver, helping to precipitate a monetary instability which would last until both metals were removed from coinage a century later. The Gold Rush inflamed tensions between North and South, two sections of the country which were already at odds over slavery and other differences in society, economy, and outlook. It became clear that California was bound to become a state in short order, and a powerful one at that. It soon became equally clear that the new state would be "free," prohibiting slavery within its borders and therefore aligned with the states of the North in foreign and domestic policy. The South was embittered, convinced that its sacrifices during the recent war (during which it had provided most of the troops and leaders) had been ignored or, worse, had benefited its northern adversaries. It was soon seeking slave-supporting lands elsewhere, a search which necessarily involved taking them from those already in possession—from Spaniards in Cuba, from Mexicans and Nicaraguans in those two countries. It failed in these attempts but managed to alarm northern opinion in the process; tensions between the sections grew. So the California Gold Rush was one of the events leading directly to the American Civil War—but it would also help to ensure that one of the participants would have the means with which to pursue it.

For numismatists, the events in California have a double meaning. First, they provide them with a fascinating series of locally-made coins, among the most interesting and historic issues in all of American history. Second, the Gold Rush and related strikes elsewhere would mean that, combined with a better coining technology, Americans would for the first time have enough coinage for their monetary needs.

These were the great days of private gold coinage. Between 1848 and 1861, makeshift mints were established in California (and in Utah, Oregon, and Colorado) to take advantage of the newly available precious metal, to make it useful for local commerce, and to send it East in a handy form for re-working there. In this, the private Western mints have points of similarity with those Spanish-American producers of the "cob" Pieces of Eight. In both instances, the idea was to create a useful, feasible coinage now; those with artistic sensibilities could improve upon it later. Consequently we should not look for great artwork on these private issues. Nor should we look for the first of them in California.

We should look instead to an isolated area where North Carolina, South Carolina, and Georgia come together. Gold was found in that part of the world shortly before 1800, and, while it sparked nothing quite comparable with the California Gold Rush, there was enough precious metal in those layers and folds of the land to inspire a sizable mining scramble in the late 1820s, the eviction of Native Americans and their replacement by white settlers—and the appearance of a couple of private coiners by the early 1830s.

The first was Templeton Reid, a sometime jeweler, watchmaker, and general handyman. Reid was extending his attentions to coining by the summer of 1830: on July 24, the (Milledgeville) *Georgia Journal* reported that he had set up a mint in that town, and had already turned about fifteen hundred dollars into two-and-one-half-dollar, five-dollar, and ten-dollar gold pieces. By the end of the month, the abysmal roads had persuaded the coiner to pull up stakes and move his operation closer to the metal supply, so he settled in the hamlet of Gainesville, where he struck a few hundred more coins between August and October. Thereafter, he seems to have abandoned coinage for nearly twenty years, relocating to Columbus, where he engaged in creating and marketing new and better types of cotton gins—an altogether safer if less glamorous way of making money.

His coins were simple affairs, featuring the origin of the precious metal and the date on the obverse, his name and the denomination on the reverse. While he was criticized for creating lightweight coins (which may have discouraged him from pursuing his new trade), Reid made his money from pure gold, and his coins in consequence were worth slightly more than their face value as

Templeton Reid, ten dollar Georgia gold coin, 1830. Courtesy the NNC.

Bechtler coins.

bullion. This helps explain their extreme rarity today: most of them were melted down and recoined at the national mint in Philadelphia.

You may be wondering how Templeton Reid managed to keep from being arrested: after all, if states could not coin money, how could an individual? The answer is that the framers of the Constitution apparently never anticipated that a private citizen would *want* to coin money, assuming instead that a new federal mint would instantly spring into action and provide plentiful coinage for everyone. As we have seen, this did not occur, and private bank notes were one result. Private gold coinage was another.

Reid had one last issue in him. Shortly after the beginning of the rush to California, he struck a ten-dollar gold coin designated CALIFORNIA GOLD. It was long assumed that the coiner had followed the lure of metal west, moving his mint one final time. But it now appears more likely that this coin (and a companion piece for twenty-five dollars, stolen from the United States Mint Collection in 1858 and never recovered) were struck in Columbus, the elderly coiner being in no condition to travel and in fact dying within a few months of his second foray into private moneying.

By 1831, Templeton Reid's pioneering effort had closed down, but a new mint was taking its place. This was run by a family of German extraction named Bechtler, which set up shop near Rutherfordton, North Carolina, almost exactly a year after Reid had struck his first coins in Milledgeville.

Located a few miles southeast of Asheville and a few miles northwest of the South Carolina and Georgia lines, Rutherfordton had become a local center for the gold trade. The Bechtlers arrived there in the spring of 1830, and their patriarch, Alt Christoph, soon made himself indispensable as the town's only jeweler and watchmaker. The local people petitioned Congress for a mint to turn their gold nuggets and dust into federal coinage; when Congress ignored them, they turned to Alt Christoph and his family for help. They got it: by July 1831, the head of the clan was striking quarter and half eagles, and by the end of the year he had created an altogether new American coin, the gold dollar. It would take the official coiner some eighteen years to respond in kind.

With one exception, the coins made by Alt Christoph and his sons did not bear dates. The exception was a five-dollar piece, bearing the precise legend AUGUST 1, 1834. This takes us back to events at the official mint in Philadelphia. In the summer of that year, Congress was about to pass a Mint Act which would reduce the gold content of the coins. The bill up for voting required that all federal gold coins be marked with the effective date of the legislation. Congress dropped that requirement at the last minute, but Bechtler placed the date on his reduced-weight half eagles anyway, just to be on the safe side.

In time, the gold area got its mint—or rather two mints, one at Charlotte, North Carolina, and the other at Dahlonega, Georgia. Neither was an unqualified success, but they were enjoying enough trade by the end of the 1830s to persuade Alt Christoph to get out of the private minting business. He transferred it to his son August in 1840. August moved the mint into Rutherfordton

proper (his father's facility had been on the family farm, some three and one-half miles north of town), and there, at a mint on the corner of Sixth and North Washington Streets, August began striking gold dollars sometime in 1842. He minted them in large numbers until his death in July 1846.

That brought a second son into the trade, Christoph, Jr. He continued to coin dollars and five-dollar pieces until the end of 1849 or the beginning of 1850. By then, the family's gold dollars were facing competition from official coins of the same denomination, and this second Bechtler son seems to have given up the coining trade to concentrate on the family's earlier profession as jeweler. But Bechtler dollars and other coins continued to circulate alongside ordinary products of

Cincinnati Mining &Trading Company, ten and five dollars, 1849. Courtesy the NNC.

Pacific Company, ten and five dollars, 1849. Courtesy the NNC.

the federal mints for many years. They generally contained the proper amount of gold, and that, and not their simple designs (the name of the coiner on the obverse, the denomination on the reverse, and nothing more) was what mattered. Most of the surviving specimens show evidence of a lengthy life in circulation.

By the late 1840s, two Eastern coiners had proved that individuals could indeed strike their own gold coinage—and probably would, if the federal government could not offer a plentiful alternative. But then gold was discovered in the West, and the scene of private issues shifted there, where it remained.

We may follow Walter Breen in dividing California private gold coinage into three main stages. The first began in the winter of 1848–49 and continued through April 1850. A number of individuals and firms struck five- and ten-dollar coins at that time, and they created a number of circulating ingots as well. The first stage came to an end after the public learned that several of these issues were debased or contained less than

Norris, Gregg & Norris half eagle.

their stated value in gold; local authorities then enacted legislation clamping down on private issues, which were henceforth restricted to ingots of at least four ounces and smaller pieces whose redemption in United States specie was guaranteed. Neither law was enforceable; both became dead letters in May 1850, as another spate of private issues entered commerce.

This second stage lasted until March 1851, brought down by a panic over rumors that the new wave of private issues was also shortweight. No further private coins appeared during the remainder of 1851.

The third and final stage of California private coinage began in January 1852 and continued through 1856. While some new coiners entered the field and placed their names on issues ranging up to fifty dollars, the most interesting event during this stage occurred on the lower end of the scale, as "fractional" gold coins (tariffed at twenty-five and fifty cents, plus a related issue of dollars) entered commerce there.

Let us examine some of the more outstanding members of the three stages. In the earliest, one of the first firms to strike coins was the Cincinnati Mining & Trading Company, which opened for business on or about January 1, 1849. This operation struck a few coins throughout that year, with a distinctive Liberty with a feather headdress for the obverse, a unique left-facing eagle with shield for the reverse. Five- and ten-dollar coins were made, but their gold content was rumored to be low; virtually all of the firm's products were soon pulled out of circulation and melted down. So were the issues of the Pacific Company, founded about a week after the Cincinnati people organized for trade. The Pacific Company's eagles and half eagles were probably struck by hand with a sledgehammer. Their designs resembled those found on contemporaneous Mexican silver coins, which may indeed have inspired the nameless artist who worked for the firm. The Pacific Company was out of business by mid-October 1849.

At one time, it was assumed that Norris, Gregg & Norris was the earliest California coiner. This assumption has since been disproved, and it now seems certain that the company's first coins were struck no earlier than May 1849. Norris, Gregg & Norris made distinctive half eagle coins near the goldfields at Benecia City through 1849; sometime before April 1850, the coiners moved to Stockton and set up shop there, an event recorded by a unique half eagle with that location named on the reverse. The Miners Bank deserves mention as well: its personnel probably had some connection with those who issued a paper note we saw in the previous chapter—although the point is still disputed. The Miners Bank struck gold eagles late in 1849 in San Francisco; public outcry over low gold content had put a stop to the enterprise by the beginning of 1850.

One of the few firms to make a lasting contribution in this early period was Moffat & Company, which began issuing rectangular specie ingots in July 1849, graduating to normal coinage later that year. The concern's five- and ten-dollar gold pieces bore a deliberate similarity to ordinary United

Baldwin & Company, ten dollars, 1850. Courtesy the NNC.

States gold coins; later issues of 1852 and 1853 (ten- and twenty-dollar gold pieces) were created after Moffat & Company had been tapped to make monetary ingots for Augustus Humbert. Humbert's "United States Assay Office of Gold" was actually a provisional federal branch mint, and it pointed the way to the future.

The second stage of California coinage saw the production of excessively rare rectangular ingots at a state assay office, headed by Frederick D. Kohler, who had earlier been involved with the lightweight Pacific Company and Miners Bank coinages; he may have been appointed to this post as a way of keeping him honest! His and other people's ingots soon yielded place to orthodox coins, fives, tens, and for the first time in California, twenties. Two firms stood out here, Baldwin & Company (whose ten-dollar gold piece depicting a *vaquero*, or Mexican cowboy, is one of the most famous of all private

United States Assay Office—Augustus Humbert, fifty-dollar slug.

The first piece struck at the new San Francisco branch of the United States Mint, twenty dollars, 1854. Courtesy the NNC

gold issues) and Schultz & Company, which set up shop behind the Baldwin Mint and struck five-dollar pieces in 1851.

The third and final stage lasted for four years, and it saw a new player enter the field: an official federal mint, which technically opened its doors on April 15, 1854. It had been coining on an *ad hoc* basis for three years prior to that, however. In the autumn of 1850, a federal Assay Office of Gold was created in San Francisco, to which was granted the right to make ingots of refined gold, worth fifty dollars each. A New York watchmaker named Augustus Humbert was appointed to assay the metal, and he in turn subcontracted the actual coining of it to Moffat & Company.

Whether or not anyone had so intended, Humbert's octagonal ingots (or "slugs," or "Californians") entered circulation as ordinary coins—indeed, they were the principal accepted currency in California between 1851 and 1853. By 1852, Humbert was producing tens as well as fifties, and he added the double eagle denomination in 1853. His ingots were better than anyone else's coins,

and these pieces, with their distinctive eagle-and-shield obverses and engine-turned reverses, led naturally to a more official coinage still. On December 14, 1853, the United States Assay Office of Gold closed its doors, and four months later a new federal branch mint opened in its place. Curtis & Perry (which, as Curtis, Perry & Ward, had bought out Moffat & Company at the end of 1851 but had retained its name) supplied the machinery and the building for the new federal branch mint. But Augustus Humbert played no part in this new institution: we eventually find him joining forces with one of the California private coiners, John G. Kellogg.

Private coining did not simply disappear with the opening of the San Francisco Mint. It persisted for some years, and Kellogg & Company alone produced more twenty-dollar gold pieces in 1854 than the new federal facility (although the United States branch mint eclipsed everyone's output once it got down to serious business in 1855). Still, Kellogg & Company's twenties filled cashiers' tills in the mid-fifties, as did gigantic round fifty-dollar coins struck by two Hun-

Private gold dollar, 1854. Courtesy the NNC.

garian veterans of the failed Revolution of 1848, Counts S. C. Wass and A. P. Molitor. Wass, Molitor & Company produced smaller coins as well, but they achieved immortality with those huge slugs, which contained over a quarter of a troy pound of pure gold each.

At the other end of the spectrum stood a motley assemblage of jewelers and dentists, people skilled with working gold in small quantities, who now proceeded to create California "fractional" coins—tiny octagonal and round half dollars and quarters, as well as dollars. Some of the makers are known, but most are anonymous, although recent research has taught us a good deal more about the coiners than we had previously known. One thing is certain, though: coiners of fractional pieces had nothing to do whatsoever with makers of larger-denomination coins; the two groups were entirely separate.

Designs for fractional gold coins were simple, a reflection of the limited space available to their designers. Halves and quarters ordinarily bore a Liberty head on the obverse, the value and origin of the gold on the reverse, although a few of the halves (and some of the dollars) displayed a reverse eagle as well, looking rather like a tiny version of the bird Augustus Humbert placed on the obverses of his ingots. The fractionals, like those ingots, were made in San Francisco.

One of the interesting things about the California Gold Rush is its ripple effect on other places and events. Earlier, I mentioned its influence on the growth of tensions between North and South, tensions which would someday lead to war between the two sections. But the Gold Rush was responsible for smaller events as well: for numismatists, events in California spawned pioneer gold coinage in two other regions, Oregon and Utah.

Neither of these areas had abundant gold of their own (although they found enough of the metal in eastern Oregon to cause the federal government to consider opening a branch mint at Baker City at the beginning of the 1860s—a consideration abruptly dropped when the gold ran out). But Oregon and Utah both had personal connections with California: many Oregon farmers had abandoned their plows and headed south at the first rumors of the gold strike, and James Marshall and Sam Brannan, of course, were recent migrants from Joseph Smith's peaceable kingdom near the Great Salt Lake—as indeed were many of the first prospectors to arrive in the Sacramento Valley.

Oregon and Utah alike had been acquired at the time of the Mexican War, but in very different ways. The Oregon Country had been first explored by British and American citizens at the end of the eighteenth century and the beginning of the nineteenth. A jurisdictional squabble between the two countries had led to a joint occupation of the area in 1818, one which was renewed regularly until 1846. By the latter year, enough settlers had come into the Columbia River Valley from the United States (most of them New Englanders) so that President Polk (who had gotten elected on an expansionist plank in 1844) felt justified in serving notice that joint occupation was at an end, that Americans were going to monopolize at least the southern part of the territory. Britain acquiesced, and the new United States possession was formally organized as Oregon Territory in 1848. Within a year, its citizens would be striking coinage from California gold.

Utah was settled by followers of the martyred Joseph Smith in 1847. Led by Brigham Young, the faithful had trekked across the "Great American Desert" in search of a land so remote and so unpromising that ordinary Americans would leave it and them alone. Their leader chose a site by the Great Salt Lake, and here the Mormons settled in July 1847. Aided by his genius and their own hard work, they would soon make the desert bloom. But they had only a limited and brief success in keeping other Americans out of Utah. The area could be a useful way station if the West Coast were ever acquired and developed, and just as Smith's people were arriving at their destination, events some fifteen hundred miles to the south were ensuring that they would not be left in solitude to enjoy it. Their compatriots were just then battling their way into Mexico City, and the victors would soon acquire title to the American Southwest, including the very area where Smith's disciples were building their theocratic state. And Americans would soon be finding the very draw which would result in thousands of them passing through Utah, on their way west, or east.

But the Mormons would stay where they were, and they would soon find that entertaining interlopers offered opportunities as well as threats. Those heading west needed goods of all sorts and were prepared to pay high prices. Mormon miners and others returning east bore gold, much of which was left behind in Utah. So money could be made, and within a few months of the California strike, authorities in Utah were preparing to make it quite literally, just as their counterparts in Oregon were.

The Mormons started first, at the end of the year 1848. When members of the flock began bringing back quantities of gold dust from California that fall, Brigham Young decided to turn it into a distinctive local coinage. He enlisted the services of a British convert named John Mobourn Kay; Kay and several Americans had gotten a makeshift mint into operation by December.

The first coins struck were ten-dollar pieces, some forty-six of them, produced during the last month of 1848 but dated 1849, probably under the assumption that coinage would continue unbroken into the new year. Production problems delayed an extension of the coinage until the following September, but from then through 1851, half and quarter eagles were struck in some quantity, as was a new denomination to American numismatic history, the double eagle or twenty-dollar gold piece.

Mormon gold, 1849.

Mormon gold, 1860.

All of these coins replicated the distinctive designs used on those first eagles: their obverses bore a three-pointed Phrygian crown, emblem of the Mormon priesthood, above an All-Seeing Eye, with the legend HOLINESS TO THE LORD. Their reverses bore hands clasped in friendship, the denomination, and the date, along with an abbreviated legend G.S.L.C.P.G., which meant "Great Salt Lake City Pure Gold." The gold in the Mormons' coins was *not* pure, however, and each denomination was only worth about eighty-five percent of its face value. Several thousand of the pieces were consequently melted down in San Francisco, victims of the same hysteria that was making instant rarities of the Pacific Company's coinage and other suspect issues.

At the end of the fifties, the Mormon mint tried again. By that time, it had a new source of gold—Colorado, where the yellow metal had been discovered a year or two previously. This time, Young's people made a single denomination, a half eagle which was as distinctive in its own way as had been the issues of 1848–51. The obverse contained a depiction of the Lion of Judah, the

date, and again the legend HOLINESS TO THE LORD, but this time rendered in a phonetic alphabet, the only coin in American history so distinguished. The reverse bore an English-language legend DESERET ASSAY OFFICE, and its type was an American eagle protecting a straw beehive. (The word "Deseret" was used by the Mormons in preference to "Utah"; it came from the Book of Mormon, where it meant "honeybee.") Around eight hundred of these coins were struck between July 1859 and March 1861, but the issue was finally quashed by an unbeliever, the "gentile" governor of Utah Territory, Alfred Cummings.

We shall speak of Colorado in more detail in a moment, for it would be the venue of the final great issue of private gold coinage. But let us return to Oregon for a moment. There, a series as interesting as the Mormon (and on the whole much rarer) was created during a few months in 1849.

The dies for this coinage still exist, housed at the Oregon Historical Society in Portland. I am a native Oregonian, but I never had an opportunity to examine them until recently. When I did so, one thing immediately became apparent: the Oregon pioneers were striking their eagles and half eagles by hand, without the intervention of an ordinary coining press. The obverse and reverse dies fit together in a kind of socket, wherein one die was actually sunk into a depression, articulated with the other. A planchet could be dropped into the hole and positioned atop the lower die. Then the "press" was closed, and the top die was struck with a sledgehammer. When the apparatus was opened, the finished coin could be tapped out with a wooden mallet. Precisely how metal was rolled and planchets were cut out largely remains a mystery, for two steel rolls are all we have left of the other machinery.

This is a primitive way to coin money, but it would work well enough *if* you had only a few coins to make, and *if* you were working with a very soft metal. And the Oregonian coiners had the advantage in both instances: they were only making a few thousand pieces (one source says six thousand half eagles and two thousand eight hundred and fifty eagles, which is almost certainly too high, based on the number of survivors), and they were, of course, making them from gold, pure gold from California.

The Oregon coinage was privately struck, but it had nearly begun as an official issue of the territory. By the beginning of 1849, nearly half a million dollars in gold dust had reached Oregon, some of it brought back by returning farmer/miners, others sent north by those still at work in the California fields. The dust caused endless disputes in its current form, because an amount valued at five dollars by one person might very well be valued at four by another and at six by a third. Inevitably, agitation began for a territorial mint. A bill was passed by the local legislature on February 16, 1849, setting up an official coiner at the capital, Oregon City. But an incoming governor named Joseph Lane arrived in Oregon before dies could be made and coins struck, and he said that such issues by a territory were illegal under the United States Constitution. Lane was on shaky ground, because the Constitution indeed forbade coinage to states but said nothing about territories. But he was the governor, and his word prevailed. There would be no official Oregon coinage, but a private one was another matter: what a territory could not do, individual citizens could and were already

Oregon gold, 1849.

doing in California and in Utah. In March 1849, Oregonians joined them.

Eight prominent businessmen founded the Oregon Exchange Company, with James Taylor as director, W. H. Wilson as assayer, William H. Rector as diemaker, and the Reverend Hamilton Campbell as main engraver. These men and the other principals achieved numismatic immortality when Campbell placed their initials on the obverse of his coin, a five-dollar gold piece. The main type on that side was a beaver, whose valuable fur had inspired some of the earliest exploration and settlement of the region. Below the animal in a simple wreath were the initials T.O. (for Territory of Oregon) and the date. The reverse bore the denomination, the weight of the gold, and the name of the issuer. Ten-dollar pieces appeared a bit later (they followed the general designs of the fives), but the location of the mint was now given as O.T. (Oregon Territory). Dies for the eagles were engraved by a newcomer, Victor Wallace, who was slightly better at his craft than had been the Reverend Campbell.

All of the "Beaver Money" was made from pure California gold dust. There was no attempt at assaying or standardization, activities which were far beyond the modest capabilities of the Oregon City coiners. To be on the safe side, they made their coins' weights well *above* federal standards: when assayed at Philadelphia, the fives were found to be worth $5.50 and the tens $11. California bankers nevertheless valued them much lower (to make a profit from melting them down), and the great majority of the pieces probably went into the melting pot within a few years of their manufacture. Actual coining came to a stop around September 1, 1849, when the two crucibles used to melt down the gold dust broke. By 1850, Californian gold coins were arriving in Oregon in fair numbers, and the monetary emergency which had led to the beaver coinage had ended. Of this coinage, less than a hundred specimens have survived.

Somewhat larger numbers are extant from the final area of pioneer coining, Colorado. This region had been acquired piecemeal between 1803 and 1848, and had been explored by Americans (Zebulon Pike, John C. Frémont, and others) over the past half century. But settlement only began in earnest after the discovery of gold on the South Platte River, near the future city of Denver. By the summer of 1858, a scramble comparable to that in California a decade previously was taking place.

And those who arrived there found conditions at least as bad as had the forty-niners, if not worse. Food was scarce, housing minimal, theft and violence rampant, law enforcement nonexistent; and the nearest secure source of many essential supplies was either Omaha, Nebraska, or St. Joseph, Missouri. Those were not the nearest areas of white settlement, of course: Kansas Territory abutted Colorado, and the latter was technically subject to a territorial governor there. But there currently was no legitimate government in Kansas, because two groups were fighting for mastery there through fair means and foul. One faction was pro-Southern and the other pro-Northern, and their adherents were currently fighting each other at the ballot box, shooting each other in the streets, and ambushing each other from behind any available cover. This was "Bleeding Kansas," a foretaste of what soon was to come on a national scale. While it ran its course, Kansas was more dangerous than Colorado, and local authorities ought not to look to their immediate eastern neighbors for help. In 1859, they took the only logical step: they organized their own government, calling it the "Territory of Jefferson," telling the federal government about it after the fact. Their response demonstrates a pragmatic and local approach to the questions of law and order. They would engage their coinage problems in the same way.

By the time Jefferson Territory was organized, gold dust and nuggets had become the universal media of exchange. As elsewhere, merchants and ordinary citizens found this an awkward system at best, and agitation for a local coinage quickly developed. In 1860 it would be met by a firm calling itself Clark, Gruber & Company.

This concern was already doing business as a bank and assay office, made up of three persons: Austin M. Clark, his brother Milton Edward Clark (who served as the firm's attorney), and Emanuel H. Gruber. Late in 1859, Milton Clark made an arduous trip back to Philadelphia and New York to purchase dies, presses, and the other necessities for a mint. In mid-January 1860, three lots were acquired in Denver City to house the new enterprise, and work on the actual two-story brick building began a couple of months later. By early July the mint was ready to strike its first coinage, and it was formally opened at a gala ceremony on the twentieth.

This was an up-to-date facility, and its output was impressive. Between July and October 1860, Clark, Gruber & Company turned some $120,000 into quarter eagles, halves, eagles, and double eagles. The two lower denominations copied ordinary federal designs (Liberty's head for the obverse, surrounded by stars, and an eagle with shield for the reverse). But for its tens and twenties,

the company proudly displayed an engraving of Pike's Peak on the obverse, along with the legend PIKES PEAK GOLD and the name of the mint town beneath the mountain. The legend was not entirely accurate, for most of the coins' gold came from the Central City region and other mining towns west of Denver. Furthermore, that mountain most certainly was not accurate: Pike's Peak is not a volcano (which is how it appears on the coins), but simply one of many mountains in a massive western range. But accurate or not, these are among the most famous of Western gold designs, the coins bearing them coveted by collectors.

Clark, Gruber's coinage slowed at the end of 1860, as heavy snows made further prospecting impossible and dried up the firm's metallic source. Coinage was resumed full speed after the spring thaw, but with new legends (without mention of the origin of the gold) and an ordinary head of Liberty in place of those marvelous peaks. This probably represented sound business judgment on the part of the firm, for its coinage would achieve a wider acceptance if it closely resembled fed-

Clark, Gruber & Company, twenty dollars, 1860.

eral issues than if it did not, but collectors regret the change nonetheless.

Clark, Gruber & Company struck approximately $131,000 in gold coin in 1860, $240,000 the following year, and $223,000 in 1862, the latter from dies dated 1861. Only a tiny percentage of these coins have survived, most of them having been melted down later in the nineteenth century. This premier private mint's days were soon numbered. The federal government never recognized the Jefferson authorities, but eventually got around to organizing the region as the Territory of Colorado (February 1861). Now national control would be tightened, and local enterprises such as private mints would face an uncertain future.

Perhaps concerned about possible retaliation, Clark, Gruber switched from coins to rectangular ingots in 1862. And in April 1863, the national government forced the sale of the mint, on the pretext that it would be wanted for a federal facility in Denver. A national branch mint would indeed come into production on the site of Clark, Gruber & Company—but not until 1906. During its first forty-three years, it would function only as an assay office.

Clark, Gruber & Company was by far the most prolific of the Colorado coiners, but there were two others, located elsewhere in the region. One of these was John J. Conway & Company, which set up shop in August 1861 at picturesquely-named Georgia Gulch, near the village of Parkeville. Conway made undated quarter eagles, half eagles, and eagles, but rumors as to their poor fineness had caused the closure of the mint by September. The other coiner was Doctor John D. Parsons, an Indiana native with a metallurgical turn of mind, who came to Denver in 1858, soon headed for Oro City (whose name suggests what the doctor was after), and finally set up a coining operation at Tarryall Mines. There he struck a few quarter eagles and half eagles, with a most distinctive obverse design, a quartz-reduction mill, used for separating gold from crushed ore. Parsons' coins are undated, but were struck in 1861, probably during the late summer. The operation came to an abrupt halt when the doctor ran out of gold. Today, no more than half a dozen quarter eagles and three half eagles are known.

The Colorado issues round out the period of private precious-metal coinage in the

John D. Parsons' coins, half eagle (left) and quarter eagle, 1861. Courtesy the NNC.

United States. There would be other strikes of gold (in the Dakotas, later in the Klondike) and silver (at Virginia City, Nevada, home of the legendary Comstock Lode), but none of them produced a distinctive coinage (unless we count regular federal gold and silver issues between 1870 and 1893 with a C C mint mark for Carson City). Why?

There are two general answers to the question. The first one is technically correct: private precious-metal coinage ceased because Congress declared it (and private base-metal coinage) illegal in 1864. But this answer explains nothing. How was Congress able to do so, and what made it think that it could achieve success now, when it would have failed even ten years previously? Here is our second answer: Congress could pass that law because times had changed.

The American Civil War was approaching its crescendo. Whether anyone in Washington wanted to admit it or not, one of the ways of life which the war was bringing to a close was the supremacy of local power and authority over national. Here is an example of what was happening: it was at this time that Americans became accustomed to saying "the United States is..." instead of "the United States *are* ..."—a small distinction on one level, an enormous one on others. The war was bringing a very old tradition to a close, that of local power, and this would inevitably have an effect on money, including the private, local coin. In the climate of opinion of 1864, such moneying would have seemed an anachronism.

But as the two sections were busily attempting to destroy each other, a curious thing was happening: the underpinnings which could bind them to each other, and to their component parts, were expanding and improving. By 1864, the North was building a transcontinental railroad, while telegraphic communications were expanding as well, fostered by the war effort North and South. What was emerging was the potential for a new, national economy, stretching from one coast to the other, an economy with communications adequate enough to send bullion to a few central points for processing, to carry it back as coinage to most if not all regions in a reasonably timely fashion. This system was not yet perfect—indeed, it would not be so during the remainder of the century—but it was and would be far better than anything Americans had previously enjoyed, and it would mean that, except at the very bottom of the monetary column, Americans would henceforth use national coins when they used metallic money for trade.

But improved communications were only one key to the disappearance of the private coinage of the American West. Had the public coiner remained as inefficient as it had been the last time we looked in on it, the private coiner would have remained in business, his wares competing with normal United States issues—and with those of foreign countries as well, just as always. But times changed here too, and the federal coiner got better at the production of money and was finally able to drive his competitors from the field. The Act of Congress of June 8, 1864, served notice that the process had been completed.

The United States Mint improved on its craft by moving in two directions. First, it upgraded its operation at Philadelphia. Second, it established branches or smaller versions of itself in key places—places whose economy or subsurface wealth promised adequate metal for coining.

It was addressing its productive capabilities by 1816. A fire at the beginning of the year had destroyed its old wooden millhouse, and Mint Director Robert Patterson used the fire as an opportunity to incorporate a steam engine into the rebuilding project. This engine was used to power a number of operations, most importantly, the rolling operation, which at last gave this crucial step the power and precision it required. A planchet-cutter was operated by the same engine. Together, these modest improvements hinted at an increase in the mint's productivity.

Its personnel got better at their craft as well. They were asking Boulton, Watt & Company for technical advice in the mid-1820s, especially concerning the production of specimen strikes, or proofs. By 1828, the minters were cautiously experimenting with restraining collars for silver coinage, their attentions extending to gold the following year. The circular collar dies surrounded the coins as they were being struck, making them more consistent and harder to counterfeit. But collars would not be used for base-metal coinage for many years, cents and half cents not being deemed to require such protection.

By the end of the 1820s, Congressional agitation to close the United States Mint had abated, and the institution now faced an altogether different problem: if it were to play the role which all agreed it should, it would have to move to larger and more modern quarters. The move to a more spacious location was accomplished between July 4, 1829 (when the cornerstone for a new mint was laid) and January 1833 (when it opened for business). The new facility was modeled after a celebrated Greek temple near Athens, designed in white marble by the talented William Strickland. But for the moment, its attractiveness was limited to the outside: inside, while the machinery now had more room, it was still the same old machinery. If the mint were to achieve the potential promised by its showy façade, it would have to modernize, and mechanize, and soon.

The key player here would be a member of a distinguished and prolific Philadelphia family, Franklin Peale. By the late 1820s, he was being employed as all-purpose fact finder by Mint Director Samuel Moore. In this capacity, Peale visited Europe, and its more modern mints, between 1833 and 1835. He examined the Royal Mint, which had been rebuilt around 1810 by Matthew Boulton's people; he may have seen Soho as well. Both places utilized a type of coining press which Matthew Boulton had patented in 1790, but which had been only slightly improved since his time. The Boulton press was essentially a machine of the traditional screw type, strengthened for connection to a new motive force, the steam engine. Peale also explored the Karlsruhe, Germany, mint. Both there and in Paris he saw a press constructed on a different principle, a machine which seemed to offer greater possibilities than those of the Boulton press. This apparatus had been patented by Diedrich Uhlhorn in 1817, and was recently improved upon by M. Thonnelier. It featured a toggle action which was easier to marry to steam power than the Boulton press, and was more miserly with the steam power it received. It did not coin by means of a screw, and, because the screw was the most vulnerable

Old ways and new: a half dollar struck in the traditional way (left), and a similar coin, struck in a new way, by the power of steam (right); both 1836. Courtesy the NNC.

part of the Boulton apparatus and the one most difficult to replace, the Thonnelier coining machine seemed a far better candidate for the rough-and-ready coining to be expected in America. Peale was sold on the Thonnelier press, and although he did not purchase one (and had not been so empowered in any case), he did manage to draw and memorize its essentials, replicating them once he returned home in mid-1835.

By March 1836, a new press had been built and was striking its first coins, powered by the mint's steam engine. These initial efforts were half dollars dated 1836, and although only twelve hundred or so of them were made that year, they gave promise of greater things to come. Even the tyro coiners of 1836 found that their new steam-powered press could make twice or thrice as many coins as the old methods from the outset. The new coins were also much more consistent in strike and finish than were the old. Providing enough metal was found,

there would be virtually no limit to the new mint's possibilities.

More coinage metal was being found. An early straw in the wind was a letter written on September 30, 1837, from Robert Maskell Patterson to Matthew Robinson Boulton. Patterson and his predecessors had been getting copper planchets from Boulton, Watt & Company for the past forty years. Now Patterson informed Boulton that no more need be sent: the mint had found an American supplier of copper. Soon it would find native supplies of gold as well, and finally silver: the way would lay open to that plentiful, national coinage which had been the dream of Alexander Hamilton, but which had eluded him and his successors for most of a century.

More straws in the wind: in 1835, Congress passed an Act (March 3) authorizing the establishment of branch mints at Charlotte, North Carolina, Dahlonega, Georgia, and New Orleans, Louisiana. The choice of the

New coins from new mints: New Orleans (above), Charlotte (left), and Dahlonega (right). Courtesy the NNC.

first two towns makes sense: they were convenient to the mines which had earlier supplied Templeton Reid with his bullion and the Bechtlers with theirs. But why New Orleans? New Orleans was convenient to a supply of precious metal too, but it came in the form of coins from Mexico and elsewhere in Latin America. The Crescent City's economy was booming by the mid-1830s, so why not help it along (and bolster local and national pride) by setting up a branch mint there as well?

By the spring of 1838, the United States had not one mint but four. And all of them were equipped with steam power and with modern coining machinery. The mints at Dahlonega and Charlotte never reached expectations—they never really went beyond the status of federal coiners for local consumers. And they only struck gold, not silver, and certainly not copper, because those metals were not found in the region. But the mint at New Orleans was a success from the beginning, coining gold and silver on a regular basis down to the outbreak of the Civil War in 1861. It reopened in 1879, and remained in business for another thirty years. Its fellows at Charlotte and Dahlonega were likewise closed at the beginning of the war, but closed they remained, overtaken by larger events.

As we have seen, a Western branch mint was opened in San Francisco in 1854, as a federal response to the Gold Rush in that area. The new mints (and the greater productivity of the parent at Philadelphia) led to a momentous decision some three years later: by an Act of Congress of February 21, 1857, "all former acts authorizing the currency of foreign gold and silver coins, and declaring the same a legal tender in payment for debts, are hereby repealed." For the first time in their history, the inhabitants of the United States felt confident enough about their money to prohibit the use of other people's within their borders. And so all those Pieces of Eight, sovereigns, Louis d'ors, thalers, and onzas assumed their present role, part of the national numismatic legacy, remembered with thanks but no longer part of an ongoing story.

That story was about to take an interesting new path, a deeply ironic one. For four years after banning other mints' coins, the United States Mint would find itself unable to keep its own in circulation. The quarreling between North and South deepened into a shooting war by the spring of 1861. War's uncertainty drove coinage into hiding, North and South; it turned the American people back to their time-honored expedient, the paper note, just as the potential seemed to have been achieved for banishing it once and for all.

CHAPTER 6

CIVIL WAR AND MONEY'S CHANGE

CHAPTER 6

CIVIL WAR AND MONEY'S CHANGE

The Civil War meant and still means many things to Americans—it has produced feelings which have clarified, deepened, and changed over the past century and a third since the guns fell silent. At bottom, there was and is a single meaning to the conflict, the way it was played out, and the way it still resonates that has overshadowed all the others. That meaning has always been there, right in front of the nation's nose—so plainly in view that it has frequently been lost sight of. When it is seen, though, it has been infernally difficult to take to heart. The greatest lesson of the Civil War was that Americans would have to pay for the fine words enshrined in the Declaration of Independence by lives lived in a new way. They would have to actually take seriously the stirring phrase about the equality of *all* men.

Abraham Lincoln saw this obligation plainest of anyone. He knew that the Republic then stood at a crossroads, that nothing less than its future identity lay in the choice of direction taken. If it were to continue to take its own words seriously, then it would have to do something about the seventh of the population whose servitude stood as a mockery of those high-minded syllables. And if it were to beg the question, well, then, it might as well admit it was a failure and rewrite its most basic document so that words now lived *down* to reality. But in either case, it was going to have to do something quickly: the question demanded an answer now, and if Mr. Lincoln was unable to evade it (and he wanted to, perhaps more than any other person then living), no one else North or South could do so either. And Americans are still wrestling with the results of the decisions taken by men dead a century and more...

The Civil War was the defining experience of American history—a true "watershed," to use a word ordinarily reserved by historians for far lesser events. The war split America's story neatly down the middle: in four short years the United States became a completely different country. It is not too much to say that, had the war not occurred, the United States would be unrecognizable to present-day Americans. They would be strangers in their own country.

In Roman mythology, there was a curious god named Janus. He had two profiles, one looking one way and one the other. Janus was the deity responsible for doors and thresholds, and he looked to the past and to the future simultaneously. The American Civil War bears apt comparison to Janus, a set of events which looked to the past for guidance but would carry the country along a path to the future that no one had ever trodden, and only a few had glimpsed.

From large events to much smaller subjects, but subjects worthy of note nonetheless, all we have been saying about the country's history might be equally applied to its money: in the four years of the Civil War, America's exchange media would begin in familiar modes, be constantly altered under pressure, and emerge with fundamentally new identities, identities which they still maintain today with minor modifications. Put most simply, the national government would acquire a monopoly on the making and circulation of *all* money within the United States of America. It already enjoyed the potential of achieving this status for coinage (and had indeed proclaimed it, in the Act of February 1857), but the war would soon force it to acquire the same powers over paper money, a medium which it proceeded to issue in amounts which made the country's eighteenth-century foray into national currency pale by comparison. The new, massive issues would have appalled Alexander Hamilton and his fiscal circle, but they helped elevate the national principle over the local, and that would have appealed to them.

The problem with wars is that no one going into them ever has the faintest idea of the identity they will eventually assume. Never was this truer than in 1861. I have spoken of the necessity of deciding how and whether to answer the equality question: the belief that the Union might be saved in spite of evading it was the first great Northern illusion, while the hope that that section would back down before a determined, disunionist South was scarcely more realistic on the other side. Both illusions would melt in the heat of the second summer of the war. In tandem with these two misapprehensions (and yielding to reality even more quickly than they did), there ran a third: that this would be a short war, and a limited one.

We can scarcely blame the participants for misconstruing the future course of events. During the past half-century, wars *had* been limited, demanding only modest amounts of treasure and blood. This was as true in Europe as it was in America, and the mind-set of 1861 simply found it difficult to imagine a longer, deeper conflict. There were a few who foresaw the possibility, and they included the new President, Abraham Lincoln. Lincoln realized that if the sectional war went beyond the stage of the set piece battle, wherein one side gained the field and the other obligingly sued for peace, all sorts of fissures might be opened. If the war could be won quickly and confined to the issue of Union, well and good, for that was a difference of philosophy, and philosophical differences can frequently be solved. But if the war lasted longer, the real issues of slavery, freedom, and race would inevitably be exposed. Mr. Lincoln had no idea how to get those djinni back into the bottle once they had been released, nor did anyone else, so it was terribly important to keep them there in the first place, to keep this a short and limited war.

If it were so restrained, it could be fought by normal monetary means, North and South. Or almost normal: specie began dis-appearing from circulation in both sections shortly after the beginning of hostilities. In the South, there had not been much coin in circulation anyway, at least in comparison with the North. The mints at Charlotte, Dahlonega, and New Orleans all closed down in the spring of 1861. Dahlonega and Charlotte had never been major coiners, and their activities had been restricted to gold in any case. But the mint of New Orleans was a distinct loss to the Confederacy: at the turn of the year, it had coined the last of its silver and gold into specie, most of it in the name of the Confederate States or in that of the state of Louisiana. It might have done much more had the bullion been at hand, but it was not. Among other things that meant that the Confederacy's total output of distinctive coinage would be confined to precisely four pieces—half dollars with a normal, United States obverse and a hastily-carved Confederate reverse. While it was hoped that half dollars of the new type would someday jingle in the pockets of Southerners, the attempt suffered the same fate as the Continental Dollar, and for the same reasons. And when the Federals captured the Crescent City and its mint in April 1862, the mechanical wherewithal for Confederate coining disappeared.

But the North was scarcely better off. By the end of 1861, Lincoln's government had suspended the payment of its own debts in specie or coin, and that encouraged the wholesale hoarding of all metallic members of the monetary system, even subsidiary coins. Less than six months after the shooting had begun, it was becoming obvious that this war must be fought and paid for, North and South, with the time-honored expedient of paper money.

But what kind? Private banks, both Northern and Southern, continued to circulate their paper. Indeed, the number of banks doing so in the South increased, as monetary need and the allure of private gain encouraged the incorporation of new banks. But the types of notes they and established firms issued, and especially the outward appearance of those notes, tells us a good deal more about

Southern prospects than the bankers and the politicians might have wished.

I have observed that the printing of American paper money had been confined to a few firms by the late 1850s. A concomitant of that was that the notes were only printed in a few places. In 1860, all of the printing locales were in the North, although at least one of the houses had a branch in the South, at New Orleans. When the war began, the border between the two sections remained extremely porous through the spring—and even longer in some places. It gradually became more and more difficult, though, to get from one section to the other, or to get commodities from one section to the other. This included bank paper money, ready for signing and circulation.

This tightening was reflected in the South in a number of odd events. Many banks used fresh, Northern-made notes through the end of 1861 and into the beginning of 1862: they had wisely ordered ahead of events or were issuing notes sparingly. Others, however, were running out or had been caught short at the outbreak of the war. With these firms, a number of interesting things happened.

Some banks issued old, engraved currency which they had ordered many years before but had kept aside for one reason or another. But these back supplies eventually ran out as well, and then the banks faced three alternatives: they could simply surrender and cease issuing paper; they could obtain notes printed by lithography, which were easier to counterfeit than engraved notes, but still offered some protection against the forger; or they could use notes printed by the old typeset method and hope for the best.

Banks made all three choices. Across the South, smaller facilities did cease to issue notes, and smaller branches of larger banks (the branch bank was a popular feature in much of the section) sometimes did likewise. Other issuers got new notes, printed by either of the two available substitutes for engraving, lithography or typesetting.

I have said nothing thus far about lithography, for it only came into prominence in the United States after engraving had reached a dominant position in security printing. Lithography had not been yet used to print ordinary money, but these were not ordinary times, and it would now be pressed into service by those banks which could afford it.

Lithography had been discovered at the close of the eighteenth century, and it had been carried to the United States by some of its earliest adherents, craftsmen from Germany. As practiced in the nineteenth century, the process involved a peculiar, exceedingly fine-grained type of limestone. This would be used in lieu of an ordinary engraving plate. The stone's peculiarity lay in the fact that its porous nature would allow it to accept the transfer of images when applied in a greasy ink. Once transferred, those images would reject water but accept ordinary printer's ink. The blank areas where no image had been transferred would reject both water *and* ink, due again to the peculiar nature of the stone. When printing began, ink was rolled on the stone and then wiped off. The greasy areas held the ink, while the untreated areas did not. A sheet of moistened paper pressed against the stone would pick up an image from the ink in the stone. This was the lithograph.

This is not an especially good way to print paper money. The lithograph allows great delicacy of line, which is what recommends it to artists. But it does not allow a bold, precise, hard line, which is desired on a bank note. Today, the classical lithographic method is used on no currency in the world. To bankers in the revolted American South, though, it must have seemed a godsend because it was far easier to make a lithographed note than an engraved one in the absence of advanced industrial technology and the technological base to support it.

That was precisely the position in which the insurgent South found itself at the outbreak of the war. The section had never needed to industrialize, for its traditional role had been as supplier of specialty agricultural products (especially cotton and tobacco) to less-fortunate regions—including England and the American North, who could in turn supply Dixie with everything it needed in the way of industrial goods far more cheaply than could the section's own modest manufacturing base. There were those in the South who drew a doleful conclusion from this curiosity: any conflict with the North had better turn out to be a war of the traditional variety, where Southern valor could quickly overcome Northern industrial potential; if not, the section was likely to lose. The ranks of these prophets grew once the war began and accelerated, but for now we merely observe that the lack of industrial base was having a deleterious effect on an admit-

tedly small portion of the Southern war effort shortly after that effort began.

Running out of engraved notes, Southern banks quickly turned to lithography. There was a firm in Richmond named Hoyer & Ludwig. Prior to the war, it had lithographed maps, sheet music, and stock certificates for local sale—the sorts of things printed by such craftsmen in ordinary times. By the late spring of 1861, bankers were coming to its doors, asking it to do its bit for the rebel war effort. They wanted it to print money for them, and it complied with their request.

Many of these banks were interested in saving face, bolstering morale, and staving off forgers to the maximum possible degree, and they wanted their new notes to look as

Bank of Pittsylvania (Chatham, Virginia), five dollars, 1861. This is a prewar Northern printing. Courtesy the NNC.

Bank of Pittsylvania (Chatham, Virginia), five dollars, 1861. This is a wartime Southern printing. Courtesy the NNC.

"normal," as similar to earlier ones, as might be currently achieved. Hoyer & Ludwig did its best to comply, and a lithographed five-dollar bill it printed for the Bank of Pittsylvania appears quite similar to an earlier, engraved one produced by the American Bank Note Company—until you look more closely. We are not speaking of the fineness or crispness of line, because as we have said, lithography is a different printing method, and its limitations in these areas should not be held against it. We are speaking rather of the images. Hoyer & Ludwig had a limited number of suitable lithographic views or "cuts" from which to choose (for it had never intended doing business as a currency printer), and while it would make a loyal attempt to give its customers what they wanted, it would be fortunate to come up with a general approximation of their earlier notes. In this case, it placed a vignette at lower-right as had the printers of the earlier note, one of George Washington, which it happened to have in stock. It also placed a larger vignette in the center, not because it was identical to what had been on the earlier note but because it was about the same size. Its border decorations were similar to but simpler than those of its predecessor, while it tried, and failed, to print with the precise bicolor registry that was the pride of the Northern printer. In short, Hoyer & Ludwig did what it could, but it would not be nearly enough to discourage any skilled forgers in the area. In time, other lithographers would join it in currency printing for private banks, and one of them would eventually drive it from the field. This firm was first known as Leggett, Keatinge & Ball, and it set up for business across town from Hoyer & Ludwig. Leggett dropped out early on, but Keatinge & Ball continued to print money for private banks through most of the remaining years of the war, and quite handsome money at that. It moved its works to Columbia, South Carolina, sometime in 1862. The exact date is not known, but it may have coincided with Confederate worries over losing the capital in the late spring of that year. These fears were dispelled when the Northern commander, George B. McClellan, proved less anxious to take Richmond than Robert E. Lee was to defend it. McClellan got the sack, but Keatinge & Ball stayed in Columbia.

Unfortunately, access to lithographic services of that firm or Hoyer & Ludwig, Bornemann of Charleston, or Howell of Savannah was often beyond banks of limited means and those located in the interior of the Confederacy, far away from the big cities and their lithographers. Such banks would repair to local, "job" printers, men accustomed to producing everything from almanacs to eviction notices, who would now add one more product to their line. No one has ever succeeded in creating a complete list of these printers, for the simple fact that many if not most of them did not sign their work. But my own research suggests that there were probably hundreds of them, scattered across the South from northern Virginia to south Texas, all busily doing their bit to keep the Southern monetary supply afloat.

There was no attempt to provide security against forgery on these notes, nor could there have been. The printers used whatever they had in the shop for decoration, not security, but because they most likely had a monopoly of any printing in the area, a would-be counterfeiter would have come to them for help! Locally and nationally, the trouble suffered by Southern currency did not stem from counterfeiting, but from more serious sources.

The typical Southern typeset private bank note would be printed in black or dark blue, and would only rarely feature a second color. It would be uniface in virtually all instances, although the section had earlier moved away from the one-sided note when it had regular access to Northern printers. The typical new typeset note would usually have the date printed in rather than written. It would probably be somewhat smaller than its prewar predecessor, for the South was beginning to run out of paper within a year of so of the onset of the conflict. Also, the paper employed may have started out as something

Bank of Chattanooga (Chattanooga, Tennessee), two dollars, 1861. Courtesy the NNC.

Bank of Chattanooga (Chattanooga, Tennessee), three dollars, 1862 (printed on earlier notes). Courtesy the NNC.

Bank of Chattanooga (Chattanooga, Tennessee), one dollar, 1863. Courtesy the NNC.

else: a number of typeset notes of the period were printed on lined notebook paper, while another source was paper upon which notes had been printed before the war, but which had not been issued then and could not be now due to the disappearance of the bank, a currently unauthorized denomination, or a badly spoiled printing. The Bank of Chattanooga used such paper, and its issues of various sorts afford us a valuable glimpse of the trials and responses of a wartime bank in the Confederacy.

This institution had opened for business in 1854. Until the spring of 1861, it had its notes made by Danforth, Wright & Company and by the American Bank Note Company after the famous merger of 1858. But it began running out of various denominations in the spring of 1861, and it then turned South to find its printers. It first investigated New Orleans, where a mediocre lithographer named Manouvrier was doing business for a number of private and public issuers. Manouvrier lithographed notes for the Bank of Chattanooga in the summer of 1861 including ones, twos, and threes, all dated 28 August 1861 in the plate. That took care of matters for the time being, but by the summer of 1862 the bank was seeking to issue more notes, and it was looking for a local printer, because Mr. Manouvrier was put out of business with the fall of New Orleans to

federal troops. It found a local person, and *he* found a most unusual paper source.

During most of the 1850s, Tennessee had enjoyed the fiscal services of the Bank of East Tennessee, whose headquarters was in Knoxville. This bank had had a branch in Chattanooga in 1854–55, but the branch had been closed in the latter year and the parent bank had failed around 1858. A goodly number of unused sheets, some printed only on the face and others on both sides, had been left over, and our unknown local printer recycled them into new ones, twos, and threes in the summer of 1862. The previous printing was a real problem: the new printer found that it was so intense and his so poor that his new notes were only marginally legible. Perhaps for this reason, or in frank recognition of the abysmal slippage of quality, the printer or the bank ordered the word "GOOD." placed vertically at the center-left of each new note, with a space below for the cashier's signature.

This makeshift recycling got the Bank of Chattanooga through another six months, and it found a final printer at the start of 1863, Keatinge & Ball. This firm was then busy with many other issuers including private banks, states, and the insurgent national government. It also lithographed notes with which to pay its own employees, one of the perquisites of the security printer!

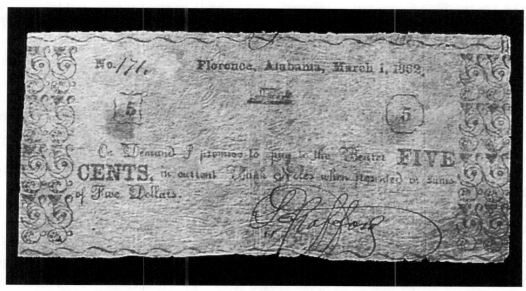

Florence, Alabama, five-cent scrip or "shinplaster," 1862. Courtesy the NNC.

The Bank of Chattanooga issued "fractional currency," notes denominated at less than one dollar, as well as larger bills. In this it reflected what was happening on the private level across the section by the first spring of the war, across the nation a few months later. When the war began, small change began going into hiding North and South. In the North, the problem did not become crucial until the autumn of 1862, after which that section responded to the problem in a number of interesting ways. But the Southern response is equally intriguing, because it was so local. Across the region, banks, insurance companies, cities and towns, merchants, soldiers' homes, even individuals issued fractional notes. In the case of private or local governments, we call them scrip. Output of the states and the Confederacy are simply called fractional currency or fractional notes. The same general rules hold for Northern issues, but at the time, those who used them had another, affectionately derogatory term for them all, "Shinplasters."

The word dates back to the Revolutionary War, when insurgent soldiers found that the squarish Continental Currency notes with which they were paid would purchase very little but would serve splendidly to bandage leg wounds. Thus shinplaster: what you used to bandage your shin. The word dropped out of favor after Yorktown but was revived during the later 1830s to describe the diminutive scrip notes issued by cities and individuals when small change was hoarded at that time. And now it was revived again, applied to fractional currency of all types.

Most of the Southern issues date from 1861 and 1862, for later in the war inflation had become such a problem that subsidiary paper made little sense. The notes—and there must have been thousands of different types—were simple affairs, almost always uniface, printed from type, with simple decoration if any. Collectors and researchers are still uncovering unknown varieties today, for we know very little indeed about the local (and not much more about the state or na-tional) monetary history of the Southern Confederacy.

The Confederacy issued paper money on both of these superior levels. On the state level, it almost had to: one of the reasons for secession had been a perceived national encroachment on local or states' rights. Modern historians tend to read "retention of slavery" into "states' rights," and they are correct in assuming that the South's "Peculiar Institution" lay at the center of the states' rights argument. But while at its core, slavery did not form *all* of the argument: the South was yearning for the good old days of unfettered local control over local affairs, and while its view of the past was not accurate in all respects, there was enough truth in it to give pause to reflective Northerners, including Abraham Lincoln. Furthermore there was enough appeal to make it somewhat difficult for the President and his followers to mount an all-out campaign against those who had rebelled on its behalf.

When the slave states seceded (and it is important to note that not all of them did so, and the four that did not—Maryland, Missouri, Delaware, and Kentucky—held the key to victory for either side) they quickly set up a provisional government of the Confederate States of America, with its capital at Montgomery, Alabama. Its chief executive was a distinguished soldier and Congressman named Jefferson Davis. Davis was elected to the office in October, confirmed there for a six-year term when the Confederate Constitution was finally ratified the following year. He was probably the most distinguished leader the South could have chosen; that he had equally distinguished flaws was not immediately apparent.

He was a states' rights man, though, and so were the members of the provisional and regular governments. When it came time to strike a balance between local and national power, they naturally came out in favor of local authority, embodied in the states. And when it came time to pay for the war upon which they were now engaged, they allowed the states to print money for the purpose.

The states had been doing so since the spring of 1861 in any case, for the issue of money was an attribute of sovereignty, and they knew they were sovereign powers, even though Mr. Lincoln might have felt otherwise. The first issues came from Virginia, whose capital, Richmond, would soon serve as proud new home to the Confederate government. The state passed successive laws authorizing such issues in March, April, and June 1861—some five million dollars' worth of notes—but the first issues only appeared late that summer, printed by the enterprising lithographers at Hoyer & Ludwig. Another $5,300,000 were authorized in December 1861 and March 1862. Hoyer & Ludwig were allowed to print the new dollar notes (the state evidently assuming that denomination would be relatively immune to counterfeiting), but production of higher notes was wisely reserved for Keatinge & Ball.

Virginia set the pattern. Over the next three and one-half years, all of the Confederate States except South Carolina issued official paper, fractional currency as well as larger denominations. Issues were printed for another slave state as well, Missouri. The state's current and future status were in doubt, for it was currently experiencing a civ-

State issues for and by Confederate Missouri: "Missouri Defense Bond," twenty dollars (top) and state note for one dollar (bottom); both 1862. Courtesy the NNC.

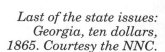

Last of the state issues: Georgia, ten dollars, 1865. Courtesy the NNC.

il war of its own, as locals bushwhacked each other in an effort to drive it into the Confederate column or keep it in the Union camp. Under much duress, Missouri chose the latter, and it is doubtful whether any of Messrs. Keatinge & Ball's attractive "Missouri Defence Bonds" ever entered circulation. But typeset notes ordered by the state's ousted pro-Confederate governor Claiborne F. Jackson did circulate in southern Missouri in 1862, and "Defence Warrants" and "Union Military Bonds" were issued by the other side between 1862 and 1864. South Carolina, the lone holdout against state issues (an odd position, considering that it was the very heart of states' rights sentiment), got around the currency question by tapping a local bank to circulate currency for it. This was the Bank of the State of South Carolina, active between 1861 and 1863, which issued notes worth five, ten, fifteen, twenty, twenty-five, fifty, and seventy-five cents, and one, two, and five dollars. Most of the state currency appeared during the first three years of the war, although Georgia was still circulating notes as late as mid-March 1865, less than a month prior to the general collapse. One wonders how it paid the printer.

How much state and local, public and private currency was issued from the Confederacy? Any answer must be an informed guess at best, because the private and local issuers kept few if any records, and those of the states were lost or destroyed in the general debacle of 1865. But I shall estimate that between fifty and one hundred million dollars' worth of state issues were authorized and that much or somewhat more printed. Say a hundred million for *all* state issues. Private banks might account for another fifty million, and scrip issues a million dollars more. So say between one hundred fifty and one hundred seventy million dollars for every state and local issuer in the Confederacy.

The central government of the Confederate States of America printed five times as much.

Mr. Davis' people at Richmond printed so much currency because they had little alternative. While they—and the states—also sold bonds to pay for the war, the great majority of Confederate finance was placed squarely on the shoulders of the man in the Southern street, whose pockets now bulged with new paper money, accepted by him out of patriotism and necessity. The Davis government knew that there was a terrible risk which accompanied such issues: for them to be redeemable at anything near face value (and this government was fiscally as well as politically conservative), the South would have to win its war of independence within a year or two at most. That should pose no problem, because everybody knew one rebel equaled at least ten Yankees, and the latter were likely to turn tail and run at the first sign of trouble. A number of New England patriots had felt the same way back in 1775, and had paid dearly for their presumption. The ghost of the national War for Independence was visited on its Southern descendant. This war was in no hurry to end, either.

The money told the story. By late 1861, the South was caught in a descending inflationary spiral. Its war was extending, deepening. There was no way to circulate coinage, so more paper had to be printed. But there was less for the paper to buy because many of the farmers and factory workers, those primary producers of goods, were off in the army. Slaves had taken many of their places, but slaves produced less willingly and produced less goods than did free men. Also, a Northern blockade which had been laughed at when imposed in the early months of 1861 was now beginning to pinch here and there. So there was less coming in from abroad as well. More dollars were chasing fewer goods, and the war was expanding as well: the value of Confederate currency began to slide, and it never stopped, as the Davis government printed more and more of it in a vain attempt to pay for the current war and anticipate an even larger one. By the beginning of 1865, it had slid so far that a holder of one of the attractive new five-hundred-dollar bills would have gladly exchanged it for a Yankee ten-dollar gold piece. But he would have found no takers.

Most Americans have seen a piece or two of Confederate money, most likely from the final issue, dated February 17, 1864. Some two hundred million dollars' worth was authorized on that date, and it has been conjectured that some ten times that amount was actually issued between then and the end of the war. This estimate is much too high: with research I conducted and published in the early 1980s, I was able to account for something less than half a billion dollars' worth of 1864-dated currency, but that is an impressive figure in and of itself, especially as much of it was printed during the final months of the war, when the Confederate authorities had rather more important matters on their minds. The 1864 notes were printed from stones prepared by Keatinge & Ball of Columbia. Many of these stones had come from Scotland, run in by blockaders under Northern noses at very great risk. The printers inevitably tried to get every last possible "pull" out of the precious stones, which accounts for the grimy quality of much of the 1864 issue.

The actual printing was done by another firm, Evans & Cogswell. This held for the bulk of the 1864-dated notes, but the very last of them, those printed after the fall of Columbia in late February 1865, were done by another Southern printer, our old friends at Hoyer & Ludwig. By that time, this firm was about the only one left in the South capable of doing the work.

It was fitting that Hoyer & Ludwig printed the last of the Confederate notes: it had very nearly printed the first of them. But not quite. There was an issue of lovely, black-and-green paper dated from Montgomery in May 1861, put into circulation during the brief period when that town served as the Confederate capital. This and a sister issue circulated a few months later from Richmond were printed by Northern printers (the National Bank Note Company, in the case of the Montgomery notes, the "Southern Bank Note Company," really the American Bank Note Company, in the case of those for Richmond). The Lincoln government made loud noises, the two New York firms soon had all the business they could handle up North, and henceforth the South was on its own.

It tapped Hoyer & Ludwig, which accordingly added a national contract to its state and local ones. The firm's work was crude, and it almost always restricted its efforts to uniface printing in black ink. Its wares were easily counterfeited by local and Northerner alike, and the Davis government was soon looking for alternative printers.

It found a good many during the first year of the war. Manouvrier of New Orleans print-

Confederate States of America, fifty dollars, 1861. It is dated at Montgomery, Alabama, but was printed in New York. Courtesy the NNC.

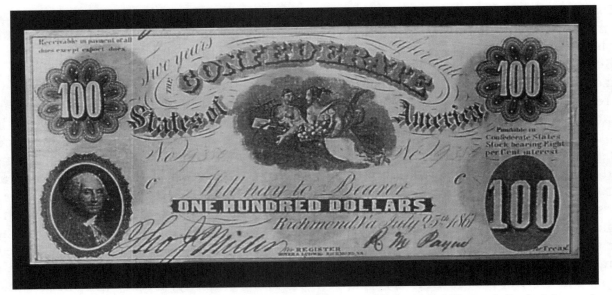

Confederate States of America, one hundred dollars, 1861. It is one of Hoyer & Ludwig's crude products. Courtesy the NNC.

A Southern Heroine: Lucy Holcombe Pickens on a Confederate dollar and a hundred-dollar bill, both 1862. Courtesy the NNC.

Confederate States of America, five hundred dollars, 1864.

ed a single issue of five-dollar bills for the Confederacy in the summer of 1861, but his lax ideas of security (as well as his inexpert lithography) persuaded Secretary of the Treasury Memminger and others to look elsewhere. They had the irascible Col. Blanton Duncan of Richmond and Columbia print some of their money in 1861–62, but they were moving to Keatinge & Ball by the latter year. They remained loyal to that firm until the final weeks, when necessity drove them back to Richmond, and to Hoyer & Ludwig.

What did the Confederacy put on its notes? It began the war with cast-off cuts from earlier printers: much of Hoyer & Ludwig's work looks like obsolete currency from the 1830s, with artful but irrelevant images of Greek goddesses, civic virtues, and the odd railway train. The resemblance ceases, though, when you look at the work more closely because Hoyer & Ludwig were far less skilled than any of the major printers of the 1830s. Within the year, as other producers were taking control of the business, more appropriate images were making their appearance.

Southern leaders were there: President Davis, R. M. T. Hunter (one of the leading proponents of states' rights), Alexander H. Stephens (Davis' Vice President, and one of the more reflective members of the government), C. G. Memminger (its treasury secretary), and Judah P. Benjamin (who served successively as its Attorney General, Secretary of War, and Secretary of State). So was George Washington, who was claimed by the North as well. Lucy Holcombe Pickens, wife of the governor of South Carolina, also graced several notes as the war went on—most notably the hundred-dollar bills of 1862–64. The portrait of this particular Southern lady was part of a growing trend toward the creation and depiction of images of Southern nationalism: she was the attractive, high-spirited wife of the man in charge at Charleston when the war began there in April 1861, and she graced more paper money than any other woman in America's history. She was joined on the hundred-dollar bill by a vignette of actual Confederate soldiers, another embodiment of aspiring nationalism. The trend reached its apotheosis with the five-hundred-dollar note of 1864: here, opposite a representation of the Great Seal of the Confederacy flanked by the Southern flag and implements of war, appears the kindly face of the South's "good soldier," the beloved Thomas Jefferson "Stonewall" Jackson. Jackson was one of the three best military leaders the Confederacy had to offer. Curiously, the other two (Nathan Bedford Forrest and the better-known Robert E. Lee) never appeared on any notes. Forrest's background may have told against him (he had started life as a slave trader, a bit too much even for the section currently fighting

Back of a Confederate twenty-dollar bill, 1863. Courtesy the NNC.

to preserve his line of work), and Lee may have simply told the Treasury he was uninterested in such honors.

In addition to named and allegorical personages, the Confederacy put anonymous people on its money including the soldiers on the hundred-dollar bill described above, as well as the slaves around which so much of the conflict revolved. Slaves appear on one of the rare Montgomery notes, a fifty-dollar bill; they are seen there hoeing cotton. Another slave picks it (on a ten-dollar note printed by Col. Duncan), a third carries it to market (on another ten, printed by Leggett, Keatinge & Ball), while several others load it on a steamboat for shipment to New Orleans (on a five-dollar note from Hoyer & Ludwig). All of these notes are scarce to rare, but the Montgomery slaves made a reappearance on hundred-dollar bills produced from late 1862 through early 1863 by Keatinge & Ball, and these bills are common.

Beyond Confederate people, the Southern government's paper depicted Confederate places—most commonly state capitols, seen on notes from late 1862 onward. Virginia, South Carolina, and Tennessee were so honored, although the South Carolina statehouse was replaced by a spirited scene of Confederate cannoneers late in the war.

These later issues were usually printed on both sides. The Confederate printers assumed that back printing would make their lithographed products more difficult to forge, and the incidence of counterfeiting does seem to have subsided after the introduction of the practice—although the declining value of the real notes may have had something to do with it as well. But counterfeiting did continue to a limited degree, the best notes being printed in Havana, Cuba, and run in by fast sloops under cover of darkness. The South chose a tint called "China blue" for the backs of Confederate notes, and this led to the name "blueback" for the issues so printed, a term which was eventually applied to Confederate currency in general, just as "greenback" was to Northern currency during the Civil War and all federal currency from 1865 to the present.

Bluebacks, state notes, private bank notes, scrip: all came tumbling down with the fall of Richmond in April 1865. Much beyond the South's bid for independence had been called into disrepute with the burning of the city, the surrender of Lee at Appomattox. The South's very identity as a separate section of the country seemed to be at risk as well, and if white Southerners proved more resilient and wedded to old ways than white Northerners had anticipated, the two sections of the country nevertheless began to move closer to one another, creating the potential of a nation altogether new, neither Northern nor Southern in outlook and complexion, but simply American. The dual journey into one country still goes on.

We have seen the types of money used by the South to wage its war, and that they were finally unequal to the task. When we turn North, we might observe that that section won its war almost despite its monetary system. Lincoln's government floundered about for a number of years in search of a reliable, stable, but expandable fiscal medium. What it and the North got was not one medium but several. Let us see what happened.

We begin on the lowest level, that of small change. It immediately becomes apparent that the Northern version of this commodity was more complex than the Southern, because it included metal as well as paper. It did *not* include many coins—at least not during the majority of the war. The Philadelphia Mint struck ten million of the new, copper-nickel "Indian head" cents in 1861, twenty-eight million more in 1862, and nearly fifty million in 1863, but it was unable to keep them out of hoarders' caches until it passed a law on June 8, 1864, forbidding private individuals to issue any metallic objects "intended for the use and purpose of current money." The law, as we have seen, served to end pioneer gold coinage, but it was primarily aimed at private competition to the lowly cent. And why such competition had arisen forms an interesting story.

As I mentioned earlier, the North hoarded coinage in the same way as the South,

Typical Northern scrip. George Bower, Catasauqua, Pennsylvania, fifty cents, 1862.

although it began to do so somewhat later. The hoarding began in earnest in 1862, when a string of federal military defeats (and a Confederate invasion of Maryland, which ended inconclusively at Antietam) made it doubtful whether Lincoln's government could defeat the Southern section, or even survive the war. By that fall, hundreds of merchants, towns, and villages in New York, New Jersey, Massachusetts, Ohio, and several other Northern states were issuing scrip, generally valued at five cents to twen-

United States postage currency, 1862 (above), and fractional currency, 1863 (below). Courtesy the NNC.

ty-five, but occasionally as low as a cent. At the same time, runs had begun on ordinary postage stamps, which represented value and had distinctive colors and designs. This annoyed the postal service, for stamps were intended for moving the mails, not for making small change. It also defrauded the unwary, for the unscrupulous quickly discovered that if you put, say, an ordinary piece of dark green paper in one of the tiny, opaque envelopes manufactured to protect the stamps from moisture and dirt, most people would accept it as ten cents—which was the value then represented by a dark green American postage stamp—without giving it more than a cursory glance.

The federal government initially sanctioned the use of postage stamps as money, passing a law in the summer of 1862 legalizing what was already being done by private citizens. But it soon reconsidered and shortly sought to address the coin shortage, and preserve its stamp supplies, in one step. It created what it initially called "postage currency," tiny notes which looked like current postage stamps, had their same color-to-denomination relationship, and were even perforated along their edges, but which bore no glue and could only be used for money, not for mailing letters. The first of the notes went into circulation on the first day of August.

The genius behind postage currency was Lincoln's Treasurer, a gentleman named Francis Elias Spinner. Spinner had once

Encased postage stamp (notice the advertisement for Arthur M. Claflin's clothing store on the back).

served as cashier of a private, note-issuing bank, the Mohawk Valley Bank of Mohawk, New York; now he was turning his attentions to another, more official sort of paper money. Postage currency was renamed and regularized by a law of March 3, 1863. Henceforth it would be known as "fractional currency." It eventually drove its private competitors out of commerce, and it was issued long after the Civil War, because much small change stubbornly remained in hiding. But the initial impact of Treasurer Spinner's notes was less dramatic: the issue of private scrip reached its height in the fall of 1862, joined by an interesting alternative use of the postage stamp.

Late the previous summer, an inventor from Boston named John Gault came up with a novel way of safely and clearly displaying a postage stamp for use in trade. He devised two round, brass shells, one with a window made of mica (one of the few durable transparent substances then known), the other solid. The stamp was placed between the two shells, which were then clamped together. The user could see the denomination of the stamp through the window, while the issuer could, if desired, place an advertisement or other message on the reverse. Thus was born the "encased postage stamp."

Gault sold his invention to a number of merchants in the East and Midwest. A well-known manufacturer of buttons named Scoville & Company made the holders, while Mr. Gault marketed them. He had a brisk business for a few weeks, because people were desperate for small change. But his invention suffered from a major disability: anyone wishing to use it must pay for it *and* the stamp, but would only be able to circulate it at the stamp's value. Gault's holders cost about two cents each, which would not be a material consideration with a ninety-cent stamp (the highest denomination so encased), but when it came to a three-cent stamp, you were talking real money, relatively speaking. One-cent stamps would be hardly worth encasing, but no fewer than twenty-nine merchants from Rhode Island to Indiana (and a thirtieth in Canada) encased them all the same, a suggestion of how scarce small change had become.

The merchants were no fools, and they would quickly switch to a cheaper substitute

Civil War "patriotic" token.

Civil War "store card."

Gustavus Lindenmeuller's one-cent token, 1863. Courtesy the NNC.

the moment it came along. By the beginning of 1863, they were getting fractional currency, at no additional cost, for everything but the lowest end of the spectrum, the cent. And by the end of 1862, that denomination was being replaced as well by the most durable legacy of the period, the Civil War token.

The move to create an acceptable substitute for the official cent seems to have begun in Cincinnati, Ohio, in the autumn of 1862. Merchants and others began to order, produce, and circulate cent-size tokens, usually made from copper (hence the affectionate name "copperheads," used to describe them then and since). Brass and copper-nickel were also used in their creation, as were white metal, zinc, and hard rubber. The movement to create cent tokens reached a crescendo in 1863 and the first half of 1864, when well over a thousand merchants circulated some 8,555 distinct types, with a total mintage of not less than twenty-five million. Several million of these pieces survive, partly because they were demonetized and thus saved for collectors.

They fall rather naturally into two categories. The first, dubbed "patriotic" by collectors, stressed national sentiments, themes, and heroes like the Union, Liberty, Abraham Lincoln, George Washington, even General McClellan (who was about to run for President against Mr. Lincoln in 1864). The second might espouse patriotic sentiments as well but also incorporated advertisements for specific merchants and their products. Members of this group are called "store cards" by collectors, and they underscore the multitude of places and people touched by the American Civil War. No fewer than twenty-three states were represented in the token roster, logical places like New York and Ohio, distinctly unlikely ones like Alabama, Tennessee, and even Virginia (with a token from Norfolk, which fell to the North in May 1862). Furthermore, every conceivable branch of human endeavor found a place here as well—from printers to stove manufacturers to undertakers to tavern owners. One of the latter was a New Yorker named Gustavus Lindenmueller, who had no fewer than a million cents struck with his bewhiskered visage on one side, a beer stein on the other. Lindenmueller's tokens circulated all over New York City, and quantities of them were paid into the Third Avenue Railroad Company for fares. The owners of the line asked Lindenmueller to redeem a large number of his pieces, which he laughingly refused

United States, two cents, 1864.

to do. The railroad had no redress, but as events such as this multiplied across the Republic, the Lincoln government determined to put a stop to such tokens at its earliest opportunity. In mid-1864, it felt ready to do so, and the fact that it was now winning its war (and producing normal cents in record numbers) made its policy feasible.

In some ways, the United States Mint was among the most junior of moneyers during the Civil War. We have referred to Indian head cents, but what else was it producing?

For most of the period, not all that much. It concentrated on coins at the lower end of the scale, cents, a new two-cent piece (introduced in 1864, the first American coin to bear the motto "In God We Trust"; the motto endured, but the new denomination did not and was not struck after 1873), and a second three-cent piece to augment unwanted supplies of the first.

The three-cent piece takes a bit of explaining. It was introduced in 1851, when the postal rate for a first-class letter was lowered to three cents. Struck in quantity between then and 1853 (first in silver whose fineness was deliberately low, later in the fineness current for all other American silver coins, ninety percent), the coiners at the United States Mint found their new, tiny coin so unpopular than few were minted sub-

sequently in silver (other than for collectors). Early in 1865, the coiners decided to try again, with a slightly larger coin struck in copper-nickel. They made a good many of the new pieces that first year, and the "trimes" did in fact perform a modest service on the lower end of the monetary scale, where they eventually played a role in redeeming three-cent fractional notes. But copper-nickel three-cent pieces eventually proved as unpopular as silver ones, and production stopped in 1889, the same year it ceased for a three-dollar coin in gold (with which one could purchase an entire sheet of three-cent stamps—the bureaucratic mind at work!).

The federal moneyers enjoyed a limited success on the base-metal end of the monetary column; but they found very little success indeed when they turned to silver and gold.

Silver coinage of the period bore a seated figure of Liberty on the obverse, an American eagle with shield on the reverse for dollars and their quarters and halves, the value in a wreath for dimes and their halves. These designs had been introduced by Christian Gobrecht in the late 1830s; they would be retained until the early 1890s for everything under a dollar, until 1873 for that coin as well. Very few pieces bearing Gobrecht's designs were struck in the early 1860s, though, and most of them came from the branch mint

United States, three cents, 1851 and 1865. Courtesy the NNC.

United States, dime, 1862. Courtesy the NNC.

United States, twenty dollars or double eagle from San Francisco, 1865. Courtesy the NNC.

at San Francisco rather than the parent facility at Philadelphia. In fact, the main mint virtually closed down at the end of 1861, only resuming meaningful activity several years after the end of the war. The only silver coin struck during the war in any quantity at all was the half dollar, and even there production slumped to less than half of what it had been before the war.

A similar pattern held for gold. Most gold coins bore a rather pedestrian Liberty head with coronet on their obverses, a stubby-winged eagle with shield on their reverses, designs for which Christian Gobrecht was again largely responsible. The major exception was the slightly more attractive double eagle, designed by the man responsible for the current cent, two cent, and both three cents, James B. Longacre. Gold coins were struck in large numbers through 1861, and in minuscule quantities after that, with the sole exception of the double eagle. Here, production actually *ascended* through the war. Virtually all of it was accounted for by the

San Francisco Mint, however, where the large gold coins were quickly struck and shipped east to bolster banking and the war effort. But the difficulties in getting, and keeping, enough double eagles in circulation to pay for a massive military effort had occurred to the Lincoln government well before the outlay of the war had reached its crescendo (in 1864, by which time it was costing over two million dollars per day). It was logistically impossible to pay for such a war on the spot, and with specie. Like it or not, Mr. Lincoln was going to have to resort to the same expedient as his Southern counterpart: he was going to have to fight his part of the Civil War with paper money. This might be completely outside the strictures so carefully laid down by the Founding Fathers nearly a century before, but there was no help for it.

His government began its unaccustomed task in the summer of 1861. There was as yet no unanimity of opinion concerning the Constitutional right of the national government to circulate paper money. It would

United States, demand note, ten dollars, 1861. Courtesy the NNC.

eventually be decided that it indeed had that authority, but while legislators and jurists debated, there was a war demanding payment. The Union government accordingly attacked the problem from an oblique angle and printed the paper it needed.

While no one was yet certain that the federal government could *print* money, everyone agreed that it had the right to *borrow* money. By a law passed on July 17, 1861, Congress sanctioned a $250 million borrowing program, and by another law it passed the same day and a third it enacted early the following month, Congress turned a portion of that quarter-billion dollars into a particular type of war matériel—federal paper money. It created the "demand note."

Specifically, it created sixty million dollars in five-, ten-, and twenty-dollar bills which promised payment of specie to the bearer "on demand"; hence the name. The

number of places where the holder of a demand note might receive coins for it was restricted to five Eastern and Midwestern cities (New York, Boston, Philadelphia, Cincinnati, and St. Louis), and the method of payment was restricted as well, to silver coin alone. But any guarantee of payment was better than none, and the value of these first forays into federal currency held up fairly well, at least in comparison with what was to come.

Demand notes are interesting from a number of viewpoints. They were not printed by the government which issued them, for the Bureau of Engraving and Printing would not be set up until the following year. Instead, these first notes were contracted out to the National Bank Note Company and the American Bank Note Company, which were printing money for the Confederacy at about the same time!

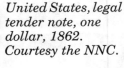

United States, legal tender note, one dollar, 1862. Courtesy the NNC.

Demand notes bore inspiratory face designs and lauded American patriots, including President Lincoln. (Lincoln and various members of his cabinet would appear on a number of Civil War-era notes while still alive, such practice not being frowned upon as yet.) The backs of these notes bore fancy designs printed in dark green, which explains the origin of the term "greenback." Alone among federal issues, demand notes bore neither the seal of the United States Treasury nor the signature of the Treasurer. Spaces were left for signatures of that gentleman and the Register of the Treasury, for it was originally expected that these two officials would personally hand-sign each note. But someone soon realized that this would be highly impractical, and the plates were amended so that lowly Treasury clerks could sign for Treasurer Spinner and his colleague. Demand notes were issued between August

1861 and April 1862, by which time the Lincoln government had concluded that much more paper would be needed and was attempting to respond with a second type of bill, the "legal tender note."

This was fiat money pure and simple. There was no provision for exchange of these new notes for coins, their wording merely stating that they were "a legal tender for all debts public and private." They grew out of legislation passed by Congress in February 1862, by which time the Union armies were securely bogged down in the mud of northern Virginia, the effort to restore the Union going absolutely nowhere. The federal government now realized that the war was going to last far longer than it had supposed, and would cost far more than the sixty million dollars it had ordered turned into demand notes. On February 25, 1862, it therefore authorized an initial issue of some $150 million dollars in legal tender notes, exchangeable for six percent government bonds and thus redeemable in five years. The notes were *not* immediately redeemable in coin, even at the five places mentioned on the demand notes—but then, the Lincoln government realized that such redemption was completely impracticable and not worth promising on the faces of its money.

The first legal tender notes bore an issue date of March 10, 1862. By early summer, the amount authorized under the February legislation had been put in circulation but a Northern victory was still nowhere in sight. Lincoln's people therefore had to secure passage of a second Act (after having solemnly promised that there would never *be* a second Act) on July 11, empowering them to circulate another hundred and fifty millions' worth of legal tender notes. A third Legal Tender Act was passed on March 3, 1863, authorizing a similar sum. But notes authorized under this final Act remained unissued during the war, the Northern government having meanwhile overhauled its inefficient tax system for better collection of extant monies from its citizens. These new taxes meant somewhat less pressure on the legal tender system, but the existence of the third Legal Tender Act meant that more of the notes might eventually be circulated if the government saw fit. Their issue resumed after the war and continued for many years, but they were eventually overshadowed by other types of currency, which will be described in succeeding chapters.

The wartime legal tender issue was printed by the same two private firms we saw earlier. (The first work of the Bureau of Engraving and Printing was confined to applying the Treasury seal and serial numbers to federal currency produced privately, and to cutting out the notes from sheets after having done so. Some of the earliest actual printing done there was the fractional currency issue of 1863, but the Bureau did not acquire a monopoly over the production of regular currency until much later.) Their designs represented something of a decline, compared with those found on the demand notes. Their green tint, once fresh, was beginning to acquire that slightly muddy quality it has retained on federal currency ever since. And while the designs used on demand notes were repeated on the new fives, tens, and twenties, the legal tender system added denominations above and below those sums, whose faces featured pedestrian portraits of living and dead Secretaries of the Treasury, including the first of them, Alexander Hamilton, who probably would have thought the legal tender note an exceedingly bad idea.

That which Hamilton had witnessed on national paper money of the 1770s repeated itself in the 1860s. Legal tender notes were not redeemable in specie at their time of issue, and their real value (against gold, as opposed to their stated value) inevitably became tied to how people felt about the government's prospects of victory on any given day. The notes never circulated at par against gold, and by early 1864 they were worth about thirty-five cents on the dollar. They later rose, as undeniable evidence began accumulating that the North was winning the war. But even at the time of Appomattox, they were worth at most three-quarters of what they said they were worth. What Mr. Davis found, Mr. Lincoln also learned: fiat money is not an especially effective way to finance a war. But Mr. Davis could do very little about his predicament, whereas Mr. Lincoln would keep searching for fiscal solutions until he found what it took to carry him and the nation through its difficulties. He would do the same with generals, raising and sacking them until he finally found the right combination.

His task was somewhat easier with paper than it was with soldiers. An obvious potential for war finance was the note-issuing private bank. This institution was still very much alive at the outbreak of the war. But it was not especially inclined to help out a beleaguered government: bankers are practical souls, and they tend to take actions more seriously than words. So while they would continue to issue their own paper currency, they would sit on the sidelines while

Mr. Lincoln issued his. Was there a way of directly engaging them in the war effort?

There was, and it became law with the National Banking Act, passed on February 25, 1863. The new law represented a half-hearted attempt at regulation of the country's chaotic banking system, but it was primarily intended as a money-raising scheme for the Union war effort. Under its provisions, private banks were encouraged to apply for federal charters, thereby becoming "national banks." They were then permitted to issue "national bank notes." They used their funds to purchase Union bonds (thus raising money for the prosecution of the war). They deposited these bonds with the United States Treasurer and were then allowed to issue national bank notes against up to ninety percent of the value of the bonds they had just deposited at Washington. Each bank's charter would run for a renewable period of twenty years.

This was all well and good: we see what the government brought out of the bargain. What did it bring into it to interest the banks? It brought prestige: any bank with the word "national" in its title would garner more local respect than one without. Again, this was all well and good, but not nearly enough. During the Act's first year, only 179 out of the many hundreds of private banks across the Republic had joined the system, with scant prospect of many more coming into the fold. That brought the second attraction into play: discriminatory taxation if banks did not join. A hint of what was to come had been suggested early in 1863—a two percent tax on state bank notes. The tax was not enacted for the time being; by the time it became law (March 3, 1865), it had ballooned to ten percent. While it was not scheduled to take effect for another eighteen months, the threat alone was enough: across the country, banks either

An early national bank note: State National Bank (Boston, Massachusetts), one dollar, 1865 (series 1875). Courtesy the NNC.

joined the new national system, ceased their own issues—or simply went out of business. By 1866, the private bank note had passed out of American history. And by that time, of course, the North had won the war whose pursuit had inspired its successor, the national bank note.

This is the most interesting and attractive form of "official" United States paper money. Its interest stems from the thousands of banks, scattered from Alaska to Puerto Rico, which would one day participate in its production and circulation. We shall be speaking of the national bank note in this respect at some length, for it will stand as one of the few remaining monuments of monetary localism in the increasingly national, conformist atmosphere of the late nineteenth and early twentieth centuries. But we are now concerned with the designs of the first, wartime national bank notes, for they

are among the most artistic renditions ever to have seen service on the nation's money.

In March 1863, an official call went out to interested artists and engravers, soliciting their help in designing the new currency. Designs for faces and backs ranging from five to one thousand dollars would be required (and eventually designs for ones and twos as well; these denominations would be added shortly). Up to two hundred dollars would be paid per note designed, and the contestants would have until the twenty-eighth of the month to submit their ideas.

A number of gifted artists responded, the attractiveness of their labors enhanced by the superb technology of the private firms who translated their designs from sketches and paintings to actual notes. For the dollar bill, T. A. Liebler designed a vignette called "Concordia," skillfully engraved by Charles Burt. The Liebler design depicted two maidens

LaCrosse National Bank (LaCrosse, Wisconsin), two dollars, 1876 (series 1875). Courtesy the NNC.

pledging amity before an altar, a most appropriate design for a nation still at war which must soon make peace. For the back of the dollar bill, F. O. C. Darley's "The Landing of the Pilgrims" was chosen, again translated into steel by Charles Burt. The scene was rendered in black, while the surrounding wording and designs were done in green. This practice was maintained for higher denominations, and it was a major contributor to the beauty of the series, especially when combined with the black designs and red seals and serial and bank charter numbers on the face.

Both sides of these notes displayed the mixed national/local, public/private nature of the system under which they were created. While signatures of the president and cashier of the local bank were affixed by hand, each national bank note bore two more, printed signatures, those of the Treasurer and the Register of the Treasury. The name of the issuing bank was given in full on the face of each note, and the back bore a state or territorial seal on the left side, an American eagle on the right. Among the most popular of all national bank note designs are those found on the two-dollar bill. There was only one version of this denomination, and it has always been avidly sought by collectors. Its green-and-black back features a scene from American history (as indeed did all backs of early national bank notes)—in this case a depiction of Sir Walter Ralegh exhibiting corn and tobacco from America in 1585. We are primarily interested in the face, though, for here is a gigantic horizontal figure "2," occupying a good half of that side of the note. This treatment gave the note its name among collectors, the "lazy two" or "lazy deuce."

It was Abraham Lincoln's hope that, once the war paid for by national bank notes and other federal currency had been won, the concord expressed on the new dollar bill could be immediately and permanently reestablished. This was not to be, and Mr. Lincoln was one of the earliest victims of his own delusion, felled by a bullet from a Southern sympathizer less than a week after Lee's surrender at Appomattox. Sadly, his policies of

a merciful peace fell with him. Still more sadly, it is unlikely that they would have survived intact in a Congress increasingly intent on making the defeated section pay dearly for its folly.

The coming years would be difficult ones for many in the North and brutal ones for most in the South, including the former object of attention from both sections, the African American. Although now legally free, he would shortly become an object of embarrassment to the victors, one of mystery, hatred, and fear to the vanquished. The twelve years after the end of the war are called the "Reconstruction" period of American history, and while it is unwise to generalize about parcels of the past, it seems safe to say that this one was more unhappy than most. The wounded country and its people might heal, but the Reconstruction period, wherein the North attempted to impose its political and racial policies on the prostrate South and finally failed, proved that the process would be painful and slow. But there were touches of green here and there, amity restored, dawning of respect between individual members of the sections and the races; not much, but a start.

And the South slowly returned to economic life. Much of the section depended on barter and federal food donations for the first year or so. Its mints remained closed (two of them forever, and the third, New Orleans, until 1879). Its banks had come tumbling down at the end of the war, and all state and Confederate currency had of course become worthless. But new national banks were being set up while the smoke of battle was still clearing. A record of sorts was held by the new First National Bank of Richmond, which received its charter on April 24, 1865, precisely twenty-two days after the fall of the city to the North! Other banks followed its lead at a more leisurely pace, and the section slowly returned to economic life. As it did so, and as the boom times already current in the North extended over the former Confederacy, the evolution and story of America's money continued, entering not a golden age but certainly a gilded one.

CHAPTER 7

THE GILDED AGE: AMERICA'S MONEY, 1865–1914

CHAPTER 7

THE GILDED AGE: AMERICA'S MONEY, 1865–1914

In 1873, two authors collaborated on a realistic novel about the newly wealthy entrepreneurs who had emerged from the Civil War and Reconstruction. Their book was highly critical of this group, whose coarseness and moneygrubbing stood in stark contrast to the ideals espoused on an official level during the same period. The two writers would go on to greater fame: one of them, Samuel Langhorne Clemens, would become America's greatest and darkest humorist, while the other, Charles Dudley Warner, would find lasting renown as an essayist if not a novelist. But if both writers are better known in other regards, the title they gave their joint production has overshadowed them both, becoming an essential signpost and slogan for an entire period of American history. They called their novel *The Gilded Age*.

The title could not have been more pointed, or more apt. This was *not* a golden age, a period when humankind was at its best, transcending limitations of class, race, sex, and world view. No, this was an age which posed as something solid and worthy, but whose plating was thin, soon revealing the bigotry and brass beneath. It was not a particularly attractive period in the nation's story, and a number of perceptive observers knew it and said so at the time.

But it was a tremendously eventful period. During the fifty years between 1865 and 1914 a number of things happened. The nation assumed its present borders when Alaska was added in 1867 and Hawaii in 1898. It gained temporary and more permanent control over other areas too: the Philippines, Puerto Rico, Guam, the Canal Zone, Guantánamo Bay. This resulted in an anomaly: a proud, annoyingly insistent republic was now an empire, a member of a club ordinarily reserved for monarchies. Messrs. Clemens and Warner saw the inconsistency and so did many other intellectuals and plain folks, but the new domains were popular with the man in the street, who therefore tended to vote for the empire-builders when election times rolled around.

Another important event occurred during the Gilded Age: the United States filled up and, as the Census of 1890 revealed, the frontier at last disappeared. New states entered the Union accordingly, thirteen of them between 1867 and 1912. The nature of those peopling the land changed: in the 1880s, the main source of immigration shifted from Northern to Southern and Eastern Europe. Between then and the First World War, millions left Catholic and Jewish areas searching for a better life or an end to religious persecution. They quickly found that the streets of America were *not* paved with gold—and many of them had the intimate, direct experience with the pavement to prove it as the sellers of goods from pushcarts and cleaners of streets. The new arrivals were received with thanks by the factory owners, and their willingness to work harder for less than older groups helped to create the greatest event of all during this Gilded Age: the nation entered it a predominantly agricultural country but left it the world's largest industrial power.

Still more changes came about: railroads extended across the country, linking West to East. Telephones and two latecomers called radio and the automobile promised to compress time and space still more. Newspapers mushroomed. Americans became more literate, in spite of the new, poorly-educated immigrants: while their first generation might not speak English, their second would indeed speak it and read it too. Cities grew. The roles of the farm, the countryside, and the small town diminished.

Thus far, the changes I have listed were for the better, or at least neutral. But events this big inevitably influenced some groups more than others, hurt other groups still, and caused immense friction and unrest virtually everywhere. Farmers, who had stood at the center of the old, prewar Republic, put up a stubborn but ultimately doomed struggle against the loss of their position at the head of the table. Native Americans got shoved away altogether, penned up on "reservations"—lands "reserved" to them because no one else had any possible use for them. African Americans saw what little they had won taken back in the South with the ending of Reconstruction; those who voyaged North found a scarcely more hospitable reception there. In both sections, they did the work which no one else would do—the sole difference being that they were less likely to be turned out of it in the South, and less likely to escape it as well.

Few African Americans went into factory work. Many of the immigrants did so, however, and the ranks of industrial labor were also swelled by women. But those who had gotten there first turned on the newcomers, alarmed lest the pittance *they* were making would be jeopardized by recent arrivals, who would work even more cheaply and for longer hours. The organized labor movement made several sputtering beginnings, including the National Labor Union, the Knights of Labor, and the American Federation of Labor, but its days of success lay far distant in the next century. There were some massive strikes all the same, in 1877, 1893–94, and again at the very end of the era. But little came of them except for sore heads for the rank and file and jail stretches for the leadership.

Those who owned the factories owned a good deal more, including major portions of the state and federal governments. They rarely served in Congress or statehouse themselves, but their needs and aspirations—ranging from antilabor legislation to protective tariffs—were assured of a favorable reception and response by those who did serve. We should not assume that the legislators were simply purchased by the men of capital, for the truth was somewhat more complex. This was a corrupt age, and a number of lawmakers were indeed for hire, but the world view of those who ran the national and state governments and those who operated the mills and owned the large farms jibed sufficiently so that much the same policies would have been enacted had politics been clean instead of corrupt. And the only lasting differences between Republicans and Democrats were two: Republicans had won the Civil War while Democrats had lost it, and Republicans favored higher tariffs while Democrats opposed them. There were other points of dispute which came and went, but the basic truth was that the two parties had an agenda which suited their and the economy's leadership but which generally ignored the real and worsening problems of the average citizen. The middle and late portions of the Gilded Age would accordingly see two movements for reform, speaking to the needs of the "forgotten man." One was staffed by the forgotten man himself: the Populist movement of the 1880s and 1890s; it would make a great deal of noise but little real headway. The other was staffed by those in the middle and upper classes who presumed to speak *for* the forgotten man: the Progressive movement of the first two decades of the new century. It would make rather more headway: by the end of the period, it would have helped eradicate some of the worst social and industrial evils of the Gilded Age.

At bottom, all of this activity was tending in one direction: the country and its people were becoming ever more interconnected, with ever fewer local variants on the general pattern. The shift from the local to the national, from the particular to the universal, had been implicit in the Northern victory of 1865; for the next half century, Americans would have civic calm at home, coupled with the ability to play a role abroad only if and

Dollar from the Carson City Mint, 1871.

when they so chose. They thus had the time and concentration necessary to explore the broad new road.

Part of the evidence that they were doing so comes from the money they were producing during the Gilded Age. It is worth, I think, a closer look than it has generally gotten, an attention paid with a due regard to larger national trends. Never has there been a closer link between American money and the larger fabric of American life than during this period.

Let us consider American coinage and currency with the larger history in the backs of our minds. What do we see? First, there is a return to coinage with the end of the Civil War. The uncertainty is over: once put in circulation specie will remain there. For most denominations, the postwar period will see an expansion of production, at least down to the harsh economic times of the middle and later 1870s, when massive unemployment will produce a decline in demand for new coins. The sole exceptions to this rule will be those pieces on either end of the scale: cents, two-cent pieces, and three-cent pieces will all see their production tail off by the late 1860s (and the two-cent piece will not be struck after 1873), while the production of the double eagle will actually *rise* through the 1870s.

The production of golden double eagles rose because there seemed to be an endless supply of the yellow metal in California, Colorado, and Nevada. This gold must be turned into a useful product, and the double eagle recommended itself: such coins were reasonably easy to strike, and they would mean less work for mints than smaller coins.

The great majority of them were struck at the San Francisco branch mint, assisted after 1870 by another federal facility at Carson City, Nevada. (The latter had been primarily set up in response to the massive Comstock silver strike near Virginia City, but it coined gold as well as silver down to its closing in 1893.) While many of the new twenties were sent back East via train and stagecoach, many more stayed near their point of origin—so many, in fact, that they were becoming a nuisance to Bay Area bankers by the beginning of the 1870s. Counting and handling of so much gold coin was time-consuming, a barrier to the efficient operation of a bank. Could Congress do something about it?

Congress could and did, with an Act of July 12, 1870, which authorized a new type of paper money, the "national gold bank note." Nine banks in California (and a tenth in Boston) were authorized to issue special paper money redeemable *only* in gold, *only* at the issuing bank. They were granted charters under the National Banking Act, and so their notes (fives, tens, twenties, fifties, hundreds, and five hundreds were authorized, but no bank issued every possible denomination) had faces identical with regular national bank notes. But their paper bore a yellow tint (for gold, of course), and their backs featured

First National Gold Bank (San Francisco, California), twenty dollars, 1870. Courtesy the NNC.

United States, hundred-dollar gold certificate, 1877 (series of 1875). Courtesy the NNC.

a unique design which displayed every federal gold denomination then in circulation.

National gold bank notes were intended as an aid for bankers, for they would obviously be far easier to handle than gold coin. From the evidence of the notes (crisp uncirculated pieces are of the highest rarity, actually unknown for several of the denominations), bankers found them useful and so did everyone else in the West. National gold bank notes were only issued in the 1870s, although gold-based federal paper money (centering on the "gold certificate," first introduced in 1863, another of Lincoln's wartime currency measures) would continue to form an important component of American currency down to the Great Depression.

Elsewhere in paper, the national banking system continued to expand. More and more charters went to Southern banks, and every state in the former Confederacy was represented in the system by 1874. National bank notes chronicled the westward movement as well, and what we saw earlier with the rise of the private note-issuing bank was replicated here with their descendants: in many cases, territories got national bank notes *before* they became states, and indeed while they were but one step removed from the frontier. And so the First National Bank of Helena received its charter in 1866, nearly a quarter of a century before Montana achieved statehood, while the First National Bank of Cheyenne was organized in 1871, some eighteen years before Wyoming became a state. But a record of sorts must surely be held by the First National Bank of Juneau, which was chartered no less than sixty-one years prior to Alaskan statehood!

What evocative names come to us from the days of the national bank note, from the Citizens National Bank of Dry Run (Pennsylvania) to the Rio Grande National Bank of Laredo (Texas) to the First National Bank of Coin (Iowa; the town is located in the southwest corner of the state, not far from the Missouri River). The national bank note is among the most avidly collected branch of American currency, and it is easy to see why: there is a localism here not seen in any other object of post-Civil War numismatics save one, the trade token. The trade token is likely to be undated, with a simple design, whereas the national bank note is beautiful and bears a real date and real signatures of the men (and a number of women) who stood behind it. Trade tokens have an interest and validity of their own, and they will be discussed later

Morgan dollar, 1878,

in this chapter, but the fact remains that for most collectors the national bank note holds a numismatic allure, a local interest, possessed by no other variety of American money from this era.

But this localism is more apparent than real. These notes were indeed signed and circulated in Oregon, Pennsylvania, Texas, and Vermont, but they were all coming from a single printer by the beginning of the 1880s: the Bureau of Engraving and Printing in Washington, D.C. They could bear such interesting names as the First National Bank of Pelican Rapids, but all of their faces were identical within any given denomination, and all of their backs exhibited only minor differences, too. In short, this seemingly most local of late nineteenth/early twenti-eth-century monies was national at heart, reflection of the homogenizing movement I mentioned earlier.

The federal government of the day might indeed respond to local monetary differences and act on behalf of influential interests on the state or regional level. It did so with the national gold bank notes, an aid to California bankers. It acted in a similar way but on a much wider scale for Western silver interests. The bankers had gotten paper money, but the silver miners would get a new coin, the "Morgan" dollar.

Named after designer George T. Morgan, the new dollar first appeared in 1878, and it spawned a new type of paper money that same year, one called the "silver certificate." But the roots of the new dollar went back

United States, ten dollars, series of 1878 (silver certificate). Courtesy the NNC

nearly twenty years. The United States had long had a "bimetallic" monetary system, one based on two precious metals rather than one, metals which were interchangeable with each other at a fixed ratio. This ratio had been established at 16:1 (meaning that weight for weight, gold was worth sixteen times as much as silver) in 1834, at which point it had remained.

The bimetallic system functioned adequately down to the end of the 1840s. Then the California Gold Rush upset the silver-to-gold ratio in favor of silver coinage, which became profitable to melt for export. Congress' response was to reduce the precious metal content of the half dollar, quarter, dime, and half dime (the silver dollar was not affected, not being struck in quantity anyway). This reduction helped get silver coinage back into commerce, and the money supply remained relatively stable until the emergency of the Civil War.

As that crisis was taking place, events far to the west were about to shape America's monetary history as well. Silver had been found near Virginia City late in the 1850s. So much of it was shortly being taken from the ground there that the Union soon acquired another state, Nevada, and the nation's monetary system a headache of monumental size and lengthy duration. The hallowed 16:1 ratio was again being upset—but this time in favor of gold. Silver's depreciation was unintentionally fostered by foreign as well as domestic events: in 1871, the new German Empire went on a strict gold standard, accordingly exporting nearly two-thirds of its silver stock—adding over two hundred million dollars to a market already glutted with silver from the American West.

Mine owners were suffering, and they and their Congressional representatives were vocal in their distress. The official reply was the Mint Act of February 12, 1873. The act gave with one hand and took away with the other. It put a slightly greater amount of silver in three subsidiary coins, the half dollar, quarter, and dime. And it gave the West and the world a completely new coin—

a "trade dollar," slightly heavier than an ordinary silver dollar, intended to compete with the Mexican peso, or Piece of Eight, in the Far Eastern trade. But it took away a great deal too, at least in the eyes of the West. It stopped production of the half dime and the silver three-cent piece (and the unpopular two-cent piece as well). And it closed out coinage of the silver dollar.

This was the famous "Crime of '73," which would soon become a rallying point for Western silver and Midwestern agrarian interests against the "goldbugs" of the East. Never mind that virtually no silver dollars had been struck during the entire decade of the 1860s. Never mind that no one wanted the three million or so which had been struck since 1870. For Western miners, the Mint Act of 1873 was outrage pure and simple, and they spent the next five years fighting to get it repealed, struggling to bring their white metal the Eastern respect which it, and they, deserved. They would see success in 1878, and the United States would see a new coin, and a new type of paper money.

Both were created by the Bland-Allison Act of February 28, 1878, which became law despite a veto from an indignant President Hayes. The act restored unlimited legal tender status to silver dollars on the traditional standard—the very coins which had been discontinued back in 1873. More to the point, it committed the United States Treasury to purchasing between two and four million dollars' worth of silver bullion each month at current market prices and turning it into new silver dollars. The coins were to have new designs, for which an English immigrant named George T. Morgan would bear responsibility. Morgan's left-facing portrait head of Liberty and reverse eagle represented a cautious attempt to bring more artistry to American coinage, a movement which gathered force as other denominations were redesigned after 1891. But for now, the dollar's new look was the last thing on most people's minds.

The reception and meaning of the Morgan dollar varied wildly from place to place:

never before or since has a single coin been so embraced and simultaneously damned by the public which used it. The West was partially assuaged, for the region's silver production now had an outlet, and the new dollars were a circulating mainstay there for many years to come. They were also popular in the South, and millions were struck in New Orleans after the reopening of the federal branch mint there in 1879. It has been said that the new coins were held in special esteem by the former slaves and their descendants: such large pieces of shiny metal suggested a dependability which paper money simply could not possess, especially to people who had witnessed its deleterious effects upon the fortunes of their former masters.

As the years went on, another group grew progressively more fond of the Morgan dollar: medium and small farmers of the Midwest, West, and South. These groups could claim to be the "forgotten Americans" of the eighties and nineties: a persistent agricultural depression robbed them of purchasing power throughout those decades, while the money they owed on land, equipment, and seed proved difficult or impossible to pay off in the normal course of affairs. They began to see the new silver dollars as a possible salvation, for if the United States Mint coined them in unlimited numbers, and if they were to enjoy free convertibility against gold coin, then so much money would flood into the economy that the price of farm products would rise. If that happened, those who raised them could pay off their debts more easily than before. This was the same general argument as had been used by impoverished farmers exactly a century before, but farmers then had wanted unlimited state paper money, not unlimited federal silver coinage. And the reaction of the moneyed interests in the 1880s was very similar to that of their ancestors in the 1780s: a dislike and distrust of one type of money (silver), a rallying around another (gold).

The Bland-Allison Act had stopped short of giving silver full bimetallic parity with gold at the old 16:1 ratio and had also offered something less than completely "free" (unlimited) silver coinage, both of which points would soon become rallying cries for miners and farmers. On the other hand, the new law did allow for a massive coinage of cheap silver at inflated prices (for the new silver dollars were intrinsically worth far less than their face value), a value-to-denomination ratio which became increasingly unrealistic as yet more silver poured from the mines and the United States Mint.

Along with Morgan dollars, the Bland-Allison Act created a new type of paper currency, the "silver certificate." This was a most specialized type of note. Originally intended to redeem the new dollars, and later extended to the redemption of the old, wartime legal tender notes, the new paper would *not* be exchangeable for gold certificates. Nor would it remotely resemble any other type of federal paper money. The words "silver" and "silver dollars" would dominate the designs of both sides of the new notes, and their backs would be printed in black, so that anyone offered one of them would know precisely what they were from the outset. All of this suggests to me the hand of silver's Eastern opposition: anyone handed a silver certificate could immediately spot it and demand payment in a gold-based medium instead. The provision for the black back was dropped in 1886, and the new currency type gradually assumed a larger role in the national economy. It might indeed be silver-based, but it was considerably easier to handle than the cumbrous coins which it represented.

But massive distrust of silver dollars and the paper currency they spawned remained strong among Eastern creditor groups, while Western and Southern debtor interests clamored for yet more of the new dollars and silver certificates. The debate over a gold versus gold-and-silver standard may strike us as academic today, but it had real and immediate connotations for those alive a century ago. When miners and small farmers clamored for "the free and unlimited coinage of silver at the rate of sixteen to one," they and the politicians who supported them were advocating much more than an abstruse economic theory which few understood and fewer still could explain. They were demanding recognition and respect for old ways of life which were now literally at risk. Those with the picks and the hoes, those who coaxed their livelihoods from the rock and soil of America, realized that their ways were becoming eclipsed by what they would have called the "Eastern Money Power"—but which we might refer to as Modern Times. The fact that they could view the unlimited coinage of a whitish metal with few practical, non-monetary applications as a panacea for everything from getting out of debt to regaining respect suggests that they were not being particularly realistic. But then, the same might be said for their opposites, who viewed the gold standard as sacred and any attempt to add silver to it as profane.

The issue came to a head in the Presidential campaign of 1896, fought out against the backdrop of a miserable, three-year-long depression which had left factory workers unemployed and farmers and miners even worse off than before. The Republicans put up William McKinley, who had no particular fire but most of the money interests on his side. The Democrats put up William Jennings Bryan, who had no new ideas but enough fire to light up a room with the old. Bryan and his partisans hammered away at the free silver idea while McKinley's spoke for gold coinage and a higher tariff. Bryan and his people gave their all, but it was not enough. "Big Bill McKinley, Advance Agent of Prosperity" got elected, and sure enough, prosperity soon followed—for which the grateful, but realistic, new President claimed little of the credit.

As prosperity returned and extended even to those who had not known it since the seventies, the issue of bimetallism faded in importance. When the Republic officially went on a single, gold monetary standard in March 1900, Bryan and the Democrats railed and ran against it that fall—but no one else cared and McKinley was reelected.

McKinley had more than prosperity on his side by that time. Since he had taken office in March 1897, the United States had acquired an overseas empire. The affable President had done little to effect the acquisition himself, but his Democratic opposition (including Samuel Langhorne Clemens, who went on the stump for Bryan) thought it had another splendid issue with which to belabor him in 1900. It discovered too late that Americans rather liked the idea of world domination and the man upon whose watch the empire-building had occurred.

In the broader view of history, the new domains (and the fact that McKinley got reelected in part because of them) represented a historic shift in emphasis on the part of America's people. Since the very beginning, they had generally looked inward, discovering enough to be done at home to keep them fully occupied. Now, whether because of the disappearance of the frontier, the achievement of a particular stage by their version of free enterprise, or other, less plausible reasons, they were ready to look outward. What they saw and how they reacted would change the nature of the country and its people and their points of view. It would also amend the nature of their numismatics—and in some very surprising ways.

There were straws in the wind by the early 1870s. That the United States was looking abroad for at least economic gain was suggested by the new trade dollar: why mint such a coin for the Far Eastern trade if you were not interested in that trade yourself? But the trade dollar did not live up to expectations. Chinese merchants accepted it readily enough, and many surviving specimens bear "chop marks," incised stamps applied by coastal merchants indicating that they found the coins of full weight and good silver. But a last-minute addition to the Mint Act of 1873 gave the "trades" legal tender status in the United States in sums up to five dollars, and a fall in silver prices in 1876 resulted in millions of the coins (which were now worth less than their face value) recrossing the Pacific and glutting commerce on the

United States, trade dollar, notice the "chops," which indicate it circulated in China.

West Coast. Their legal tender status for American use was hastily revoked, and the coins were no longer struck for commerce after 1878. They were formally repudiated by the federal government some nine years later—the only American coins so dishonored.

Another straw: you will recall that prior to 1857 the United States Mint had neither expertise enough nor bullion enough to safely prohibit the use of foreign coin. By 1876 this same institution was actually beginning to coin for other countries, having received Congressional approval to do so back in 1874. It first struck minor coinage for Venezuela, gradually extending its production to coinage for other small nations in the Western

Foreign coins struck at the United States Mint, late nineteenth and early twentieth centuries. Courtesy the NNC.

Hemisphere (the Dominican Republic in 1897, El Salvador in 1904, and Costa Rica in 1905). By 1906, it was supplying Mexico, in an interesting case of historical reciprocity: Mexico had provided the United States with coinage for two centuries, and now Americans would return the favor. The United States Mint would extend its coinage production across Latin America during the first half of the twentieth century—a move matched country-for-country by the American Bank Note Company's paper money. That firm might no longer serve as a printer of United States federal paper money, but it would enjoy a golden age as a supplier of Latin American nations and their banks, a position it would not relinquish until the 1970s.

In the 1880s, the United States Mint extended its attentions in another overseas direction: Hawaii. The islands formed an independent kingdom in those days, but American missionaries had been going there since 1820, shortly followed by Yankee traders and businessmen. In 1847, an issue of copper *keneta* (cents) had been prepared for King Kamehameha III by a private mint in Attleboro, Massachusetts. The issue was poorly received: the monarch's portrait was almost unrecognizable and the reverse denomination was mis-

spelled! Indignant natives threw these first Hawaiian coins into the sea, and it took fifteen years for the Royal Treasury to disperse the hundred thousand pieces of the issue.

American penetration of the islands increased pace after 1849. In the early 1880s, King Kalakaua I desired another issue of Hawaiian coinage, and after a two-year search the United States Mint was brought into the islands' numismatics. The King's representative, sugar baron Claus Sprekels, approached the Americans with preliminary designs and a proposal to coin a million *dala* (the dollar of Hawaii, on an exact par with the United States coin) in silver for the island chain. The issue would consist of dala, "hapalua" (half dollars), "hapaha" (quarters), and "hapawalu" (eighth dollars, for Hawaiians used the Spanish-American real for small change). This last denomination was abandoned in the pattern stage in favor of a dime, or "umi keneta" (ten-cent) piece—which would make it possible to strike the entire coinage issue on planchets left over from regular American coining. The King's right-facing portrait would grace the new coins' obverses, the national arms their reverses (except in the case of the ten-cent piece, whose reverse would feature a wreath). This distribution of designs replicated that

Hawaiian dollar and its quarter, 1883. Courtesy the NNC.

found on contemporary United States silver coins, and it was likely deliberate.

While proof coinage was made at Philadelphia, the "business strikes" were made by the branch facility at San Francisco. Coinage went on between September 1883 and June 1884, but all of the coins bore the 1883 date. By now, the American Bank Note Company was producing the islands' paper money and postage stamps, another indicator of a growing American interest and presence there. So was the leasing of Pearl Harbor as a base for the nascent United States Navy (in 1887). And so was the decision of a group of American businessmen, led by Sanford B. Dole (the Pineapple King), to overthrow the native dynasty and seek admission to the United States.

This took place in 1893; a Queen (Liliuokalani, who was seeking to reassert native control) was replaced by a Provisional Government (led by Mr. Dole), which would only exist for as long as it took to get the islands annexed by the United States. Unfortunately, incoming American President Grover Cleveland was against the idea (on the grounds that the average Hawaiian did not favor it, which was probably true). He vetoed the annexation treaty, and the rebuffed businessmen hastily organized the Republic of Hawaii, which would reapply for admission at a more favorable time. That moment came some five years later, with a new American President, and a new, more ambitious foreign policy. Hawaii was annexed in 1898, the fact obscured by much larger events that same year.

Hawaiian coinage was an exception: most of the United States Mint's foreign coining forays were accomplished in Spanish America. Two of the other nations there for which the United States would shortly coin were Cuba and Panamá, and there was a very good reason for the connection: it had helped create those countries.

It has become fashionable to dismiss American concern for other peoples' welfare as pious claptrap masking nefarious intentions. And certainly Americans have tended to view foreign policy more in black-and-white, right-and-wrong terms than most nations—especially in cases where American self-interest is at stake. So when we see what happened at the end of the last century (American eviction of several nations from Caribbean lands) we are tempted to impute it to simple covetousness. But while desire for an empire, for new markets, even for spreading the Protestant Gospel to "heathen" (long-Catholic) areas, undoubtedly helped shape the course of events, it did not explain everything. Sincere altruism and an affectionate regard for the underdog also had their say.

In the case of Cuba, they had a very large say indeed. The island had interested American Presidents from John Quincy Adams to Ulysses S. Grant, during whose tenure Cubans fought a revolt against Spanish mismanagement. The rebellion did well for a few years, and it initially appeared likely that the United States would intervene on behalf of the insurgents. But Spain gradually gained the upper hand, promising reforms which were not kept but which did dampen patriot ardor. The United States decided to stay out of the affair. The revolt ended in 1878, but the peace was surface-deep. Cubans wanted their independence, and the island was likely to flare up again upon any reasonable pretext.

Pretext came in the mid-1890s. These were years of economic depression across the globe, and any land whose economy depended upon a single commodity (whose popularity and sales rose with good times and fell with bad) would suffer greatly. Cuba was such a land, for when no one bought its sugar, what had been seasonal employment in the best of times now became simply intolerable. Revolts broke out in eastern Cuba, supported by an exile group in New York City. A band of exiles returned to their island to lead the campaign, among them José Martí, a radical journalist and tireless apostle for freedom. Martí was one of the first to fall in battle, but his death gave the revolution its martyr, just as his years of pamphleteering in the

United States had established a solid base of American sympathy for the Cuban cause.

The rebels did well enough at first, but a determined Spanish counterattack (centering on the dreaded *reconcentraciones*, concentration camps) had dampened the fires in most places by the end of 1896. But the initiative was now passing from Spain to the United States, where it would remain.

It was doing so in part because of a war between two moguls of the American press, Joseph Pulitzer of the New York *World* and William Randolph Hearst of the New York *Journal*. Pulitzer and Hearst were struggling for domination of the lucrative penny newspaper market, and the bloody Cuban revolt was a yellow publisher's dream, offering everything from sex to heroism to brutality and death. The two publishers sent their writers and artists to the scene of battle, with instructions to bring back the latest on Spanish atrocities even if they had to make them up. By 1897, American sentiment was solidly anti-Spanish, and Madrid now decided to tone down the worst aspects of its campaign. It recalled General Valeriano Weyler ("Butcher" or "Beast" Weyler, as he was

called by Messrs. Pulitzer and Hearst), who had devised the concentration camp system, and offered Cuba home rule.

But events had now moved beyond official control in Washington or Madrid. Early in 1898, a Cuban agent purloined a letter of the Spanish Minister to Washington, wherein President McKinley was characterized as "weak and a bidder for the admiration of the crowd, besides being a common politician who tries to leave a door open behind himself while keeping on good terms with the jingoes of his party." A number of Americans privately harbored the same opinion of their President, but when the agent thoughtfully turned the letter over to William Randolph Hearst (who published it in the *Journal* with appropriate banner headlines), citizens of all political persuasions rallied to the standard of their vilified Chief Executive. Then came the final act. On February 15, 1898, the U.S.S. Maine was blown sky-high in Havana harbor. The vessel had been anchored there to protect American lives in case of emergency; now some 266 Americans perished while guarding the safety of others. There was no evi-

Cuban peso, struck at Philadelphia, designed by Charles Barber, 1915.

dence that Spain was behind the explosion, and to this day no one knows who or what caused it. But Americans in 1898 were certain that they knew the answer, and they demanded war. A stronger man than McKinley would have acceded to their will, and hostilities were declared on April 25, 1898.

The war was to have been fought *only* for the liberation of Cuba, but it somehow ended with American acquisition of Puerto Rico, Guam, the Philippine Islands, and Cuba, which was occupied from the autumn of 1898 to the spring of 1902. It then became an independent country, but American influence remained strong—and the ability to intervene in the island's internal affairs remained a part of the Cuban constitution until 1934.

Between 1898 and 1915, American money circulated freely in Cuba. In the latter year, a new, distinctly Cuban coinage appeared, with the island's arms and a large star on the new pesos and their subdivisions, the national arms and José Martí on the gold peso and its multiples. Cuban coinage, struck in Philadelphia and designed by Chief Engraver Charles T. Barber, was established on a par with that of the United States. The United States continued to strike the country's coins and print its paper money until the rise of Fidel Castro.

By a logical succession of events, the Spanish-American War extended United States minting activities into two other areas. America acquired the Philippine Islands by force from Spain, agonized whether to keep them or not, and finally decided to do so—over the objections of Filipino insurgents, who had been in the field against Spain and remained there against the United States. They had been put down by 1902, and from that time until the mid-1930s, the Philippines would have an uneasy and anomalous status as an American colony. Granted an increasing measure of home rule after 1910, they became a self-governing "commonwealth" in 1935, their independence promised but postponed until 1946 by the Second World War. During the days as colony and commonwealth, Filipino

coinage and currency were supplied by the United States Mint and the Bureau of Engraving and Printing. Coins were struck at every current American mint except for New Orleans, and after 1920 at a new, special branch facility set up in Manila. The anomalous nature of the islands' status was demonstrated by the designs seen on their coinage: for obverses, a seated Filipino or a standing Filipina, for reverses, an American eagle surmounting an American shield. The coins were created by a local artist named Melecio Figueroa, and they were denominated in centavos and pesos.

The acquisition of an empire naturally carried with it the necessity of defending it. Under ideal conditions such a defense should be both speedy and economical. The travails of the battleship "Oregon" (which almost didn't reach Cuba from the American West Coast before the Spanish-American War ended) showed the virtue of celerity in movements of the United States Navy, while practical considerations suggested that a single fleet rather than two (one each to patrol the Atlantic and Pacific) would be both politically and economically preferable. The obvious answer to America's defensive needs was an interoceanic canal cut through Central America, either on or near the Isthmus of Panamá.

Talk of a canal had begun in the days of Cortés, and it had periodically resurfaced during the succeeding centuries. By the time of the Spanish-American War, a costly private attempt using French capital had bogged down, and the two powers with the greatest interest in the project (Great Britain and the United States) were still abiding by a treaty they had concluded back in 1850, denying each the sole right to build and fortify any interoceanic waterway which might be contemplated.

The war changed a good deal, demonstrating the importance of a canal. Then McKinley was assassinated in the summer of 1901, and his Vice President succeeded. The new leader was Theodore Roosevelt, and the words "patience" and "self-effacement" were not to be found in his vocabulary. Teddy Roosevelt concluded that a canal across the Isthmus would be a simply splendid idea, and he did his best to nudge the project along.

He had to act as midwife to a new country in order to get his way. The backers of the moribund canal across Panamá were keen to sell Roosevelt on their particular route (for they could hope to salvage something from their earlier investment by turning their rights over to the Americans). But Colombia owned the area, which meant that the United States would have to compensate that country as well before American work on the canal could begin. An agreement with Bogotá proved difficult to achieve: the Colombians were aware that Roosevelt wanted his canal as quickly as possible, and they stalled negotiations in order to extract the last dollar out of the Americans. The fact that the French company's concession would expire at the beginning of 1904 added a piquant note to the proceedings: if Colombia stood firm, it might expect to extract still more largess from the Americans, for it could charge them at least a portion of what the French entrepreneurs would have charged for *their* rights. And the latter were by now becoming hysterical, for obvious reasons.

Thus matters stood at the beginning of November 1903. Secretary of State John Hay had earlier secured the abrogation of the 1850 treaty with the British; the United States could now have the canal across Panamá, if Colombia agreed—which it would not, at least for another two months. Its attitude was understandable, but it ignored two of Theodore Roosevelt's primary character traits: impatience and an insistence on having his own way once he had set his course. If Colombia would not sell Americans the right to build a canal across its territory, perhaps an independent Panamá would do so.

Theodore Roosevelt did not foment the rebellion which broke out at the end of 1903. Those responsible were members of the Interoceanic Canal Company and their local political allies, who viewed Colombian intransigence as exceedingly bad for local business. But if not behind the revolt, Roosevelt certainly helped it along: he sent the United States Navy to the area, directing it to prevent Colombian troops from landing and putting down the revolution. And he quickly recognized the new country and concluded a canal treaty with it.

And so a new nation was added to the world's constellation. A new nation needs a new coinage, and America acted as midwife here as well. In 1904 and succeeding years, the Philadelphia Mint struck distinctive new coins for Panamá, coins again designed by Charles Barber. They featured a mailed bust of Vasco Nuñez de Balboa, the first Spanish explorer to cross the Isthmus and catch a glimpse of the Pacific Ocean. Balboa's portrait appeared on no fewer than six new coins, ranging from one-half to fifty *centesimos*, and the country's new coinage unit was named in his honor, the *balboa*. The national arms graced the other sides of most of these coins, a practice still followed today. But the first issues of 1904 were minuscule, as have been most succeeding coinages: for the majority of business, the country has preferred to use American coinage—and American currency as well.

Theodore Roosevelt may be said to be the father of Panamanian numismatics, but numismatists know him far better in an American capacity: more than any other person, he was responsible for an artistic awakening on the early twentieth-century United States coin, an awakening which briefly placed it on a par with the best efforts of other nations, and which occasionally elevated it to the status of great art.

Roosevelt became involved in numismatics because he was deeply disgusted with the appearance of the coins then in circulation. The old Gobrecht silver designs had been abandoned after 1891 in favor of new images for the dime, quarter, and half dollar, but these did not represent much of an improvement. Designer Charles Barber's Liberty head was acceptable, but his

Philippines Islands, peso, 1906. Courtesy the NNC.

Panama, fifty centesimos and two-and-one-half centesimos, 1904. They were struck at Philadelphia and designed by Charles Barber. Courtesy the NNC.

United States, half dollar, 1892.

United States, five cents, 1866.

United States, five cents, 1900 (the V-nickel).

United States, ten dollars, pre-Saint-Gaudens design, 1906.

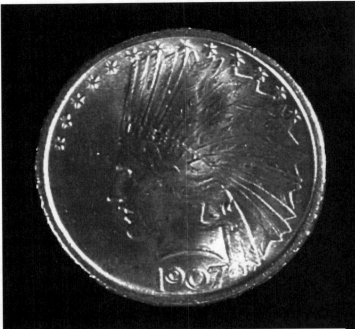

United States, ten dollars, 1907, designed by Augustus Saint-Gaudens. Courtesy the NNC.

United States, twenty dollars, 1907. It highlights Augustus Saint-Gaudens' design in high relief. Courtesy the NNC.

eagle was completely heraldic and appeared outdated even at the time it was introduced. For minor coinage, Longacre's Indian still graced the cent, over forty years after she had first appeared there. A copper-nickel five-cent piece, or "nickel," had been introduced in 1866, but its designs similarly failed to inspire: a fancy obverse shield and a reverse numeral by James Longacre (used until 1883), a trite obverse Liberty head and a large reverse "V" by Charles Barber (used thereafter). Barber's left-facing goddess bore a peaked coronet, and she looked rather like a waitress. Furthermore, he had to add the word "cents" to his reverse design after thousands of coins without it had been gold-plated and foisted on the unwary as half eagles. We have already been introduced to George T. Morgan's dollar.

That left gold, whose designs annoyed Mr. Roosevelt most of all. Ideas introduced by Gobrecht in 1838 and by Longacre in 1850 were still present on coins ranging from the quarter eagle to the double eagle. Surely, reasoned the President, the nation could do better than that. Once reelected in 1904 (and beyond considerations of the politically immediate), the energetic leader swung into action.

He knew of a gifted sculptor and medalist named Augustus Saint-Gaudens, who had been responsible for an attractive medal of a modern style portraying Christopher Columbus, created in conjunction with the four-hundredth anniversary on the discovery of America. (The enthusiastic celebration of the great event, culminating in a world's fair held at Chicago in 1893, was an early indication of a greater American interest in hemispheric affairs, which would help lead to war some five years later.) The politician and the artist had maintained contact over the years, and soon after his reelection, Roosevelt turned to Saint-Gaudens for help in coinage redesign.

Saint-Gaudens responded magnificently. His eagle featured a simple, left-facing Liberty with a feathered warbonnet (the latter added at the insistence of the President), and a naturalistic, striding eagle inspired by an ancient Egyptian silver coin. Saint-Gaudens' double eagle was still more ambitious, and it is his best-known creation and arguably the most beautiful American coin. We see a figure of Liberty on the obverse, striding toward us in the dawn, holding the torch of freedom and the olive branch of peace. On the reverse, another eagle, this time in flight above the sun. Saint-Gaudens' designs inspired jealousy on the part of Mint Engraver Charles Barber, whose own design for the double eagle, while an improvement on the past, was demonstrably not in the same league with that of Roosevelt's outsider friend. Saint-Gaudens died in the summer of 1907, and he never saw the completion of his project, never knew that the envious Barber would succeed in reducing the high relief of his prototypes, thereby robbing them of a portion of their artistry. But even amended for the worse, they were still splendid coins, heralding a sea change in the direction of American numismatic art.

Roosevelt left office at the beginning of March 1909, but he secured the redesign of the quarter and half eagle before he departed. These coins featured designs somewhat reminiscent of those on Saint-Gaudens' eagle, but struck *into* rather than *onto* the planchets, so that the fields of the new coins became their highest point. The innovative treatment engendered criticism (largely because it was assumed that it would trap dirt and spread disease), but like the designs by Saint-Gaudens, these by Bela Lyon Pratt would serve on America's gold coinage down to the end of the medium itself.

Roosevelt's successor William Howard Taft continued the drive for greater numismatic artistry. A redesigned cent appeared in the summer of his first year, and the fifty-year-old Longacre Indian head was allowed to retire. The year 1909 happened to be the centenary of the birth of Abraham Lincoln, and a Lithuanian immigrant named Victor David Brenner paid the martyred leader a lasting tribute, in the form of a sympathetic obverse portrait for the new one-cent piece.

Slightly amended, Brenner's portrait is still in use, although his pleasant if uninspired reverse (featuring "ears" of wheat, with the name of the country and the denomination of the coin between them) was abandoned in 1959 in favor of an ambitious but unsuccessful attempt to replicate the entire Lincoln Memorial within the space of a coin less than an inch across.

Numismatic redesign continued after the Democratic party, which had largely been out of power since the beginning of the Civil War, finally regained national office in the election of 1912. The five-cent piece was modified the following year, and America's most artistic minor coin resulted. Struck until 1938, the "Indian head," or "buffalo," nickel showed what a gifted designer (in this case

United States half eagle with new incuse design.

United States, Lincoln cent, 1909.

*United States, five cents, 1913
(the buffalo nickel).*

James Earle Fraser) could do with a humble coinage in a base metal. The remaining new designs fall beyond the scope of this chapter. Before leaving our discussion, though, we must briefly glance at two other events in American numismatics during the Gilded Age. Both had early roots in other places, and while one would reach its zenith in America later in the twentieth century, the other saw its golden age during the period covered by this chapter.

The first event was the creation of a coin for celebration rather than for commerce. This was the commemorative, and its origins in America go back slightly more than a century, to 1892. The concept has much deeper roots elsewhere, however. Coinage celebratory of a particular event or personage was known to the ancient Greeks, while one could make a good case that the great majority of Roman imperial coinage had a commemorative purpose—to celebrate virtues and advertise triumphs with one of the few vehicles available to the ancient state. Commemora-

tive coinage passed from the scene with the decline of Rome, but it was revived here and there in the Renaissance, in Germany and Italy, and occasionally elsewhere. By the nineteenth century, it was growing in popularity in Europe, extending its attraction to the Americas as well.

While the 1848 CAL. quarter eagle was a commemorative coin in one sense, collectors begin the American series with a half dollar and quarter issued in conjunction with the World's Columbian Exposition, held in Chicago between May 1 and October 30, 1893. Half dollars with an imaginary head of Columbus on the obverse, a representation of the *Santa María* on the reverse (a collaborative effort between Charles Barber and George T. Morgan) were produced for sale in 1892 and 1893, while a quarter with Queen Isabella on the obverse, a female figure with a distaff and spindle on the reverse, appeared in 1893. The work of Charles Barber, the obverse looked nothing like the real queen, while the reverse may

United States, commemorative quarter dollar struck for the Colombian Exposition, 1893. Courtesy the NNC.

be taken to neatly summarize the perceived role of women at the time. Five million of the half dollars were minted in Philadelphia, along with about twenty-four thousand of the quarters.

From these modest beginnings, a numismatic industry would someday grow. Charles Barber was responsible for a silver dollar dated 1900 but struck during the last month of 1899 (celebrating George Washington and the Marquis de Lafayette), while the busy designer also tried his hand on a series of tiny commem-

orative gold dollars made for the Louisiana Purchase Exposition (dated 1903) and the Lewis and Clark Exposition (dated 1904 and 1905). All of these coins were throwbacks to the artistic concepts of an earlier day, but they kept the commemorative idea alive until more gifted hands could be found to take advantage of it. The latter would appear by 1915, and the United States commemorative coin would soon enter an age of excellence.

But the career of another American monetary form, the token, would by then be in

Elks Club (Redding, California), twelve-and-one-half cents, c. 1890. Courtesy the NNC.

decline. Like the celebratory coin, the private substitute for the regular coin had roots in the classical world. We have seen this monetary form during the colonial period and the time of the Civil War. In those eras, it was primarily an Eastern and Midwestern phenomenon, but during the Gilded Age, the locus of the token shifted west.

It appeared there because the Far West was chronically short of small change. There were silver dollars and gold coins aplenty—after all, the federal mints at San Francisco, Carson City, and Denver (which began striking money in 1906) had been set up to take advantage of local silver and gold. But these mints made far fewer small coins than large—and they struck no cents until 1908 and no five-cent pieces until 1912. Furthermore, what smaller members of the silver series were struck tended to stay in large Western cities, to the detriment of merchants in small Western towns.

The latter responded as Americans had always addressed a numismatic shortage: they obtained and circulated alternative money. Across the West, thousands of tokens, struck in brass, copper, zinc, aluminum, and even hard rubber, were called into service to expand the money supply. Because of the federal law of 1864 (which you will recall made private coinage illegal), these merchants' tokens generally promised payment in a specific article (a five-cent cigar, for instance) or "in trade," meaning that the customer might use the token as he pleased for the amount indicated on the piece. A number of these tokens bore denominations of twelve-and-one-half cents, suggesting that a portion of Americans were still thinking in Spanish-American monetary terms, decades after their government had passed a law to wean them from such thoughts. Many of these coinage substitutes bear the names of the establishments and towns where they passed as money. Many others do not: collectors call them "mavericks," from Samuel A. Maverick, a nineteenth-century Texas rancher who refused to brand his cattle. It is pleasant to think that Mr. Maverick might have used some of these nameless tokens himself.

Nameless and named, Western trade tokens formed a vital part of numismatic Americana during the Gilded Age, but like the national bank notes which circulated in the same towns, their localism was more apparent than real. A handful of firms in New York and Chicago struck for the majority of them, just as the national bank notes all came from the same printer. Here as elsewhere, diversity was yielding place to uniformity in the matter of America's money, a trend accelerated in the twentieth century.

CHAPTER 8

ISOLATION, DEPRESSION, INTERVENTION: AMERICA, 1914–1945

CHAPTER 8

ISOLATION, DEPRESSION, INTERVENTION: AMERICA, 1914–1945

In the summer of 1914, much of the world entered what has aptly been called the Second Thirty Years' War. Like the first, which had disfigured much of the seventeenth century, this new conflict consisted of hellish fighting punctuated by armed truces. The fighting took place in two acts, one of them lasting from the late summer of 1914 to the end of 1918, the other from the late summer of 1939 to that of 1945. These two episodes were separated by a much longer period of anxiety and armed peace. Perhaps a hundred million perished in the cauldron of the fighting, and from that cauldron, our world would emerge.

During much of the first and third acts (and during virtually all of the second), the United States was distinguished by its absence from the play. Contemporary Americans are accustomed to thinking on a global scale, at least to a degree, and they are aware of at least some of the effects of their actions on the world scene and of the influence that wider world has upon their own lives. They tend to assume that their ancestors held the same world view. They are wrong.

Prior to 1940, a combination of distance, spread-eagle nationalism, and problems and prospects at home kept Americans' attention firmly fixed on domestic affairs (where there seemed so much to do, so much profit to be made) rather than on foreign affairs (where there seemed few practical prospects, where virtuous Americans would probably be mulcted by clever Europeans anyway). Their national tendency to mind their own business was never more vibrant than it was in the summer of 1914. When citizens of the New World heard that a conflagration had once more erupted in the Old, they heartily congratulated each other on staying clear of it.

And they had problems enough at home, matters they wished to solve there. The President at the time was Thomas Woodrow Wilson, a reforming educator and governor who had been elected in 1912 when the two wings of the Republican party had obligingly turned on each other rather than the Democrats. Wilson was elected over William Howard Taft and Theodore Roosevelt. The fact that both vanquished and victor were reformers tells us much about the spirit of the times: Wilson was elected by a "progressive" movement which wanted domestic reform, which was ready and eager to address the problems which the feverish capitalism of the Gilded Age had created or worsened.

"Trusts" were everywhere—those faceless octopi who restricted trade, held down wages, and squeezed the "little guy" to death. And along with oil trusts, sugar trusts, steel trusts, and the like, there was, it appeared, a "money trust."

In 1912, an investigation by Louisiana Congressman Arsène Pujo uncovered a shocking fact: a tiny group of Wall Street banking houses (led by J. P. Morgan & Company, the National City Bank, controlled by the Rockefellers, and the First National Bank, owned by George F. Baker) wielded control over a huge agglomeration of other banks, insurance companies, and manufacturing enterprises. Between them, the partners of the three banks held 341 directorships in 112 corporations with a combined capitalization of twenty-two billion dollars. The Pujo Committee—and the Republic—did *not* find fault with the moral conduct of these financiers; what was appalling was the sheer extent of their power.

By the time President Wilson was inaugurated (March 4, 1913), public opinion was demanding a dismantling of the "money trust," or at least its containment by the federal government. One way to keep it within bounds might be by exerting a greater federal control over the sinews of the banking system, the paper money employed in its operations. Thus was born the Federal Reserve Act of 1913, and thus, in the following year, was born a new type of paper money, the Federal Reserve note.

The Federal Reserve Act divided the nation into twelve districts, each with a Federal Reserve Bank at its heart. The twelve districts (and their cities, and the symbols which each must employ on the notes they issued) are as follows:

District	City of Issue	Identification Symbol Appearing on notes
1	Boston	1 or A
2	New York City	2 or B
3	Philadelphia	3 or C
4	Cleveland	4 or D
5	Richmond	5 or E
6	Atlanta	6 or F
7	Chicago	7 or G
8	St. Louis	8 or H
9	Minneapolis	9 or I
10	Kansas City, MO	10 or J
11	Dallas	11 or K
12	San Francisco	12 or L

Let it be noted that the great majority of the Federal Reserve Banks existed in Eastern and Midwestern cities, rather faithfully following population distribution at the time; they are still there today. Early Federal Reserve notes bore a number and its letter appropriate to the issuing authority in a seal,

United States, Federal Reserve note, ten dollars, series of 1914. Courtesy the NNC.

surrounded by the name of the issuer spelled out in full in two concentric lines (e.g., "2-B," along with "Federal Reserve/Bank of/New York/New York"). Beginning with the 1928 series, only the number appeared in the center of the seal, and from 1934 to the present, only the letter. These seals have always appeared on the left-hand side of the face.

Working in tandem with the Federal Reserve Board in Washington, each of the member banks had the theoretical power and obligation to advise on and act as a watchdog over banking activity within its district. In time, the Federal Reserve System would acquire real regulatory teeth, but for the present, it merely seemed to suggest that localism—or at least regionalism—in American numismatics was alive and well and had acquired an enhanced vitality.

The acquisition was more apparent than real: like their better-established competitors, the Federal Reserve notes of 1914 and later were printed in Washington at the Bureau of Engraving and Printing, and their black faces and green backs—even with distinctive designs—were undeniably products of the national government. Their uniqueness of design would disappear in time as well. But the Federal Reserve note remains unique in another way: among all of the different types of federal, state, and local currency issued in America over the past three centuries, this is the only one which has survived down to the present.

A peculiar combination of political and economic forces would bring this to pass. As I hinted above, the American participation in the "Great War" (renamed the "First World War," when it became apparent that it would not be the last of its kind) was limited; the Yanks came in in time to see some of the last battles on the Western Front. But they had not been there for the first, and worst, of them: their vision of the fighting was therefore tinged with an aura and a romance which the Allies and Central Powers had had burned out of them by the time the Americans appeared. This idealism was extremely important to what followed, however, both at home and abroad: it represented a shifting of the reforming drive from attention to domestic problems to a crusade to save Europe from itself, "to make the world safe for democracy" in the words of the American leader. When United States hubris and optimism collided with European reality (a desire to parlay the Allied victory in 1918 into a settling of old scores through a harsh victors' peace), the outcome was the worst of several possible combinations. Disillusioned, Americans would reject any substantive role in the new, postwar world order, but their disillusionment would extend to matters domestic as well, and the zeal for public reform be replaced by one for private enrichment. Thus the "Roaring Twenties," a supposedly golden age of unparalleled industrial growth, sexual liberation, and new social, economic, and cultural icons: the automobile, the radio, the flapper. Caddies became millionaires, cleverly following advice they picked up from wealthy clients on the links. An advertising man named Bruce Barton had a best-selling book in 1925 called *The Man Nobody Knows*, wherein he proved that the success of Christ's Gospel lay in His following sound business principles. Inventors and captains of industry were held up for the veneration of the crowd; they replaced statesmen and politicians there, who received even less respect than they perhaps deserved. Booze, bathing beauties, and ballyhoo—it was quite an era, but not quite a golden age.

Its golden dust was not scattered equally across the Republic, touching all of its people. Accustomed to high commodity prices during the war, Midwestern and Southern farmers saw their incomes shrink and their debts rise after the beginning of the 1920s. Factory workers did poorly too, their wages held down by a new, antilabor stance on the part of public officials (one of whom, a governor of Massachusetts named Calvin Coolidge, handled a Boston police strike with such draconian aplomb that he eventually became President of the United States in 1923, and something of an American icon himself). A determined managerial attempt to sell the concepts of the company union and the open shop kept wages depressed as well. African Americans did still worse: those who had migrated North before and during the war finding that they were no more welcome in Omaha, Nebraska, than they had been in Opelika, Alabama. Women did slightly better: at least they now had the vote, and they could exert some influence on the national scene. But all in all, as the 1920s roared on, a disturbing fact became slowly apparent to those who wished to see it: much of the economic boom was based on hot air. And all of those new buildings, automobiles, radios, and other appurtenances of the new era might someday go begging, when everyone's credit, and hence their ability to purchase them, became stretched to the limit. If that ever happened, matters would become very interesting indeed.

And it happened, of course. In 1928, one of the architects of the prosperous twenties, Herbert Hoover (who had served as Secretary of Commerce under the still-more-popular Mr. Coolidge) was elected President of the United States. He was inaugurated in March 1929. Some seven months later, he reaped the whirlwind.

While not directly responsible for it, Hoover bore the blame for the worst depression in all of United States history. In terms of individual misery, the hard times of the late 1830s might have been worse—for some people. But the Great Depression occurred at a time when the nation and its citizens were far more connected to each other, much more dependent on each other, than had been the case a century before. In the 1830s there were entire sections of the country which escaped unscathed from bad times; in the 1930s, no one was exempt.

And nothing was exempt: the Great Depression would leave an indelible trace on America's coinage and currency. It would both give and take away: it would create a last flowering of localism, of individualized money of various types, while the seeds were being simultaneously planted for a greater monetary centralization and conformity than ever before seen. In essence, America's present money

dates from the 1930s, and it was shaped in the workshop of the Great Depression.

Hard Times had a variety of effects. For coinage, the years between 1929 and 1933 saw a progressive decline in production, for those out of work would hardly need abundant new coinage for their diminishing purchases in the marketplace. In the year of the stock market crash, no fewer than eight coinage denominations were in current production at the United States Mint (cents, five-cent pieces, dimes, quarters, half dollars, quarter eagles, half eagles, and double eagles); the only American denominations not struck that year were dollars and eagles. In 1930, the total was six, and in 1931, four, where it remained in 1932 and 1933. It only began rising in 1934, both in terms of denominations struck and numbers coined. And in 1932 and 1933, two of the four denominations minted were gold coins, of no earthly value to the average citizen whose weekly wages were likely less than the value of the smaller denomination, the eagle, if they were being received at all.

Paper money was still being printed, of course, but currency was now made on a new, smaller module, as the thrifty Mr. Hoover meditated on the reams of paper which could thereby be saved and acted accordingly. The types of notes in circulation remained what they had been prior to the crash—Federal Reserve bills, silver certificates, legal tender notes, and the rest—but there now set in a standardization of design if not of type, one which augured ill for the future of diversity in American money. But for now, the nation's people were far more concerned about the soundness of their currency than the sameness of its designs. And there was growing indication that a goodly portion of it might be shaky indeed.

Worry centered on the national bank notes. Originally created as a wartime fiscal measure by Abraham Lincoln, these descendants of the private currency issues of earlier days had rendered reasonably adequate service since the time of their introduction, even though the level of federal management applied to them was limited by statute and by the philosophy of the party currently in office. There had been failures during previous economic downturns—in the depression of the early 1890s, the banking panic of 1907, and the recession of 1921—but the system had managed to right itself with a minimum of federal assistance. The Great Depression was another matter. Banks began failing immediately after the Wall Street crash in the autumn of 1929, and, despite Mr. Hoover's increasingly-optimistic utterances to a dwindling audience, the number of failures grew. In 1930, nearly 1,200 banks failed, and in 1931, that many went under during the single month of October! Despite Hoover's utterances concerning the fundamental soundness of America's banks and other fiscal institutions, average citizens were voting with their feet, taking their savings (if they had any) out of the bank and stuffing them under the mattress, where they could at least keep an eye on them.

By late 1932, a crisis had been reached. That November, Hoover lost his bid for re-election to Franklin Delano Roosevelt (whose campaign was as vague as possible on ways to fight the Depression: Roosevelt knew that he need not say much of anything to win, so great was the antipathy to Mr. Hoover). But Hoover would remain uncomfortably in office until the following March, for that was the current wording of the United States Constitution. During the last four months of the discredited Hoover administration, a growing sense of panic gripped the nation. No one knew what Roosevelt would do (and he scarcely knew himself because Roosevelt was one of those people who make up their policies—and themselves—as they go along), and if he had concrete ideas to fight hard times, he was hardly likely to share them with Herbert Hoover. Everybody knew that Hoover himself would do nothing—and would probably earn a rebuke if he presented economic legislation for Congressional consideration. And so the crisis deepened.

On the state level, governors began doing their bit to stop the hemorrhaging of the banking system. They began proclaiming "banking holidays," a period during which every bank within their jurisdiction would be forced to close its doors, preventing a run upon it by panicky customers and creditors. When the time of anxiety had passed, the bank could resume business. The first state to take this action was Nevada, which did so a few days before the November elections. The state's closure was only supposed to last for twelve days, but uneasiness had worsened rather than abated at the end of that time, and the moratorium was lengthened and finally extended indefinitely. This action spurred worry elsewhere, and by February 1933 other states were following in Nevada's wake, the panic spreading across the nation. By the time Hoover finally left the White House and Roosevelt finally moved in, virtually every bank in the country had shut down or was operating under extreme difficulties. We shall see what the incoming administration did in a few moments. For now, though, let us look at a truly extraordinary phenomenon, as the American people triumphantly coped with the worse monetary crisis they had ever had to face.

A recurring theme of this study has been the ingenuity of the American people in the face of shortages of "normal" money. In the seventeenth century, they had taken over Native American commodities, adapting them to their own purposes; they had incorporated other people's silver to make New England coins; they had used crops—even nails—to get the buying and selling done which their growing economies demanded. In the fourth decade of the twentieth century, they made money of their own once again.

Their elaboration of it began in 1931, extended in places down to 1939, but its core period coincided with the banking crisis of late 1932 and early 1933. During those brief months, Americans gave their money a vitality and variety it had rarely seen before and has never seen since.

They made their makeshift money from a variety of materials, including paper, wood (there really were "wooden nickels" during those days), base metal, leather, fish skin, vulcanite, and (in a marvelous instance of history repeating itself) clamshells. They

Chamber of Commerce (Tenino, Washington), fifty cents, 1932. It was printed on wood. Courtesy the NNC.

Heppner, Oregon, five dollars, 1933. It was printed on sheepskin. Courtesy the NNC.

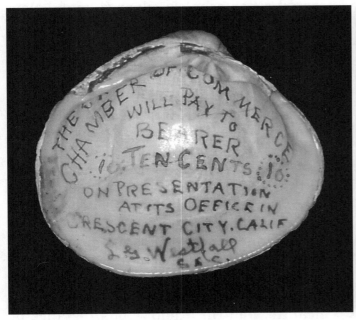

Chamber of Commerce (Crescent City, California), ten cents, 1933. It was inked by hand on a clamshell. Courtesy the NNC.

made it according to a variety of plans, ranging from a simple substitute for ordinary coinage and currency to a far more sophisticated idea, wherein to remain "good" the currency had to be spent at regular intervals, those who received it affixing small stamps to the back, along with the date of the transaction; in this way, money could be pumped into and kept in ailing local economies. Americans made their emergency money by a variety of methods, ranging from engraving to lithography to linoleum-block printing to pen and ink.

A bewildering number of authorities stood behind those issues, including large cities, small towns, companies and firms within those cities and towns, and mutual aid associations—and the Fox Meadow Elementary School, of Scarsdale, New York, which emitted hand-made issues printed on oilcloth early in 1933 for internal consumption.

But most of all, Americans made and employed their new money in a variety of places. Citizens in *every one* of the current forty-eight states—and residents of Alaska, Hawaii, and the District of Columbia—used the medium in the early thirties. While New York City and other Eastern centers were well-represented as we might expect, so were places better known for wide vistas than as crowded urban centers, such as Heppner, Oregon, and Riverton, Wyoming. I am not certain that a final tally of all issuers of "Depression scrip" (to give this money the name collectors most commonly apply to it)

can ever be done, but Ralph A. Mitchell and Neil Shafer, authors of the basic reference, *Standard Catalog of Depression Scrip of the United States* (1984), list around eleven hundred distinct issuers, many or most of whom circulated more than one denomination of scrip. In short, what we have here is a period of localism in currency fully comparable with that obtained during the nineteenth century, if of shorter duration.

The incoming Roosevelt administration would take very determined steps to end the banking crisis which had inspired the scrip. Upon entering office (and surveying the wreckage of the banking system) the new leader simply carried the bank closure idea to its logical conclusion: on March 6, 1933, he proclaimed a national bank holiday, to last everywhere until the end of the ninth of March. During the days of the banking ban, the finances of each bank would be carefully examined. Those institutions found sound would be allowed to reopen. Those found unsound would stay closed.

Solvent banks gradually reopened their doors between the thirteen and fifteenth of March, and this bold stroke (as well as Roosevelt's programs for other aspects of the economy, and his sheer attitude: the new chief executive always *sounded* like he knew what he was doing, whether he actually did or not) brought a return of confidence to the nation, a return of normal money to the channels of commerce. But scrip issues would hardly disappear overnight, lingering

United States, Federal Reserve Bank note, five dollars, 1933. Courtesy the NNC.

through the middle of the decade in portions of the South, Midwest, and Far West.

Coping with the banking emergency meant getting more money into circulation. The proclamation of March 6, 1933, was one way of doing so. Another was the creation of an interim national currency, the last form of federal paper currency adopted in the United States, and the shortest-lived.

This was the Federal Reserve *Bank* note, as opposed to the Federal Reserve note. Created by the National Emergency Banking Act of March 9, 1933, the new currency was intended to act as a temporary replacement for ordinary Federal Reserve notes, many of which had been hoarded during the fiscal crisis. But a return of confidence brought normal currency back into circulation more quickly than anticipated, and the new notes were not really needed, their issue curtailed later in 1933.

Other types of money were being curtailed as well. Between 1933 and 1935, other types of national paper currency were eclipsed by the Federal Reserve note. The Roosevelt administration looked at the circulatory landscape as it took office, and what it saw displeased it. Several thousand national banks were still issuing notes, over which the federal government had only an approximate control. These institutions had closed their doors along with everyone else, and many of them, concluded Roosevelt, had better stay closed, their right to issue currency revoked. And other forms of currency were hardly better. Roosevelt had determined to demonetize gold coinage, a policy he and a Democratic Congress would accomplish with successive laws passed in 1933 and 1934. If gold coinage were to be removed from circulation, it only made sense to remove currency redeemable in gold coin as well.

Under the new philosophy, the printing of the venerable national bank note came to a close in 1935, while the Gold Reserve Act of January 1934 demonetized gold certificates (and also made most United States currency "redeemable in lawful money" rather than spelling out precisely what sort of coin might be received for each note). Production

of silver certificates was restricted to lower denominations, while legal tender issues were similarly curtailed. What Roosevelt and his advisors sought was a plausible currency which was also manageable, manipulable, and capable of expansion in times of depression, of contraction in times of inflation. They found it in the Federal Reserve System, with the Federal Reserve note. Henceforth, this type of currency would reign supreme, and America's paper money would lose much of its individuality and (with the disappearance of emergency scrip issues as better times returned) much of its localism. But the long-lived localist thread in the American tapestry would enjoy one last hurrah before yielding to complete numismatic conformity, and the hurrah would be heard on the coinage.

One of the favorite avocations of the Roosevelt administration was a celebration of the diversity and richness of American history. This partiality was sincere, even as economic and social pressures and prospects (as well its own policies) were creating the bases of an increasing homogeneity, a greater national conformity which would come to full fruition in the years immediately following Roosevelt's death. His celebration of the local and historical led to such useful products as the state guides produced by the Federal Writers' Workshops in the 1930s and 1940s, but it found one of its most lasting expressions in the commemorative coin.

As was noted earlier, commemorative coinage came to the United States with the Columbian Exposition celebrations of 1892–93, and it had taken root in America by the first years of the new century. Commemoratives were issued from time to time during the teens and twenties. In 1915, the Panama-Pacific Exposition saw no fewer than four denominations of commemorative coinage, three of which were in gold, including huge round and octagonal fifty-dollar pieces, reminiscent of the "slugs" of pioneer days. A new silver dollar was introduced at the end of 1921, intended to commemorate the reestablishment of peace with the former Central

United States, commemorative gold dollar for the Panama-Pacific Exposition, 1915. Courtesy the NNC.

Peace dollar, 1921.

Oregon Trail commemorative half dollar, 1926.

Cincinnati commemorative half dollar, 1936.

Powers. (An isolationist Congress feared giving the voters the wrong idea by actually signing a peace treaty with the vanquished, and so it simply declared the resumption of peaceful relations with them by joint resolution in October 1921.) Designed by Anthony de Francisci, the new "Peace" dollar would be incorporated into the range of normal coinage, struck each year through 1928 and again in 1934 and 1935.

Commemorative coinage continued through the administrations of Harding and Coolidge, now ordinarily restricted to a single denomination, the half dollar. Issues of that period tended to focus on events rather than places—battles of the American Revolution, the sesquicentennial of independence, the centenary of the Monroe Doctrine—although the most successful and longest-lived of them pointed the way, for it celebrated a place as well as an epoch, the Oregon Trail.

The collapse of 1929 brought celebratory coinage to an abrupt end for four years. True, a commemorative was mooted for the bicentennial of George Washington's birth in 1932, but it soon transmogrified into that most pedestrian of twentieth-century American circulating coins, the Washington quarter—which is still in production today. The real resumption of commemorative coinage began in 1934, accelerated in 1935, crested in 1936, and continued to enliven America's money through 1939, after which concern with possible warfare (and simple overproduction, with a consequent criticism on the part of public and Congress) put a damper on such numismatic enthusiasm.

While it lasted, though, what a time it was! A fundamental shift had taken place, and while events would still receive their commemorative due, the real emphasis was now on the places, and the individuality and historicity of those places, where the events had occurred. Such celebration of local themes and people was underscored by the employment of local artists to create the designs for the new issues. Some of the places and persons celebrated were perhaps less than epochal (the supposed fiftieth anniversary of the musical importance of Cincinnati comes to

mind, especially as the commemorative struck for that celebration depicted a man who had never set foot there; and so far as anybody knew, nothing had actually happened in Cincinnati's musical life in 1886, the date commemorated on the half dollar). Some of the artistic attempts were more successful than others: Henry Kreis' Connecticut tercentenary coin definitely succeeds as an artistic endeavor, while Benjamin Hawkins' Wiscon-

Connecticut Tercentenary half dollar, 1935.

sin centennial half dollar fails as resoundingly, perhaps because the Wisconsin Centennial Commission chose the designs. But the overall effect of the multiplicity of commemorative coins (and in the peak year, 1936, there were no fewer than sixteen new ones, added to another five members of earlier series, also struck that year) was a positive one: these coins are one of the final metallic suggestions that the celebration of the local,

Wisconsin Centennial half dollar, 1936.

the nonstandard element of American life, was alive and well, and still had a vibrant, acceptable role to play in the numismatic life of the Republic. American collectors, at least, now look back to those days as a golden age of national numismatics, even though their parents and grandparents may have thought that the spate of commemoratives was becoming too much of a good thing, was getting out of hand. There would be time enough for reconsideration in the grayer days to come.

The period of the American commemorative coincided with one of the high points of American numismatic artistry on circulating coinage. True, the daring incuse designs of Bela Pratt and the overarching beauty of those of Augustus Saint-Gaudens had passed from the scene (gone the way of gold coinage itself in 1933), but for silver and base-metal coinage, these were great days indeed—with a single exception.

The exception was the quarter, whose pedestrian imagery has already been mentioned. The designs it replaced had been devised during the period immediately prior to America's entry into the First World War, products of the talented Hermon MacNeil. On the obverse of MacNeil's quarter, a cautious Liberty emerges from a gateway. She holds an olive branch in her right hand, suggesting her (and America's) preference for peace. But her left hand holds a shield: she is prepared to defend herself if need be. An eagle in flight adorns the reverse of the MacNeil quarter.

These designs rather nicely reflected popular opinion at the end of 1916, the time when they were introduced to American coinage—except for one thing. The artist had depicted the goddess without a crucial bit of drapery, her right breast thus exposed to the viewer—and to the Society for the Suppression of Vice, who immediately launched a vigorous campaign against this latest assault on national decency by the 1916 equivalent of secular humanists. Lady Liberty was rather quickly covered (by a bodice of chain mail, which may have been more appropriate at that). With minor alterations on the reverse, the "standing liberty" quarter was struck until 1930. In 1932, it was replaced by the unexceptionable

Standing Liberty quarter, 1916.

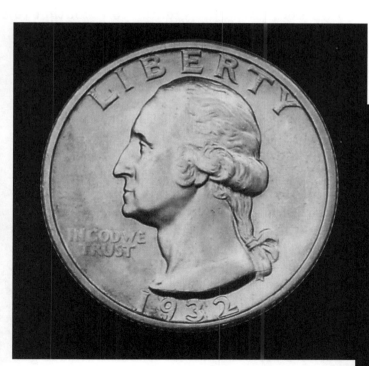

Washington quarter, 1932.

"Mercury" dime, 1916.

if mediocre Washington design, the product of John Flanagan.

For other circulating denominations during the thirties, the artistic flowering which Theodore Roosevelt had engendered (and which had come to full fruition some years after he had departed office) still held sway. We have already been introduced to Brenner's cent and Fraser's five-cent piece, or nickel; the dime and half dollar were both redesigned in 1916, Charles Barber's trite renditions now replaced by magnificent, authentically "patriotic" images by Adolph Alexander Weinman.

As with MacNeil's quarter, Weinman's dime and half dollar were designed just prior to American entry into the First World War, and the themes they incorporated indicated as much. For the dime, a realistic, left-facing head of Liberty imparted a new freshness to American numismatic design, although the wings on the deity's cap, which the artist had intended to symbolize liberty of thought (a precious commodity in times of uncertainty) were mistaken for the attributes of a god, and the coin became known as the "Mercury" dime. Weinman's reverse brought an altogether new concept to American coinage: the fasces, emblem of

unity, an obvious desideratum in the face of international danger.

Attractive as was his dime, this artist's half dollar was his greater contribution to United States numismatics, and it stands as the most beautiful circulating half dollar design ever created. We see a Liberty who actually wears the American flag, striding toward the dawn, with a bundle of oak and laurel branches (symbols of honor in civilian and military activities) held in the crook of her left arm. On the reverse is the usual American eagle, but a splendidly naturalistic bird this time, posed before a sapling of Mountain Pine, symbol of America. Weinman's dime was struck through 1945, his half dollar through 1947, each replaced by designs representing a descent in artistry from the great days of the early twentieth century.

James Earle Fraser's "buffalo" or "Indian head" nickel had already passed from the scene. Public law mandates that coin designs can be changed after a quarter-century of service, and in 1938, this policy was employed to create a new five-cent piece, honoring Thomas Jefferson. Designed by Felix Schlag, the new coin marked a deepening of the trend away

Walking Liberty half dollar, 1916.

from symbolic representations and toward real people, a move already seen with the Lincoln cent of 1909 and the Washington quarter of 1932. The Schlag designs can in no way be considered an improvement over their predecessors (although in fairness it must be said that much of what artistry had been placed there by the artist had been removed at the United States Mint before production got under way in the late summer of 1938). The "Jefferson" nickel is still in production, although it has seen minor modifications in design over the years—and a major modification in metallic content, a response to larger events in American history.

Those larger events centered on the final act of the Second Thirty Years' War. After an uneasy armed truce of twenty-one years' duration, the old adversaries of 1914 lined up once again. This time the sons finished what their fathers had begun. War broke out in September 1939, as a revanchist Germany (which had made a recent career of bluffing Great Britain and France out of areas deemed worth worrying about but not worth fighting to defend) attempted one final bluff and found at last found that there was a point beyond which the Allies would not retreat.

As in 1914, most Americans were quite happy to stay out of the conflict. For the first two-thirds of a year, the war seemed to have degenerated into nothing more than hot air, as Hitler absorbed Poland (whose guarantee had led Britain and France to declare hostilities in September) into the Greater German Reich—and his theoretical adversaries were only too glad to allow him to do so unmolested. This convinced Americans of the essential bluff and posturing which they had always known lay at the heart of the European mind; enlisting in such a war was certainly not worth their consideration. Then *Blitzkrieg*, as Hitler overran Norway, Denmark, the Low Countries, and finally one of the prime players, France. And now the war looked very real indeed, one which America must avoid at all perils.

But the nation was schizophrenic as the 1940s began. It did not desire an Axis victory, even as it began to look like its own deep involvement would be the only possibility of avoiding such an event. Ties of language, blood, and faith naturally bound the country to Great Britain, which was seen by many as a gallant David, struggling on alone against Hitler's Goliath. Others saw England as the oppressor, trampler on the rights of the Irish and other unfortunate neighbors. But the deepest division was this: in 1940, virtually no one in the United States wanted to go to war, but the ranks of those who believed that they would soon be doing so grew steadily.

When war finally came to the United States, it originated in a quarter which Americans regarded as a sideshow, when they regarded it at all: on December 7, 1941, Japan, of all nations, attacked the United States at Pearl Harbor (that splendid naval base the Navy had acquired from the Hawaiian monarchy back in 1887). Average Americans were greatly shocked, their president somewhat less so: the Japanese attack had come about in part because of Roosevelt's intransigence on issues which Tokyo considered life-or-death but which, viewed from the other side of the Pacific, looked rather more like simple expansionism. But whoever bore ultimate responsibility for Pearl Harbor, the essential point was that it united Americans overnight, destroyed twenty years' worth (or far more, depending on where you start counting) of isolationism at a single stroke—and ensured that Americans would henceforth be as deeply involved in the world conflict as anyone else. The Japanese were allied to Hitler's Germany and Mussolini's Italy, and those two nations promptly declared war as well.

American participation in the Second World War lasted some forty-five months and left 292,131 dead and 671,801 wounded of the 16,353,659 men and women who served in its armed forces. During its course, defense expenditures multiplied by a factor of fifty. The war changed America abroad, as the nation reluctantly abandoned most of its determination to chart a separate path, a determination it had cherished since the days of the thirteen colonies. Henceforth, its voice would be heard on the international scene, whether anyone wished to hear it or not.

But American participation in the Second World War changed even more at home than it did abroad. It planted seeds for the future: having been told they were important during wartime, America's women would not indefinitely allow their men to shape the sex's destinies once the war was over. And African Americans, having bled and died at Anzio, naturally and inevitably began to question why they could not vote in Alabama. The beginning of a war is like the lid on Pandora's box: once you lift it, you have no way of knowing what will come out, or what it will do once it gets out.

Wars commonly act as forcing beds for technological development, and this one was no exception. Some of the new products were welcome, and Americans wondered how they had ever survived without them: plastics, synthetic fibers centering on nylon, artificial lubricants, new food products. Some of them were otherwise, and Americans soon wondered whether they would be able to survive them at all: the Bomb stands out here.

The Second World War had a greater and longer impact on some areas of American life than on others. It changed the way average people viewed themselves and their nation in relationship to the rest of the world, and that change endured. But it also spawned a number of interesting developments in their money, and none of them was permanent.

Changes took place on coins and currency alike. For coinage, copper was removed from the cent at the end of 1942, 1943 issues being struck in zinc-plated steel. But public outcry (the new, pale cents were confused with dimes, and their zinc coating yielded quickly to rust) caused the United States Mint to abandon the experiment at the end of 1943; it would turn unwanted shell casings into cents during 1944, 1945, and 1946 and finally resumed normal production in 1947. Upon careful examination, collectors will see that 1944–46 cents are slightly yellower than those struck prior to the war, for shell casings contained a slightly different alloy from that ordinarily used for cent coinage.

The second coin to see major wartime changes was the five-cent piece. Nickel was deemed a critical war material (as was copper, which explains why the United States Mint removed it from the cent in 1943), but could the nickel be struck without nickel? It could, but to no one's satisfaction. A nightmarish combination of copper (56 percent), silver (35 percent, thereby giving the five-cent piece an intrinsic value approaching its stated one), and manganese (9 percent) was introduced in October 1942. Through 1945, all five-cent pieces would be struck from the new alloy, precious nickel thereby saved for more important uses.

But the alloy was a great disappointment. Tarnished coins turned an unappetizing grayish-yellow, and the metallic mixture made for a large percentage of "planchet laminations," wherein parts of the design simply separated from the coin after it had been placed in circulation, leaving unsightly peels on its faces. The threefold alloy satisfied no one, but more than half a billion coins were made from it. Beyond their color and the problem of their appearance, they could also be distinguished from their prewar brethren by a large mint mark over the dome of Monticello rather than a small one at its right side. And for the first time in American history, the main Mint at Philadelphia received a mark of its own, a letter "P." Its distinctive mark was taken away from it after 1945 (and the other two mint marks migrated back to their earlier position); but the "P" was restored to the nickel and extended to most other denominations some decades later.

There were changes on American currency as well, although most citizens were unaware of them at the time. This was because they took place in peripheral areas (in Hawaii and in parts of the theater of war). The Hawaiian issues were simply ordinary silver certificates, upon which a brown seal was substituted for the blue one appropriate to that type of currency, with the word "Hawaii" overprinted twice in small letters on the face and once in gigantic ones on the back. Ones, fives, tens, and twenties were so issued, and they grew out of the fear early in the war that the Hawaiian Islands were in imminent danger of falling to Japan. Special currency such as these notes could be disavowed if that event took place. It never did, of course, but the notes rendered good service as ordinary currency in Hawaii and the Pacific during the remainder of the war. Notes were also issued for use of American troops in Europe and North Africa: one-, five-, and ten-dollar silver certificates whose yellow seal indicated their special nature.

These notes were denominated in dollars, for they were for the use of Americans,

1943-P nickel.

whether or not they happened to be in the United States at the time. But they foreshadowed a far larger issue of paper denominated in other currencies: the francs, schilling, mark, lire, and yen of France, Austria, Germany, Italy, and Japan, respectively. Collectors call such issues "AMC" for Allied Military Currency, and they were created for and used by those in the nations defeated by the Allies. They were not American currency, even though they were handled by many thousands of American troops overseas, both during and after the war. But they were largely printed in the United States by the Bureau of Engraving and Printing in Washington and by two private firms, Forbes in Boston and Stecher-Traung in San Francisco. British printers supplied some of the Austrian notes, while Russian ones created some of the issues circulated in Germany. But all the notes closely resembled each other, regardless of country and regardless of printer, a deliberate attempt to show the unity of the Allied forces in small matters as well as large.

Official American-made paper money for other nations was joined by coinage. The United States Mint's earlier activities in supplying Latin America were mentioned in the last chapter. During the war, these enterprises expanded dramatically, and they moved in a variety of directions. The

mint continued to supply a number of old customers in Latin America and elsewhere. But it also provided "liberation" issues of several types. For the Philippines (which had had its own mint in Manila since 1920, but which had fallen to Japan early in the war), massive coin issues of the prewar type were prepared in Denver and San Francisco in 1944–45, placed in Philippine commerce as the islands were liberated by United States troops during those years. (And the Bureau of Engraving and Printing, which had been supplying Philippine paper currency ever since 1903, prepared similar, and massive, note issues for the newly-liberated islands, all of it proudly overprinted VICTORY on face and back.)

The United States Mint also served as temporary coiner for the Netherlands, supplying its possessions with money of the prewar type when the mother country was unable to do so. American-made coins on the Dutch model were shipped to the Netherlands Antilles (which were never occupied by the Axis) and to the Dutch East Indies (which were, being overrun by Japan early in the war, only liberated at its end). Finally, coins were prepared for liberated France and Belgium, the urgency of the times when they were made manifested in their extreme simplicity of design. A two-franc coin was struck in brass for France, while the mint

France, Allied Military Currency, one thousand francs, series of 1944. Courtesy the NNC.

American wartime coinage for the Dutch Empire. Courtesy the NNC.

American coinage for France, two francs, 1944. Courtesy the NNC.

American coinage for Belgium, made from recycled cent steel planchets (two francs, 1944). Courtesy the NNC.

found a handy way of recycling the unwanted steel cent planchets of 1943, turning them into Belgian double francs of 1944. These two coins are the simplest issues ever struck by the United States Mint: just simple words, a wreath or two, and the date. But they may have been the most welcomed of mint issues as well, when we consider what they would have meant to the hard-pressed peoples for whom they had been struck.

Thus the coinage and currency of an America at war. For all of the diversity of metals and types, for all of the interesting experiments, the numismatic expedients of the Second World War left no permanent imprint on the story of the nation's money. When the fighting had ended, reality snapped back into its earlier, prewar mold:

paper money resumed its normal seal colors, coinage its normal alloys. Commemorative issues soon resumed, now that the United States Mint had leisure time to think about them. But an unintended and doleful new coin entered the monetary spectrum as well, and it might serve to symbolize the war and the events which had led up to it.

The new coin was a dime, approved late in 1945, introduced early in 1946. And it bore the head of the man who had dominated the American war effort and who had died in its pursuit, Franklin Delano Roosevelt. The coin is still in circulation today, linking Americans who have never heard of him (and only approximately of the war for which he perished) with the man and the events. And with this coin, we move into the present period of United States numismatics.

Roosevelt dime, 1946.

CHAPTER 9

COLD WAR AND BEYOND
(1946 TO THE PRESENT)

CHAPTER 9

COLD WAR AND BEYOND (1946 TO THE PRESENT)

The years since the end of the Second World War have been among the most eventful in American, and indeed human, history. From 1946 through the time of this writing, the average middle-aged United States citizen has lived through the following: the breakup of the wartime alliance with Russia, and the resulting Red Scare; the civil rights movement; the relative empowerment of women; the space crusade, and the landing of a man on the moon; the assassination of one president and the forced resignation of another; the murder of respected leaders of reform; student unrest; small wars (not so small at that, if you were involved in them) in Korea, Vietnam, the Persian Gulf—and military engagements in more places than one can readily remember; several recessions; the longest economic boom in American history; television; the computer; the rise of the suburb and the decline of the central city; rock and roll; the Pill; the final divorce between the average citizen and high art; the binding of the American physical landscape into the closest connection ever seen; the fragmentation of the people living in that landscape to a degree never before seen. Changes indeed, changes everywhere, except one place: with very few exceptions, America's money has not changed at all. The half century or so since the end of the Second World War has been the most curious passage in the entire story of American numismatics. Throughout this book, I have attempted to illustrate the dynamism at work in the coinage and currency of the United States, a dynamism spurred by and reflective of the larger events of the period. Yet here, against a background of some of the greatest alterations ever seen in ways of life, interpersonal relationships, and the foreign and domestic outlook of the United States government and those it serves, we still see American coinage and currency which would not only be recognizable to the average man and woman of 1946, but would probably escape their notice altogether.

What happened? Why did the money become fixed in a single, changeless pattern? And what does this say about larger issues? Let me tell you what I think.

Americans have tended to be an insular people, largely concerned with domestic problems and prospects, and so it was during most of their history, down to the days of the Second World War. That conflict convinced them that they must look outside their walls, and pay greater attention to, take larger responsibility for, international affairs. There was very little missionary zeal here (at least, not after the first few years); rather, Americans were now more fully involved in the world because it appeared that they could no longer safely ignore it.

Their new relationship meant hot war in Korea and Vietnam, cold war with Russia, and an inability to enjoy the promised fruits of their earlier victory in 1945. When an individual suffers one threatening situation after another, a perpetual stress results: the subject tires of always being on guard, seeks to take pleasure in those elements in life which promise stability and hark back to better times, times more predictable and reliable. Countries are aggregations of individual citizens: what takes place on a personal scale may also take place on a national one.

I believe that the last five decades of national stress have played a major role in the unusual continuity of America's money. When people are constantly bombarded with threats and predictions of Armageddon (I am old enough to remember regular drills in my primary school, wherein we were taught to duck under our desks in the event of a nuclear attack; wise nine-year-olds, we knew at the time that this was unlikely to help, but it was possibly better than nothing), they tend to take what comfort they can in prosaic objects which have "always" been with them in the same blessedly reliable form. Coinage and currency can fall into this category, and did, I think, in the case of the United States. My surmisal is strengthened by a curious succession of events: between 1989 and 1991, the major perceived foreign threat (the Soviet Union) removed itself from contention, and now, for the first time since 1945, a real debate seems to be rising over the designs on American coinage and currency—not only on the part of collectors but on that of the wider public. In the case of currency, of course, most of the popular concern stems from worry over counterfeiting rather than concern over esthetics, but American paper money was nearly as vulnerable ten years ago as it is now, and no one expressed a concern at that time. Put most simply, Americans had more important matters on their minds until fairly recently: now that they have the leisure to look at their coins and notes with a more critical eye, changes may be on the way.

You may observe that other nations have also gone through stressful periods since the end of the war—and in many cases, the hardships they have borne have dwarfed anything seen in the United States—but monetary experimentation has flourished elsewhere, experimentation in coinage and currency alike. All of this is quite true, but with a disclaimer: on the foreign scene, at least, the period after 1945 was the first time that average Americans had had to contemplate, day after day, year after year, the wider world in its full, terrifying sense. They had not been gradually introduced to it, had not known about it all along, but were presented with it all at once. Their shock and stress were therefore greater than they might have

been, their desire for stability where available somewhat more pronounced than might have been expected. And their predilection for safe, unchanging money was thus, I think, greater than would have otherwise been the case.

I cheerfully admit that all this is speculation, and that other forces have been at work even if my speculations are correct. One of the reasons why America's money has remained the same for half a century is the natural indolence of any bureaucracy, in the United States and elsewhere. In the case of coinage, contemporary minters are mainly concerned with technological considerations: designs are adopted or rejected, not primarily because of their looks, but because they will or will not translate well onto an easy-to-mass-produce piece of metal. And the arrangements which grace American circulating coinage are relatively successful from that standpoint. They are well-balanced, obverse to reverse, so that designs on each side come up reasonably well in a single, quick blow of the press. And to the cry of the artist for reform of design comes the response of the minter: if it works, leave it alone. Thus one reason for continuity on American coinage.

Another is the amount of verbiage which must, either by force of law or by force of tradition, be placed *on* the coinage. The elements which each coin must bear include the name of the country, a national motto ("E Pluribus Unum"), a second national motto ("In God We Trust"), a third national motto ("Liberty"), the denomination, the date, and the place of mintage, as evidenced by a mint mark. Once you get all that onto a coin, you have precious little room for anything else, and if you have been bequeathed a design which managed to cram everything in and which still proved easy to coin, you will hold onto it very tightly.

When we turn to paper money, we see an even greater continuity, one which has been even more deliberate. Even to the practiced eye, the only substantive changes which have taken place on most denominations since 1945 are the addition of the motto "In God We Trust" to the backs of the bills (introduced in the late 1950s, completed by the early 1960s) and the retiring of other types of paper currency in favor of the Federal Reserve note. But designs remain what they were: faces are black, backs green, and signatures lie exactly where they were when we last looked for them. The issuing authority prefers it that way because it perceives that those it serves desire it that way: paper is an incredibly delicate exchange medium, and the United States Treasury realizes that the introduction of new designs and obvious technological changes may alarm the public, may render earlier, perfectly legitimate, issues suspect. So no change is best, or a change so subtle that it will foil the forger without alarming the legitimate user of the currency (which explains recent addition of microprinting and security threads, changes so subtle and so diffident that they have neither alarmed nor protected the public).

Thus it has been, but the possibilities of the color photocopier and the threats of counterfeiting on the parts of unfriendly nations are at last forcing changes on printer and public alike: a hundred-dollar note with substantive new design arrangements was introduced at the end of March 1996, a harbinger of change across the paper spectrum. In 1997, it was joined by a new fifty-dollar bill. Thus far, the public seems to have generally accepted the reforms, although there have been predictable columns in the Washington *Post* and elsewhere, decrying the departure from the strict bilateral symmetry of earlier times.

From generalities and theories, let us turn to the numismatic items themselves. We have seen many of these pieces prior to 1945, and one of them prior to 1914—the Lincoln cent. In 1959, the cent was changed, in commemoration of Lincoln's hundred-fiftieth birthday and the half-century mark of the Lincoln cent itself. The martyred president continued to form the obverse type. But on the reverse, Brenner's sensible if pedestrian "wheat ears" gave way to an attempt to depict the entire Lincoln Memorial, an attempt which found some success from a technological perspective, rather less from an artistic one. Thus amended, the Lincoln cent is now approaching its ninetieth year.

Its comrades, the Washington quarter and the Jefferson nickel, are growing gray as well, the quarter having achieved a design age of

Lincoln cent, 1959.

Franklin half dollar, 1948.

Kennedy half dollar, 1964.

sixty-five years and the nickel sixty. Both the dime and the half dollar were redesigned shortly after the end of the war: Franklin Delano Roosevelt was placed on the obverse of the former in 1946, and a design featuring a torch now replaced Weinman's fasces as the reverse type. The new dime's design was neat and compact, which was about the most flattering thing to be said about it.

But we might be far less charitable about the half dollar. In 1947, the last coins using the Weinman designs were struck, replaced the following year by new coins of a lesser artistry. The products of John R. Sinnock (who had recently produced the Roosevelt dime), the new half dollars featured a bust of Benjamin Franklin on the obverse, the Liberty Bell on the reverse. In order to comply with the Mint Act of 1792, Sinnock added a tiny eagle to the right of the bell. This odd placement neatly summarizes the somewhat ungainly concept of the entire design. Sinnock's dime is still very much alive, but his half dollar came to an abrupt end in 1963, replaced by a new coin by Gilroy Roberts which paid homage to the martyred president, John Fitzgerald Kennedy. Roberts' work still ap-

pears on half dollars, although changing usage patterns have restricted the circulation of his coins to a few spots in the Far West.

Another coin which saw its usage progressively restricted was the dollar. No members of this denomination were released between 1935 and 1971 (although 1964-dated dollars of the "Peace" design were indeed struck, then melted down once the price of silver rose; predictably, a few specimens are rumored to have escaped the melting pot and may one day emerge on the collecting market). Also, in 1971, a new coin with new designs appeared. In one of the few recent instances wherein larger events have found reflection on American coinage, Frank Gasparro's new dollar featured a rendition of the Apollo IX insignia (which had been worn by the first humans to walk on the moon) on the reverse, a left-facing head of Dwight David Eisenhower (during whose tenure in office the race into space had begun) on the obverse. The result was a spectacularly ugly coin, but one with an undeniable logical unity between obverse and reverse subjects. Struck intermittently through 1978, the unity was lost the following year.

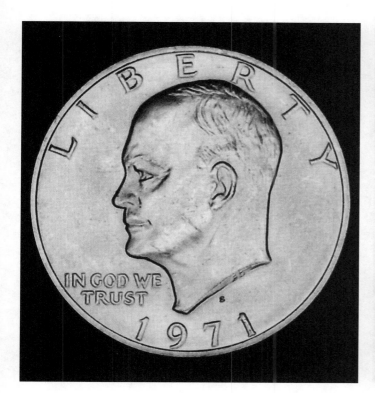 

Eisenhower dollar, 1971.

By the late 1970s, the dollar was not circulating except in certain restricted portions of the Far West. In an attempt to increase the coin's convenience and appeal (and to create a more durable dollar than the circulating paper one) the United States Mint decided to reduce the coin's size, bringing out a smaller piece in the spring of 1979. For his new obverse, Frank Gasparro abandoned Eisenhower (and hence the unity and logic of his full-size coin), placing the noted feminist Susan B. Anthony there in the famous general's place. There she reposed in uncomfortable juxtaposition with the eagle on the moon for the next two years.

The "Anthony" dollar was a fiasco, ammunition for those officials who opposed change on American coinage. But they themselves bore part of the blame. The coin had originally been planned as eleven-sided rather than round (so that confusion with the quarter would not occur). But this helpful idea had been abandoned by the time the Anthony dollar went into production, as had the sole realistic suggestion for ensuring its success in circulation, halting production of the paper dollar.

The United States Mint made nearly two-thirds of a billion Anthony dollars in 1979, an output reduced to less than ninety million in 1980 and ten million in 1981; the institution then gave up the attempt, and the coins were put into storage, where most of them still remain. At the time, I suggested another possible reason for the public rejection of the coin: on a visceral level, it simply didn't look like it was *worth* a dollar. It was small. And it contained not a trace of silver.

To be sure, no other American coin contained silver by that point either, and virtually none had since the mid-1960s. But the dime, quarter, and half dollar owed some of their continuing acceptance to their continuity of size and design (plus the fact that they were the *only* dimes, quarters, and halves provided by the government for public use). At the time of the introduction of the Anthony coin, the public already had a paper dollar, as well as a coin of a "real" dollar size—the Eisenhower dollar, which was reassuringly heavy, if base. Once base metal was combined with a reduced size and a changed design, trouble was inevitable.

Susan B. Anthony dollar, 1979.

The United States removed silver from most of its coinage by the Act of July 23, 1965. It had seen no choice, for the price of the precious metal had risen to the point where it nearly paid to melt down American coins for their silver. This figure was actually reached and surpassed a few months later. That event, and new issues of a clad, copper-nickel composition for dimes and quarters and "billon" (a copper-silver mixture, wherein copper predominates) for halves, had driven silver coins out of commerce by 1967. The remainder of the half dollar's silver was removed in 1970, and from that time to this, every circulating American coin above five cents has consisted of the same metallic composition, with outer layers of 75 percent copper and 25 percent nickel, bonded to a core of pure copper. To add insult to injury, the makeup of the cent was downgraded as well in 1982: at that point, a rise in the price of copper led to a new cent made of pure zinc, with a thin copper plating to maintain appearances.

The changes in metallic composition, the melting of earlier issues, and the freezing of designs to save face have all contributed to a curious fact in American numismatics. Fewer and fewer young people are becoming interested in the hobby, for there is less and less to attract them in the coinage of their own country.

Any collecting must be predicated upon the availability of objects with discernible differences and the attractions of rarity and age. But when the oldest coin one is likely to see in circulation (and the coinage in one's pocket is the traditional cradle of the collector) is dated 1965, when it looks like every other coin in one's pocket and elsewhere, and when its numbers are counted in the billions, there is no reason to look at one's change, no reason to collect it, no reason to venture deeper into numismatics.

The commemorative coin serves as a partial solution to the dilemma, both from the standpoint of the aspiring collector and from that of the government. The celebratory coin can give the hobbyist the variety and rarity he or she craves, and provision of this type of "special" coinage may simultaneously please a segment of the public at little expense, keep normal coinage in circulation, and turn a profit for the coiner, if handled intelligently.

And so the commemorative coin was resumed after 1945. Three such issues were struck over the next few years, celebrating

Washington / Carver half dollar, 1951.

the centenary of the state of Iowa (issues of 1946), paying homage to the educator Booker T. Washington (issues of 1946 through 1951), and granting recognition to Booker T. Washington again, in conjunction with the scientist George Washington Carver (issues of 1951 through 1954). These two individuals were African Americans, and the commemoratives bearing their portraits suggested that members of this race were at least beginning to receive a measure of their due on American coins, anticipating their progress in wider matters.

There was rather more to the Washington/Carver coin than appeared at first glance. It was promoted by an engaging character named S. J. Phillips to provide funds "to oppose the spread of communism among Negroes in the interest of National Defense" (the coin appeared at the height of the Cold War, and the government was concerned about subversion in all aspects of society at the time). Phillips promoted this particular half dollar because he was deeply in debt from promoting the earlier one for Booker T. Washington and needed the money raised to pay off creditors and avoid lawsuits. In time, the real purpose of the Washington/Carver coin became common knowledge in Congress, and it cast a pall over the American

commemorative which would last for a quarter of a century. Commemorative coinage came to a halt.

In 1975–76, the reverses of the quarter, half, and dollar were redesigned to celebrate the bicentennial of the declaration of American independence. Of the three designs chosen (a Revolutionary War drummer boy for the quarter, Independence Hall for the half, and the Liberty Bell superimposed on the moon for the dollar), only the quarter design represented a real success, its artist (Jack L. Ahr) taking the pains necessary to fit his concept into the circular constraints of a coin. Significantly, all three coins were released into commerce as normal issues, even though special presentation pieces could be purchased if desired: the Washington/Carver commemorative still influenced thinking in the federal government and the mint which served it. The Bureau of Engraving and Printing made its own contribution to the festivities with a two-dollar Federal Reserve note (the first of that denomination) with a depiction of the signing of the Declaration of Independence.

The commemorative coin had been rehabilitated by the early 1980s. In 1982, the two hundred-fiftieth anniversary of George Washington's birth was recorded on a new

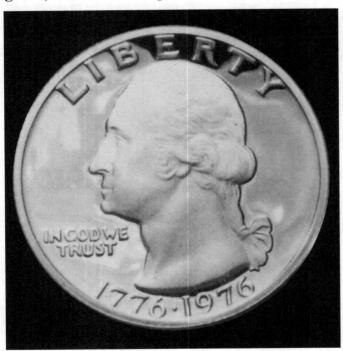

Bicentennial quarter dollar, 1976.

Olympic Games commemorative, one dollar, 1992.

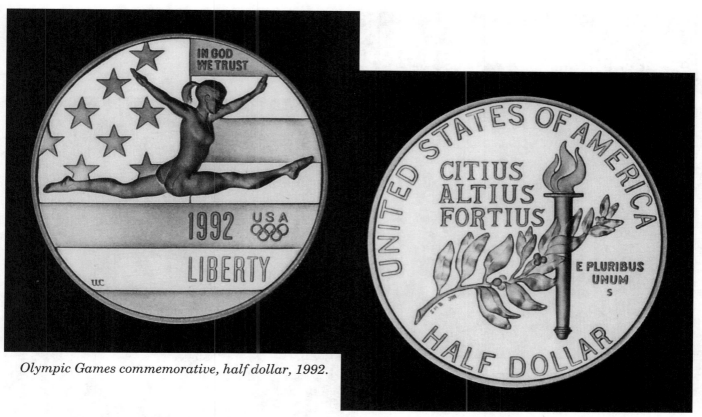

Olympic Games commemorative, half dollar, 1992.

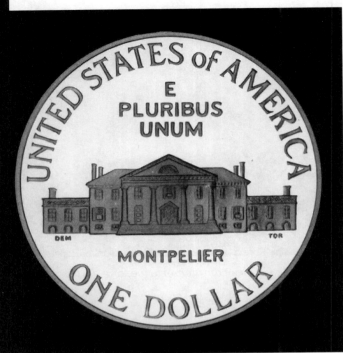

Bill of Rights commemorative (featuring James Madison), one dollar, 1993.

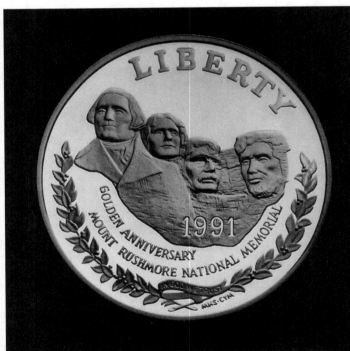

Golden Anniversary of Mount Rushmore National Memorial, one dollar, 1991.

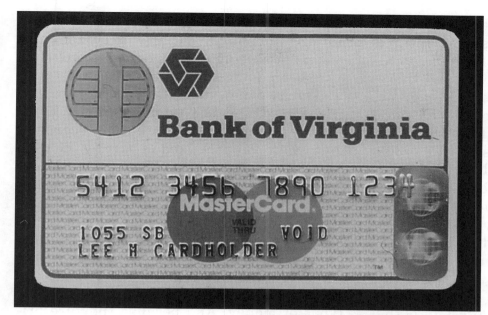

An early "smart" credit card from the Bank of Virginia, c. 1986. This specimen stores medical information about its holder. Courtesy the NNC.

"Affinity" credit card (Mercantile Bank, St. Louis, Missouri, c. 1992). Courtesy the NNC.

Telephone debit card, 1994. Courtesy the NNC.

half dollar, struck only for collectors and not for circulation. That forecast the future: since then, a large number of commemoratives have been struck in silver, and there has been a resumption of gold coinage as well. But during the course of this new activity, an important difference has emerged. Most of the issues of the 1930s paid homage to places as well as people and events, injecting a note of localism into a national coinage. But the issues of the 1980s and 1990s have swung back, away from localism and toward events and persons of national significance. Their subject matter proclaims as much: the Olympic Games, American immigration, the Korean War, the bicentennial of Congress, etc. One of the few exceptions is an issue of dollars and half dollars in silver and half eagles in gold commemorating Mount Rushmore; a cursory examination of any of the three suggests that this particular bit of localism might have been better left unsung!

It might be said that, along with ordinary circulating coinage and currency, these special coins mark the disappearance of the concept of place from American numismatics. The nation's coinage may come from four mints (a facility at West Point, New York, was added to Philadelphia, Denver, and San Francisco in 1974), and the nation's notes may come from twelve Federal Reserve branches, scattered from New York to San Francisco, but at bottom, all American money now comes from the same source, which is perfectly obvious whenever one looks at it. This is perhaps inevitable in a modern nation of the wealth and size of the United States of America, and we might have forecast the event long before it took place. But the collector and the historian are at liberty to regret it all the same.

And yet there are two types of money where the spirit of the nonstandard and the local are still alive and well, and growing in strength as I write. Neither of them are "official," in the sense of a public authority standing behind them, but an examination of the American numismatic past suggests that there is nothing new, and certainly nothing unusual, about private citizens and groups producing monies of their own; they have been doing so for centuries.

The two new monetary forms are the credit card and the telephone debit card. Both represent a new concept, an economic unit whose value is fixed in part by the user rather than the issuer. That is, while my credit card or telephone card may indeed have an arbitrary charge or call limit, *I* choose how much of its value to employ, and where it will be employed, at any given time; I may reuse it as well for successive purchases. These new forms give their patrons far greater flexibility than orthodox, "official" types of money. And because they are privately-produced and -distributed, they are not subject to the standardization seen on coinage and currency.

They can bear any design desired by the issuer, and there can be, and now are, a very great variety of issuers. This is particularly true for credit cards: it now seems that every bank from one coast to the other is issuing credit cards. The cards combine availability with distinction and attractiveness; they combine, in fact, most of the elements of collector appeal. And the collector is beginning to take notice: there is now a vibrant hobbyist market in credit cards, which are written about and collected by state, by type of issuing institution (for organizations ranging from colleges to charities are also entering the arena), and of course by design. And interest in telephone debit cards is also mounting in the United States, having already caught the fancy of collectors in Europe and Asia.

These developments are exciting for the hobbyist, but they are perhaps more important for the historian and student of numismatics, for they proclaim in no uncertain language that the exceptional, the unusual, and the local have by no means disappeared from America's media of exchange, and that what appears at first glance to be a closing door may in fact be one which is opening. Who knows where it may lead this people—and their money.

SUGGESTED READING

SUGGESTED READING

A) On Numismatics

America's Copper Coinage, 1783–1857. New York: American Numismatic Society, 1985.

America's Currency, 1789–1866. New York: American Numismatic Society, 1986.

America's Gold Coinage, 1795–1933. New York: American Numismatic Society, 1990.

America's Silver Coinage, 1794–1981. New York: American Numismatic Society, 1987.

Bischoff, William L. (ed.). *The Coinage of El Perú*. New York: American Numismatic Society, 1989.

Breen, Walter. *Walter Breen's Complete Encyclopedia of U.S. and Colonial Coins*. New York: FCI Press/Doubleday, 1988.

Criswell, Grover C. *Confederate and Southern States Currency*. 3d. ed. Port Clinton, OH: BNR Press, 1992.

Crosby, Sylvester S. *The Early Coins of America*. 1875. Reprint. Lawrence, MA: Quarterman Publications, 1983.

Davies, Glyn. *A History of Money, From Ancient Times to the Present*. Cardiff: University of Wales Press, 1994.

Doty, Richard G. "Early United States Copper Coinage: The English Connection." *British Numismatic Journal*, 57 (1987), pp. 54-76.

Doty, Richard G. "Recycling Artistic Capital: Security Printing and Silversmithing in Colonial America." <u>Proceedings</u> of the XIth International Numismatic Congress (Louvain-la-Neuve, Belgium: Séminaire de Numismatique Marcel Hoc, 1993), 4, pp. 171-183.

Doty, Richard G. (ed.). *The Token: America's Other Money*. New York: American Numismatic Society, 1995.

Fuld, George and Melvin Fuld. *Patriotic Civil War Tokens*. 4th ed. Iola, WI: Krause Publications, 1982.

Fuld, George and Melvin Fuld. *U.S. Civil War Store Cards*. 2d ed. Lawrence, MA: Quarterman Publications, 1975.

Haxby, James A. *Standard Catalog of United States Obsolete Bank Notes, 1782-1866.* 4 vols. Iola, WI: Krause Publications, 1988.

Hessler, Gene. *The Engraver's Line: An Encyclopedia of Paper Money & Postage Stamp Art.* Port Clinton, OH: BNR Press, 1993.

Hickman, John and Dean Oakes. *Standard Catalog of National Bank Notes.* 1st ed. Iola, WI: Krause Publications, 1982.

Kagin, Donald. *Private Gold Coins and Patterns of the United States.* New York: Arco, 1981.

Kleeberg, John M. (ed.). *Money of Pre-Federal America.* New York: American Numismatic Society, 1992.

Krause, Chester L. and Robert F. Lemke. *Standard Catalog of United States Paper Money.* 12th ed.; ed. Robert E. Wilhite. Iola, WI: Krause Publications, 1993.

Low, Lyman H. *Hard Times Tokens.* New York: The Author, 1899.

Mitchell, Ralph A. and Neil Shafer. *Standard Catalog of United States Depression Scrip.* 1st ed. Iola, WI: Krause Publications, 1984.

Mossman, Philip L. *Money of the American Colonies and Confederation.* New York: American Numismatic Society, 1993.

Mossman, Philip L. (ed.). *Coinage of the American Confederation Period.* New York: American Numismatic Society, 1996.

Newman, Eric P. *The Early Paper Money of America.* 3d ed. Iola, WI: Krause Publications, 1990.

Newman, Eric P. and Richard G. Doty (eds.). *Studies on Money in Early America.* New York: American Numismatic Society, 1976.

Noyes, William C. *United States Large Cents, 1793–1814.* Bloomington, MN: The Author, 1991.

Noyes, William C. *United States Large Cents, 1816–1839.* Bloomington, MN: The Author, 1991.

Pollock, Andrew W., III. *United States Patterns and Related Issues.* Wolfeboro, NH: Bowers & Merena Galleries, 1994.

Rulau, Russell. *Early American Tokens.* Iola, WI: Krause Publications, 1983.

Rulau, Russell. *Tokens of the Gay Nineties, 1890–1900.* 1st ed. Iola, WI: Krause Publications, 1987.

Rulau, Russell. *U.S. Merchant Tokens, 1845–1860.* 3d ed. Iola, WI: Krause Publications, 1990.

Rulau, Russell. *United States Trade Tokens, 1866–1899*. 2d ed. Iola, WI: Krause Publications, 1988.

Schilke, Oscar G. and Raphael E. Solomon. *America's Foreign Coins*. New York: Coin and Currency Institute, 1964.

Taxay, Don. *The U.S. Mint and Coinage*. New York: Arco, 1966.

B)On Larger Matters

(**NOTE:** I make no pretensions of giving the reader a comprehensive bibliography for *all* of American history, but I have enjoyed and been instructed by the following books, among others.)

Allen, Frederick Lewis. *The Big Change: America Transforms Itself, 1900–1950*. New York: Harper, 1952.

Arciniegas, Germán. *Latin America: A Cultural History*. Trans. Joan MacLean. New York: Knopf, 1972.

Ball, Douglas B. *Financial Failure and Confederate Defeat*. Urbana and Chicago: University of Illinois Press, 1991.

Bathe, Greville and Dorothy Bathe. *Jacob Perkins: His Inventions, His Times, & His Contemporaries*. Philadelphia: Historical Society of Pennsylvania, 1943.

Bowers, Claude. *The Tragic Era: The Revolution After Lincoln*. New York: Halcyon House, 1929.

Branch, Taylor. *Parting the Waters: America in the King Years, 1954–63*. New York: Simon and Schuster, 1988.

Burns, James MacGregor. *The American Experiment: The Vineyard of Liberty*. New York: Knopf, 1983.

Burns, James MacGregor. *The American Experiment: The Workshop of Democracy*. New York: Knopf, 1986.

Campbell, Charles S. *The Transformation of American Foreign Relations, 1865–1900*. New York: Harper & Row, 1976.

Catton, Bruce. *The Army of the Potomac*. 3 vols. Garden City, NY: Doubleday, 1951–1953.

Chesnut, Mary Boykin. *A Diary from Dixie*. Ed. Ben Ames Williams. Boston: Houghton Mifflin, 1949.

Davis, William C. *Jefferson Davis: The Man and His Hour*. New York: Harper Collins, 1992.

DeVoto, Bernard. *The Course of Empire*. Boston: Houghton Mifflin, 1952.

DeVoto, Bernard. *The Year of Decision: 1846*. Boston: Houghton Mifflin, 1989.

Draper, Theodore. *A Struggle for Power: The American Revolution*. 1st ed. New York: Times Books, 1996.

Ellis, Edward Robb. *Echoes of Distant Thunder: Life in the United States, 1914–1918*. New York: Kodansha International, 1996.

Fischer, David Hackett. *Albion's Seed: Four British Folkways in America*. New York: Oxford University Press, 1989.

Fleming, Thomas. *1776: Year of Illusions*. 1st ed. New York: Norton, 1975.

Fleming, Thomas. *The Man Who Dared the Lightning: A New Look at Benjamin Franklin*. New York: William Morrow, 1971.

Foote, Shelby. *The Civil War: A Narrative*. 3 vols. New York: Random House, 1958–1974.

Garraty, John A. *The Great Depression*. Garden City, NY: Anchor Press/Doubleday, 1987.

Herring, Hubert. *A History of Latin America*. 3d ed. New York: Knopf, 1968.

Innes, Hammond. *The Conquistadors*. New York: Knopf, 1969.

Kammen, Michael. *A Season of Youth: The American Revolution and the Historical Imagination*. New York: Knopf, 1980.

Klingaman, William K. *1919: The Year Our World Began*. New York: Harper & Row, 1987.

Klingman, William K. *1929: The Year of the Great Crash*. New York: Harper & Row, 1989.

Klingman, William K. *1941: Our Lives in a World on the Edge*. New York: Harper & Row, 1989.

Leach, Douglas Edward. *The Northern Colonial Frontier, 1607–1763*. New York: Holt, Rinehart & Winston, 1966.

Leckie, Robert. *None Died in Vain: The Saga of the American Civil War*. New York: Harper & Row, 1990.

Leech, Margaret. *In the Days of McKinley*. New York: Harper, 1959.

Leech, Margaret. *Reveille in Washington, 1860–1865*. New York: Harper & Brothers, 1941.

Leuchtenburg, William E. *Franklin D. Roosevelt and the New Deal, 1932–1940*. New York: Harper & Row, 1963.

Magill, Frank N. (ed.). *The American Presidents: The Office and the Men*. 3 vols. Pasadena, CA: Salem Press, 1986.

Malone, Dumas. *Jefferson and His Time*. 6 vols. Boston: Little, Brown, 1948–1981.

Malone, Dumas and Basil Rauch. *Empire for Liberty: The Genesis and Growth of the United States of America*. 2 vols. New York: Appleton-Century-Crofts, 1960.

Marzio, Peter C. (ed.). *A Nation of Nations: The People Who Came to America as Seen Through Objects and Documents Exhibited at the Smithsonian Institution*. New York: Harper & Row, 1976.

McCullough, David. *The Path Between the Seas: The Creation of the Panama Canal, 1870–1914*. New York: Simon & Schuster, 1977.

Nevins, Allan. *Ordeal of the Union*. 8 vols. New York: Scribner, 1947–1971.

Nevins, Allan. *Ordeal of the Union: Selected Chapters*. Comp. E.B. Long. New York: Scribner, 1973.

Nye, Russel Blaine. *The Cultural Life of the New Nation, 1776–1830*. New York: Harper, 1960.

O'Toole, G.J.A. *The Spanish War: An American Epic-1898*. 1st ed. New York: Norton, 1984.

Parmet, Herbert S. *Richard Nixon and His America*. Boston: Little, Brown, 1990.

Patterson, James T. *Grand Expectations: The United States, 1945–1974*. New York: Oxford University Press, 1996.

Perkins, Edward J. *The Economy of Colonial America*. New York: Columbia University Press, 1980.

Peterson, Merrill D. *The Great Triumvirate: Webster, Clay, and Calhoun*. New York: Oxford University Press, 1987.

Pollard, Edward A. *Southern History of the War*. 2 vols. in 1. 1866. Reprint. New York: Fairfax Press, 1977.

Schlereth, Thomas. *Victorian America: Transformations in Everyday Life, 1876–1915*. New York: Harper Collins, 1991.

Schlesinger, Arthur M., Jr. *The Age of Jackson*. Boston: Little, Brown, 1945.

Schlesinger, Arthur M., Jr. *The Coming of the New Deal*. Cambridge, MA: Harvard University Press, 1958.

Smith, Page. *A People's History of the United States*. 8 vols. New York: Penguin Books, 1989–1991.

Terkel, Louis. *Hard Times: An Oral History of the Great Depression*. New York: Pantheon Books, 1970.

Thomas, Gordon and Max Morgan-Witts. *The Day the Bubble Burst: A Social History of the Wall Street Crash of 1929*. Garden City, NY: Doubleday, 1979.

Valentine, Alan. *1913: America Between Two Worlds*. New York: Macmillan, 1962.

Van Doren, Carl. *Benjamin Franklin*. New York: Viking Press, 1938.

Ward, Barbara McLean and Gerald W.R. Ward (eds.). *Silver in American Life*. Boston, MA: D.R. Godine, 1979.

Williams, William Appleman. *Contours of American History*. New York: Norton, 1989.

Willison, George F. *Saints and Strangers*. New York: Reynal & Hitchcock, 1945.

INDEX

A

African Americans, 45, 70, 115, 170, 198, 210, 224
Alabama, 101, 147–148, 151, 158, 198, 210
Alaska, 8, 165, 169, 173, 201
Allied Military Currency (AMC), 212
American Bank Note Company, 101, 145, 147, 151, 161, 179–180
American Revolution, 59, 205
Anthony dollar, 222
Arizona, 119
Arkansas, 101
Articles of Confederation, 48, 51, 66, 69, 71

B

Baldwin & Company, 125–126
Bank of Chattanooga, 146–148
Bank of North America, 72–73, 92
Bank of the United States (first), 71, 92, 94
Banking holidays, 199, 201
Barber, Charles T., 181–184, 187, 190–191, 208
Barry, Standish, 72
Barter, 26, 32, 39, 41, 72, 166
Bath metal, 40
Bechtler family, 122–123, 138
Bill of exchange, 27
Bimetallic system, 175
"Birch," 175–176
Bland-Allison Act, 175–176
Bluebacks, 154
Boudinot, Elias, 82, 84–85
Boulton, Matthew Robinson, 137
Boulton, Matthew, 65, 74, 81–82, 84, 94–96, 136
Boulton, Watt & Company, 82–83, 135, 137
Branch mints, 126–128, 134–135, 137–138, 143, 159, 171, 176, 180, 182, 228
Brasher doubloon, 57–58
Brenner, Victor David, 187, 208, 219
Broome, Samuel, 65
Bryan, William Jennings, 177
Buell, Abel, 65

Buffalo nickel, 188–189, 208
Bureau of Engraving and Printing, 161, 163, 174, 182, 197, 212, 224

C

Cacao beans, 9
California, 102, 119–122, 124–129, 131–132, 171–172, 174–175, 191, 200
Calvert family, 33
Chain cent, 76
Chalmers, John, 60–61
Charles I, 32, 34
Charles II, 24, 32, 34
Cincinnati Mining & Trading Company, 125
Civil War tokens, 157–158
Civil War, 101, 107, 116, 120, 135, 138–139, 141, 154, 156–160, 162, 169–171, 173, 175, 188, 192
Clad coinage, 223
Clark, Gruber & Company, 133–134
Cobs, 13–14, 121
Cold War, 215, 217, 224
Colombia, 86, 183
Colorado, 119, 121, 130, 132, 134, 171
Columbus, Christopher, 27, 187, 190
Commemorative coinage, 32, 42, 72, 190–191, 202, 205–206, 214, 223–224
Commodity money, 28
Comstock Lode, 135
Confederate States of America, 148, 150–152
Confederatio patterns, 62–63
Connecticut, 24, 28, 41–42, 56–57, 65, 71, 92, 97, 99, 111, 205
Constellatio Nova coppers, 60, 63–64
Constellatio Nova patterns, 61, 64
Constitution, 51, 69–71, 74, 85, 88, 122, 131, 148, 199
Continental Currency, 48–52, 55–56, 71, 97, 148
Continental Dollar, 65, 142
Conway, John J. & Company, 134
Copper planchets, 137
Coram, Thomas, 50, 52, 55
Cortés, Hernán, 9, 182
Counterfeiting (paper money), 49, 95, 97–98, 100, 145, 149, 154, 218–219

N

O

P

Q